W9-BVL-634

Also by Calvin Trillin

Trillin on Texas
Deciding the Next Decider
About Alice
A Heckuva Job
Obliviously On He Sails
Feeding a Yen
Tepper Isn't Going Out
Family Man
Messages from My Father
Too Soon to Tell
Deadline Poet
Remembering Denny
American Stories
Enough's Enough
Travels with Alice
If You Can't Say Something Nice
With All Disrespect
Killings
Third Helpings
Uncivil Liberties
Floater
Alice, Let's Eat
Runestruck
American Fried
U.S. Journal
Barnett Frummer Is an Unbloomed Flower
An Education in Georgia

QUITE ENOUGH OF CALVIN TRILLIN

QUITE ENOUGH OF CALVIN TRILLIN

Forty Years of Funny Stuff

Calvin Trillin

RANDOM HOUSE
NEW YORK

Published in the United States by Random House,
an imprint of The Random House Publishing Group,
a division of Random House, Inc., New York.

RANDOM HOUSE and colophon are registered
trademarks of Random House, Inc.

All of the pieces that appear in this work have been
previously published, some in different form.

LIBRARY OF CONGRESS CATALOGING-IN-PUBLICATION DATA
Trillin, Calvin.
Quite enough of Calvin Trillin / by Calvin Trillin.
p. cm.
ISBN 978-1-4000-6982-8
eBook ISBN 978-0-679-60480-8
1. Trillin, Calvin. 2. Authors, American—20th century—Biography. I. Title.
PS3570.R5Z475 2011
814'.54—dc22 2011004050
[B]

Printed in the United States of America on acid-free paper

www.atrandom.com

2 4 6 8 9 7 5 3 1

FIRST EDITION

Book Design by Dana Leigh Blanchette

My wife, Alice, appears as a character in many of these pieces. Before her death, in 2001, even the pieces that didn't mention her were written in the hope of making her giggle. This book is dedicated to her memory.

Contents

LIFE AMONG THE LITERATI

MADLY MAKING MONEY

THE YEARS WITH NAVASKY

TWENTY YEARS OF POLS—ONE POEM EACH

NYC

FAMILY MATTERS

BEASTS OF THE FIELD, FISH OF THE SEA, AND CHIGGERS IN THE TALL GRASS

ENGLISH AND SOME LANGUAGES I DON'T SPEAK

BAGELS, YIDDISH, AND OTHER JEWISH CONTRIBUTIONS TO WESTERN CIVILIZATION

THE SPORTING LIFE

SCIENCE, TECHNOLOGY, AND THE HEALING ARTS

FOREIGNERS

ISSUES AND OTHER IRRITATIONS

SEEING THE WORLD

NATIONAL HOLIDAYS

Author's Note

These pieces have appeared in, among other places, *The New Yorker, The Nation,* a newspaper column syndicated by King Features, *The New York Times,* and various books. Some of them have been trimmed or merged or otherwise altered, but they remain in their period. Salaries have not been multiplied to account for inflation. VCR references have not been transformed into TiVo references.

BIOGRAPHICALLY SPEAKING

"I've found that a lot of people say they're from Kansas City when they aren't. Just for the prestige."

Chubby

It's common these days for memoirs of childhood to concentrate on some dark secret within the author's ostensibly happy family. It's not just common; it's pretty much mandatory. Memoir in America is an atrocity arms race. A memoir that reveals incest is trumped by one that reveals bestiality, and that, in turn, is driven from the bestseller list by one that reveals incestuous bestiality.

When I went into the memoir game, I knew I was working at a

horrific disadvantage: As much as I would hate this getting around in literary circles in New York, the fact is that I had a happy childhood. At times, I've imagined how embarrassing this background would be if I found myself discussing childhoods with other memoirists late at night at some memoirist hangout.

After talking about their own upbringings for a while—the glue-sniffing and sporadically violent grandmother, for instance, or the family tapeworm—they look toward me. Their looks are not totally respectful. They are aware that I've admitted in print that I never heard my parents raise their voices to each other. They have reason to suspect, from bits of information I've let drop from time to time, that I was happy in high school. I try desperately to think of a dark secret in my upbringing. All I can think of is Chubby, the collie dog.

"Well, there's Chubby, the collie dog," I say, tentatively.

"Chubby, the collie dog?" they repeat.

There really was a collie named Chubby. I wouldn't claim that the secret about him qualifies as certifiably traumatic, but maybe it explains an otherwise mysterious loyalty I had as a boy to the collie stories of Albert Payson Terhune. We owned Chubby when I was two or three years old. He was sickly. One day Chubby disappeared. My parents told my sister, Sukey, and me that he had been given to some friends who lived on a farm, so that he could thrive in the healthy country air. Many years later—as I remember, I was home on vacation from college—Chubby's name came up while my parents and Sukey and I were having dinner. I asked why we'd never gone to visit him on the farm. Sukey looked at me as if I had suddenly announced that I was thinking about eating the mashed potatoes with my hands for a while, just for a change of pace.

"There wasn't any farm," she said. "That was just what they told us. Chubby had to be put to sleep."

"Put to sleep!" I said. "Chubby's gone?"

Somebody—my mother, I think—pointed out that Chubby would have been gone in any case, since collies didn't ordinarily live to the age of eighteen.

"Isn't it sort of late for me to be finding this out?" I said.

"It's not our fault if you're slow on the uptake," my father said.

I never found myself in a memoirist gathering that required me to tell the story of Chubby, but, as it happened, I did relate the story in a book. A week or so later, I got a phone call from Sukey.

"The collie was not called Chubby," she said. "The collie was called George. *You* were called Chubby."

1998

Geography

Geography was my best subject. You can imagine how I feel when I read that the average American high school student is likely to identify Alabama as the capital of Chicago. I knew all the state capitals. I knew major mineral resources. Missouri: lead and zinc. (That's just an example.) I learned so many geographical facts that I've had to spend a lot of time in recent years trying to forget them so I'll have room in my brain for some things that may be more useful. I don't hold with the theory that everyone is just using a little bit of his gray matter. I think we're all going flat out.

For instance, I've worked hard to forget the longest word in the English language, which I had to learn for a high school club. Pneumonoultramicroscopicsilicovolcanoconiosis. It isn't a word that's easy to work into conversations. There are only so many times you can say, "Speaking of diseases usually contracted through the inhalation of quartz dust . . ." I finally managed to forget how to spell it, and I was able to remember my Army serial number.

I think my interest in geography grew from the long automobile trips across the country I used to take with my family as a child. I grew up in Kansas City, which is what the real estate people would call equally convenient to either coast. We usually went west. My father would be in the front seat, pointing out buttes and mesas, and my sister, Sukey, and I would be in the back, protecting our territory.

We had an invisible line in the center of the seat. At least, Sukey said it was in the center.

There were constant border tensions. It was sort of like the border between Finland and the old Soviet Union. I played Finland. Sukey played the Soviet Union. Then my father did something that we now know was politically retrograde and maybe antifeminist. He told me, "We do not hit girls. You will never hit your sister again." Sukey was not visited with a similar injunction. So I became a unilaterally disarmed Finland, while she was a Soviet Union bristling with weaponry. If I hadn't had to be on constant alert because of Sukey's expansionist backseat policy, I might now know the difference between a butte and a mesa.

If I had followed my geographical bent, I would have become a regionalist, a geographer who decides where to draw the lines dividing the regions of the United States, like the Midwest and the South and the New England states. Actually, I do the same sort of thing, without a degree, except I only use two regions—partly because of my math. Math was my worst subject. I was never able to convince the mathematics teacher that many of my answers were meant ironically. Also, I had trouble with pi, as in "pi r squared." Some years ago, the Texas State Legislature passed a resolution to change pi to an even three. And I was for it.

The way I divide up the country, the first region is the part of the United States that had major league baseball before the Second World War. That's the *Ancien* United States, or the Old Country. The rest of the United States is the rest of the United States—or the Expansion Team United States.

For those of you who didn't follow baseball closely in 1948, there's an easy way to know whether you're in the Old Country or the Expansion Team United States. In the Old Country, the waiters in an Italian restaurant have names like Sal or Vinnie. If you're in an Italian restaurant and the waiter's name is Duane, you're in the Expansion Team United States.

1988

Spelling Yiffniff

My father used to offer an array of prizes for anyone who could spell yiffniff. That's not how to spell it, of course—yiffniff. I'm just trying to let you know what it sounds like, in case you'd like to take a crack at it yourself. Don't get your hopes up: This is a spelling word that once defied some of the finest twelve-year-old minds Kansas City had to offer.

The prizes were up for grabs any time my father drove us to a Boy Scout meeting. After a while, all he had to say to start the yiffniff attempts was "Well?"

"Y-i . . . ," some particularly brave kid like Dogbite Davis would say.

"Wrong," my father would say, in a way that somehow made it sound like "Wrong, dummy."

"How could I be wrong already?" Dogbite would say.

"Wrong," my father would repeat. "Next."

Sometimes he would begin the ride by calling out the prizes he was offering: ". . . a new Schwinn three-speed, a trip to California, a lifetime pass to Kansas City Blues baseball games, free piano lessons for a year, a new pair of shoes." No matter what the other prizes were, the list always ended with "a new pair of shoes."

Some of the prizes were not tempting to us. We weren't interested in shoes. We would have done anything to avoid free piano lessons for a year. Still, we were desperate to spell yiffniff.

"L-l . . . ," Eddie Williams began one day.

"Wrong," my father said when Eddie had finished. "Next."

"That's Spanish," Eddie said, "the double *L* that sounds like a *y*."

"This is English," my father said. "Next."

Sometimes someone would ask what yiffniff meant.

"You don't have to give the definition to get the prizes," my father would say. "Just spell it."

As far as I could gather, yiffniff didn't have a definition. It was a word that existed solely to be spelled. My father had invented it for that purpose.

Occasionally some kid in the car—usually, the contentious Dogbite Davis—would make an issue out of yiffniff's origins. "But you made it up!" he'd tell my father, in an accusing tone.

"Of course I made it up," my father would reply. "That's why I know how to spell it."

"But it could be spelled a million ways."

"All of them are wrong except my way," my father would say. "It's my word."

If you're thinking that my father, who had never shared the secret of how to spell his word, could have simply called any spelling we came up with wrong and thus avoided handing out the prizes, you never knew my father. His views on honesty made the Boy Scout position on that subject seem wishy-washy. There was no doubt among us that my father knew how to spell yiffniff and would award the prizes to anyone who spelled it that way. But nobody seemed able to do it.

Finally, we brought in a ringer—my cousin Keith, from Salina, who had reached the finals of the Kansas State Spelling Bee. (Although Keith, who eventually became an English professor, remembers the details of his elimination differently, I'm sure I was saying even then that the word he missed in the finals was "hayseed.") We told my father that Keith, who was visiting Kansas City, wanted to go to a Scout meeting with us to brush up on some of his knots.

"Well?" my father said, when the car was loaded.

"Yiffniff," my cousin Keith said clearly, announcing the assigned word in the spelling bee style. "Y-y . . ."

Y-y! Using *y* both as a consonant and as a vowel! What a move! We looked at my father for a response. He said nothing. Emboldened, Keith picked up the pace: "Y-y-g-h-k-n-i-p-h."

For a few moments the car was silent. Then my father said, "Wrong. Next."

Suddenly the car was bedlam as we began arguing about where

our plans had gone wrong. "Maybe we should have got the guy who knew how to spell 'hayseed,' " Dogbite said. We argued all the way to the Scout meeting, but it was the sort of argument that erupts on a team that has already lost the game. We knew Keith had been our best shot.

1986

Doing My Talent

I can whistle and hum at the same time. It's my talent, in the way the Miss America people use the word talent—as in "Miss Minnesota will now do her talent." If the Miss America people announced that I would now do my talent, I would whistle and hum at the same time. I would probably whistle and hum "Stars and Stripes Forever," although I've also prepared "Buckle Down, Winsocki" in case of an encore. It's a secure feeling, knowing that you're ready if the Miss America people call.

I hate to use the phrase "God-given talent"—like a lot of people with God-given talent, I have always prided myself on my lack of pretense—but it's true that whistling and humming at the same time came to me naturally. I didn't work at it, the way I worked at being able to blow a hard-boiled egg out of the shell. It's more like my other talent, the ability to bark like a dog: One day I just realized I could do it.

I can whistle/hum anything, but I prefer "Stars and Stripes Forever" because it's a traditional song for people doing my sort of talent. On Ted Mack's *Original Amateur Hour,* a program whose passing I lament, "Stars and Stripes Forever" was a staple. I once saw a man play it on his head with two spoons, varying the notes by how widely he opened his mouth. I suspect he had "Buckle Down, Winsocki" ready as an encore, even though they never did encores on Ted Mack's *Original Amateur Hour.* "Buckle Down, Winsocki" is also traditional.

You might think that my ability to whistle and hum at the same time has always been a matter of pride in my family. I know the sort of scenes you're imagining. You see my wife at lunch with one of her friends. "It must be exciting being married to someone who can do a talent," the friend is saying. My wife smiles knowingly. You see my daughters as kindergartners bringing other kids home and begging me to show little Jason and Jennifer and Emma how I can whistle and hum at the same time. "Do 'Stars and Stripes Forever,' Daddy," they say. "Then do 'Buckle Down, Winsocki.' " I do both. Even little Jason looks impressed. "Jesus," he says. "I thought I'd seen everything."

That's not the way it has been at all. When my daughters were kindergartners, they never asked me to whistle and hum at the same time for their friends. Little Jason, I know for a fact, still hasn't seen everything, even though he's now sixteen years old. Now that my daughters are teenagers themselves, their response to a bit of spontaneous whistle/humming in a restaurant or an elevator tends to begin with "Daddy, please."

I don't know what my wife and her friends say to each other at lunch, but I have to consider the possibility that my wife rolls her eyes up toward the back of her head as her friend asks, "How's the old spoon player these days?" All this reminds me of what used to be said about the kid in my fourth-grade class who couldn't seem to catch on to math: "He doesn't get much encouragement at home."

Not that I expect special treatment. I'm not just being modest when I say that I think many people have similar talents, even if they don't always demonstrate them. I've always thought that of world leaders, even though a lot of them act as if they might have had too much encouragement at home. When I used to see pictures of General de Gaulle, I'd always think, "I bet that man can play 'Lady of Spain' on his head with a spoon. He may not want to, but he has the capacity." I believe that if you gave Helmut Kohl an ordinary pocket comb and some waxed paper, he could turn out a credible rendition of "Pop Goes the Weasel." I've always thought that Margaret Thatcher must be able to throw a lighted cigarette in the air and catch it in her mouth. I sometimes think that we would have been better off, and she would have been better off, if she had just gone ahead and done it.

Actually, I don't do my own talent in public anymore. Here's what happened: I was in Milwaukee on a book tour. Some people who had read about my talent came in the store and said that they had a man with them who could also whistle and hum at the same time. They suggested that the two of us might like to do a quartet. He was the chairman of the neurology department at the local medical school, although I don't think that had any connection to his talent. The talent I do is not deeply neurological. It's more like a God-given talent. At any rate, it turned out that this man could not simply hum and whistle at the same time. He could hum one tune while he whistled another tune. He could, to be specific, whistle "Goodnight, Irene" while humming "I'm in the Mood for Love." Well, right then, I packed it in.

But I still daydream about doing my talent. Sometimes, I imagine that Ted Mack's *Original Amateur Hour* has been brought back to network television. I'm on the first show. I've whistled and hummed "Stars and Stripes Forever." They call for an encore. I'm ready.

1990

People in Charge

In all of the theories about why so many people have attacks of wackiness when they reach middle age—resign from the bank to go live in a van with a teenage mushroom-gatherer, and that sort of thing—one factor has been neglected: When someone reaches middle age, people he knows begin to get put in charge of things, and knowing what he knows about the people who are being put in charge of things scares the hell out of him. If he's one of the people put in charge of things himself, it may scare him all the more. In his heart of hearts, he knows how he made it through English 137, and he suspects others may know. He's right. I know. I'm not in charge of anything, but I'm scared anyway. I know some of these people.

The neglect of the old-acquaintance factor has meant that some manifestations of middle-age behavior are misunderstood. For instance, there came a time when I seemed to lose interest in reading the morning paper. "He's at that age," the United Parcel Service deliveryman explained to my wife. "His hormones are starting to act up on him." Wrong. My hormones are just fine, thank you. Look to your own hormones, United Parcel Service deliveryman. "He's depressed because he sees himself slipping," another lay analyst said, after observing me while he was in the house to unstop a clogged drain. "I've seen it on a lot of jobs lately. He knows he's starting to throw a step behind the runner."

Wrong again. That is not why I quit reading the morning paper. I quit because I was starting to come across the names of people I knew, and it was scaring the hell out of me. Sure, I had borne up under it stoically for a while. I didn't say anything when I read that the trustee chosen to preside over some important estate was a childhood neighbor of mine who had regularly cheated his little sister at Old Maid. People change. Maybe selling answers to the ninth grade algebra test—answers, I happen to know, that were worked out by the weird but brilliant Norton Gonsheimer on a promise (never kept) of 40 percent of the action—does not indicate a deep, immutable streak of dishonesty. Who was I to interfere? I remained calm when I read that the new chief of surgery at a fancy hospital uptown was someone who, I happen to know, was held back in the third grade for klutziness. I certainly didn't say anything when I read that one sector of the U.S. Army's missile-alert force was under the command of someone I knew in college as Dipso Dick Donnigan. What the Russians don't know, I figured, won't hurt them.

When I read that Dalt Durfee had been sent over to work out our trade difficulties with the Japanese, I said a little something. I said, "Dalt Durfee! That pea-brain! Jesus Christ Almighty!" Or words to that effect. I might have said more, I'll admit, if my wife hadn't shot me an odd look and told me I was frightening the children. The reason that the news about Dalt Durfee pushed me over the edge was that I finally realized what was happening. When people around the country read in the morning paper that L. Dalton Durfee, Deputy Undersecretary of State for Asian Economic Affairs, was going to sort things out with the Japanese, they felt reassured that somebody as important as a deputy undersecretary was looking into the matter, and they continued breakfast secure in the expectation that they'd soon be able to buy something that was actually made in America besides hairspray and trash bags. I realized, though, that the person walking around in the role of Deputy Undersecretary of State was, in fact, Dalt Durfee, the fourth-dumbest guy in my college class—someone whose most penetrating display of intellectual curiosity had been when he asked a professor of geology whether A.M. means morning or afternoon. I realized that the Japanese would have California before the year was out. Worse than that, I finally realized that every deputy undersecretary was known way back when by someone like me. At that point I gave up reading the morning paper.

Why, then, did the symptoms persist? Why did I continue in a funk that inspired the postman to explain to my wife that many men grow listless at a certain age because their thoughts start to dwell morbidly on the future of their prostates? The symptoms persisted because I realized that the people I knew back when were not simply in the newspaper; they were in the Yellow Pages. When I was staring out the window and the postman thought I was thinking of prostates, I was actually thinking of all the people listed in the Yellow Pages under Attorneys. I know some of those people. It scares me.

In Toledo, the listing includes Ralph W. Moshler, Esq. It's really Blinko Moshler, the dumbest guy in my class—a man who could stand in the intellectual shadow cast by Dalt Durfee and never see the sun. When Durfee asked the professor of geology whether A.M. meant morning or afternoon, Blinko, who was pushy as well as dumb, waved his hand and shouted "Afternoon! It means afternoon!" How, you ask, did someone as dumb as Blinko Moshler get through law school? If law school is hard to get through, I answer, how come there are so many lawyers?

Blinko is with a respectable firm. People who don't know any better think he's a lawyer named Ralph W. Moshler, Esq. I worry about that. Sometimes, when I'm waiting to fall asleep at night, I imagine a decent, hardworking young man from a very small town in Ohio who goes to Toledo to get factory work. He lives quietly in a boardinghouse. He's saving his money so he can go back to his little town and open a Burger King franchise. One day, his landlady is brutally murdered. Circumstantial evidence points to the young boarder, although he is, of course, completely innocent. He has no money for a lawyer. The judge says, "I have appointed an attorney to represent you—a prominent member of the bar named Ralph W. Moshler."

"Stop!" I shout. "It's not a lawyer! It's Blinko! He's a mushhead! It's Blinko!"

My wife shakes me awake. "You were talking in your sleep again," she says. "You must be getting to that age."

1983

Cow Town

I think I've reached a détente with the boosters in Kansas City, my hometown. The trouble started some years ago, when the boosters were possessed for a while by the notion that Kansas City was not a cow town but "the glamour city of the seventies." I'm certain that the boosters—I took to calling them the glamour gang—loved Kansas City in their own way, but sometimes it seemed that they mainly just hated cows.

I appointed myself the protector of all that is bovine. I was lobbing in my opinions from New York, of course—like a Free French officer, as I saw it, engaged in the issues of his homeland while living in London during the occupation. I jeered at whatever evidence was presented to demonstrate that Kansas City—"a cow town no longer," they kept saying—was sophisticated and up-to-date. When the glamour gang boasted about Kansas City's new quarter-of-a-billion-dollar "international airport" that had been built somewhere in the direction of Nebraska—the city council's policy on accumulation of noncontiguous land having been inherited intact from the British Colonial Office of

1843—I pointed out that no flights took off from said international airport and landed in another country. Yes, things got ugly.

We had a strong disagreement over the city's motto. When I was a boy, Kansas City was known as "Gateway to the West" or "The Heart of America." Then St. Louis built a "gateway arch" 235 miles from the real gateway and starting calling itself "Gateway to the West." That left "The Heart of America"—which I rather liked but which must have reminded the glamour gang of one of the internal organs of a cow. They decided that the city needed a new motto and the one they got the city to adopt was "More Boulevards than Paris, More Fountains than Rome."

So I wrote somewhere that if we had so many fountains, we could tear one of them down and use the materials to build a statue of Henry Perry, who brought barbecue to Kansas City in the early twenties. As I said, things got ugly.

After a study had shown that the Kansas City economy was indeed based on agriculture, though, the glamour gang recanted its anti–cow town views in front of the Rotary Club, and for a while, Kansas City had as its motto "World Food Capital." I quit jeering. I even started feeling a little forgiving toward St. Louis for having stolen "Gateway to the West." It's understandable that St. Louis would have been sort of desperate for an impressive motto, since it had previously been known as "Mound City." Kansas City people try to get along.

Not many years ago, I spoke at the Chamber of Commerce banquet in Kansas City, and I tried to reach out for some common ground. I said that when I recommended tearing down one of the fountains, that depended on how many more fountains than Rome we had. If we had only one more, I was not in favor of tearing it down. I didn't want to lose the edge. I didn't want to show up in Rome someday and see a sign on the city limits that said PIÙ FONTANI DI KANSAS CITY.

The Chamber people seemed to accept that. I think we're okay now.

1997

My Tuxedo

I am often mistaken for the sort of person who does not own a tuxedo. Once or twice, I regret to say, this mistake has been made even though I happened to be wearing a tuxedo at the time ("My goodness, are they still renting that kind?"). More often, it is part of a general impression. "I don't suppose you own a tuxedo . . . ," people sometimes say to me, the way an English country gentleman might say to the Hasidic scholar he has met on the train, "I don't suppose you own a shooting stick. . . ." The general impression is incorrect. I do own a tuxedo. I have owned a tuxedo for nearly thirty years. The same tuxedo. If you were planning to invite me to an event at which tuxedos are required, rest assured that I would show up properly dressed.

Don't ask me for New Year's Eve. I'm busy. I go to the same party every New Year's Eve, and one reason it gives me great pleasure is that it presents me with an opportunity to wear my tuxedo. I bought the tuxedo in 1954, when I was a thrifty young undergraduate, because I had added up the number of black-tie events I would have to attend during college, divided the cost of a tuxedo by that number, and concluded that I would be better off buying a tuxedo than renting one. As you must have gathered, this was a fancy college. I am often mistaken for the sort of person who did not attend a fancy college, but that's another story.

As it turned out, there have been a number of occasions to wear the tuxedo since graduation—that possibility hadn't even figured in my tuxedo management scheme in 1954—and every time I wear it, the cost per wearing decreases. This New Year's Eve, for instance, wearing my tuxedo is going to cost me only about forty-eight cents. Try renting a tuxedo for forty-eight cents these days. Knowing that my tuxedo becomes cheaper every time I wear it may influence me in the direction of showing up in a tuxedo now and then at events where black-tie is not strictly necessary, like a hog roast or a divorce hearing or a meeting where people are planning the overthrow of the government by force and violence.

"Oh, you shouldn't have bothered," the hostess often says, while gazing admiringly at my cummerbund.

"It's nothing, really," I tell her. "A matter of approximately fifty-five cents."

When I tell people about my tuxedo ("Guess how much this tuxedo is costing me tonight. Go ahead—don't be afraid to guess. Just take a guess. How much do you think?"), they often tell me that I should be proud of being able to fit into something I bought in college. True. I would be prouder, though, if I did not have reason to believe that the pants of my tuxedo actually belong to Joe LeBeau. Joe was a college classmate of mine—a rather rotund college classmate of mine, if you must know. I have reason to believe that just before graduation, at a black-tie party for which a large room was converted into a dormitory for a number of out-of-town guests who were wearing nearly identical tuxedos, Joe LeBeau and I came away with each other's pants. That's the sort of thing that can happen at a fancy college.

When somebody who sees me in my tuxedo asks a question that leads to the subject of Joe LeBeau ("Say, are you by any chance wearing somebody else's pants, or what?"), I am often asked why I did not simply exchange his pants for my own once the mistake was discovered. Anybody who asks that never knew Joe LeBeau, for whom the phrase "not vulnerable to reason" was invented. As an example of LeBeauesque conversation, I repeat an exchange between LeBeau and an earnest fellow from down the hall who happened to be taking the same course in modern history:

JOE LEBEAU: The French and Germans were fighting on the same side then.

EARNEST FELLOW: But that's impossible! The French hated the Germans!

JOE LEBEAU: Do you blame them?

I haven't seen Joe LeBeau since graduation—I understand he's a judge in California—but I occasionally run into other classmates who, as graduates of a fancy college, tend to be Wall Street financiers, impatient with those of us who have not just depreciated a factory or written off an airline. "What are you up to?" they always say.

"I am amortizing my tuxedo," I tell them. "I am amortizing the hell out of my tuxedo."

I can see my New Year's Eve now. I am dressing for the evening. I calculate what my tuxedo is going to cost me to wear to the same party one year hence, assuming I wear it occasionally during the intervening months—to a turkey shoot, say, or a bris. Even taking the voluminous pants off the hanger gives me pleasure. I find it a bit awkward putting on Joe LeBeau's pants, of course, but I love to start the new year by thinking of him trying to put on mine.

1983

THE MEDIA—LIBERAL ELITE AND OTHERWISE

"When I was a writer at Time, *I tried to escape from the Religion section by writing 'alleged' in front of any historically questionable religious event—the 'alleged parting of the Red Sea,' say, or 'thirty years after the alleged crucifixion.'"*

Corrections

JANUARY 14—Because of an editing error, an article in Friday's theater section transposed the identifications of two people involved in the production of *Waiting for Bruce,* a farce now in rehearsal at the Rivoli. Ralph W. Murtaugh, Jr., a New York attorney, is one of the play's financial backers. Hilary Murtaugh plays the ingénue. The two Murtaughs are not related. At no time during the rehearsal visited by the reporter did Ralph Murtaugh, Jr., "sashay across the stage."

MARCH 25—Because of some problems in transmission, there were several errors in yesterday's account of a symposium held by the Women's Civic Forum of Rye on the role played by slovenliness in cases of domestic violence. The moderator of the symposium, Laura Murtaugh, should not have been identified as "an unmarried mother of eight." Mrs. Murtaugh, the president of the board of directors of the Women's Civic Forum, is married to Ralph W. Murtaugh, Jr., an attorney who practices in Manhattan. The phrase "he was raised with the hogs and he lived like a hog" was read by Mrs. Murtaugh from the trial testimony of an Ohio woman. It did not refer to Mrs. Murtaugh's own husband. Mr. Murtaugh was raised in New York.

APRIL 4—An article in yesterday's edition on the growing contention between lawyers and their clients should not have used an anonymous quotation referring to the firm of Newton, Murtaugh & Clayton as "ambulance-chasing jackals" without offering the firm an opportunity to reply. Also, the number of hours customarily billed by Newton, Murtaugh partners was shown incorrectly on a chart accompanying the article. According to a spokesman for the firm, the partner who said he bills clients for "thirty-five or forty hours on a good day" was speaking ironically. There are only twenty-four hours in a day. The same article was in error as to the first name and the background of one of the firm's senior partners. The correct name is Ralph W. Murtaugh, Jr. There is no one named Hilary Murtaugh connected with the firm. Ralph W. Murtaugh, Jr., has at no time played an ingénue on Broadway.

APRIL 29—Because of a computer error, the early editions on Wednesday misidentified the person arrested for a series of armed robberies of kitchen-supply stores on the West Side of Manhattan. The person arrested under suspicion of being the so-called "pesto bandit" was Raymond Cullom, twenty-two, of Queens. Ralph W. Murtaugh III, nineteen, of Rye, should have been identified as the runner-up in the annual Squash for Kids charity squash tournament, in Rye, rather than as the alleged robber.

MAY 18—Because of an error in transmission, a four-bedroom brick colonial house on Weeping Bend Lane, in Rye, owned by Mr. and Mrs. Ralph W. Murtaugh, Jr., was incorrectly listed in Sunday's real-estate section as being on the market for $17,500. The house is not for sale. Also, contrary to the information in the listing, it does not have flocked wallpaper or a round bed.

JUNE 21—In Sunday's edition, the account of a wedding that took place the previous day at St. John's Church in Rye was incorrect in a number of respects. The cause of the errors was the participation of the reporter in the reception. This is in itself against the policy of this newspaper, and should not have occurred. Jane Murtaugh was misidentified in two mentions. She was neither the mother of the bride nor the father of the bride. She was the bride. It was she who was wearing a white silk gown trimmed in tulle. The minister was wearing conventional ministerial robes. Miss Murtaugh should not have been identified on second mention as Mrs. Perkins, since she will retain her name and since Mr. Perkins was not, in fact, the groom. The number of bridesmaids was incorrectly reported. There were eight bridesmaids, not thirty-eight. Their dresses were blue, not glued. The bridegroom's name is not Franklin Marshall. His name is Emory Barnswell, and he graduated from Franklin and Marshall College. Mr. Barnswell never attended Emory University, which, in any case, does not offer a degree in furniture stripping. Mr. Barnswell's ancestor was not a signer of the Declaration of Independence, and was not named Hector (Boom-Boom) Bondini. The name of the father of the bride was inadvertently dropped from the article. He is Hilary Murtaugh.

1990

On the Assumption that Al Gore Will Slim Down if He's Intending to Run for President, a Political Reporter Is Assigned to Watch Gore's Waistline

This job means sometimes digging up the dirt
On if a pol has stolen or he's cheating
With some cute waitress from a D.C. bar.
But who knew I'd be tracking what he's eating?

My editor, the clever dog, decided
The way to check that presidential itch is
To follow Gore, especially at meals,
And see if he stays too big for his britches.

Last week, I told my desk that Gore might run,
Though he appeared to be at least full-size.
A waiter at a Georgetown place revealed
Gore's order had included "hold the fries."

But now a source will swear that he was there
When Gore demolished half a cow, then stowed
Away in sixty seconds gobs of pie.
Two pieces. Apple crumble. À la mode.

My major back in school was poly-sci—
Quite valuable, I thought, for this position.
I know now, though, for covering Al Gore,
I should have studied diet and nutrition.

2007

Presidential Ups and Downs

Washington Pundits Take Their Analytical Skills to the Ranch

CRAWFORD, TEX., AUG. 20—President George W. Bush's failure to catch a fish after he spent two hours on his heavily stocked bass pond this afternoon was considered a defeat for Mr. Bush by most observers here, and one that would weaken his position in swapping fish stories with Democrats and Republican moderates in Congress. A White House spokesman's comment that the President, being a serious conservationist, had "done catch-and-release one better" may have only worsened matters, since most of the press corps dismissed it as a desperate attempt at spin.

CRAWFORD, TEX., AUG. 21—The President scored a solid victory today by working on the clearing of his nature trail for an hour and a half without injuring himself.

CRAWFORD, TEX., AUG. 22—Eating scrambled eggs this morning for breakfast was seen as a victory for the President, who had been having his eggs sunny-side up for more than a week. The President prefers his eggs scrambled. White House officials have been unwilling to discuss the reasoning behind the apparently contradictory sunny-side-up policy. However, they are not directly denying a story that the Crawford ranch's cook, Rosa Gonzales, had refused to serve scrambled eggs ever since the President, in an effort to compliment her, tried to pronounce the dish in Spanish—*huevos revueltos*—and came out with something that Ms. Gonzales understood as "very revolting." It is not clear how the situation was resolved in a manner that permitted a return to scrambled eggs this morning, but White House officials did little to hide their jubilation.

CRAWFORD, TEX., AUG. 23—White House spokesmen refused to elaborate on a terse announcement this morning that a two-year-old Hereford steer on the Bush ranch had stepped into a gopher hole and broken its leg—a defeat for the President.

CRAWFORD, TEX., AUG. 24—Even George W. Bush's harshest critics are acknowledging today that the weather has given the President an important victory. "The entire country has been suffering from a heat wave," said a member of the White House staff who has been at the President's ranch for three weeks, "but there can't be any place quite as miserable as this." Daniel Jonas, a Democratic pollster who specializes in issues of empathy, said, "Let's face it: This is a big one for Bush."

CRAWFORD, TEX., AUG. 25—George W. Bush was served *huevos rancheros* for breakfast today—a serious defeat for the President, who does not like highly spiced food.

CRAWFORD, TEX., AUG. 26—Republicans both here and in Washington were glowing today after George W. Bush apparently scored a big victory by losing at golf. "He's just a regular guy with a bad slice," one party loyalist said. "He knows loss. He understands loss." The low scorer in the foursome, a wealthy oilman from Lubbock, won ten dollars from each of the other players. Late this afternoon, Democrats were saying that the episode might prove to be a defeat for Mr. Bush now that it is known that longtime family friends of the President's parents came forward on the eighteenth green to cover his losses.

CRAWFORD, TEX., AUG. 27—President Bush scored his biggest victory of the week this morning when Rosa Gonzales, his cook, posed, smiling, for a picture with him in the kitchen of the Crawford ranch. Although Ms. Gonzales has not been made available for interviews, the White House has formally denied that she ever referred to the President as "*la boquita de un gringo puro*"—roughly, "little gringo mouth." In response to reporters' questions at the photo opportunity, the President explained his views on how best to prepare eggs by saying that he is a uniter, not a divider. H. Cole Knudnik, an expert on presidential diet at the Brookings Institute, said, "The President was overdue for a clear-cut victory on this one, and he got it."

2001

"Whatta We Got for the Folks This Week?"

The office of Pete Smithers, a senior editor whose responsibilities include the Lifestyles section. Among the magazine's writers, it is assumed that Smithers's only conceivable qualification for high office is his unique ability to lean back from his desk at a terrifyingly drastic angle—his legs absolutely straight, his heels hooked precariously on the edge of his desk, and his Bass Weejuns spread at the toes to form a perfect V-shaped frame through which he can regard the writer standing before him, like a man sighting very carefully through a large gunsight.

The writer whose duty at the Lifestyles story conference is to serve up potential stories for Smithers's approval is Fred Becker, a "floater" who moves from section to section, depending on which regular writer is away—and who feels himself in imminent danger of being switched suddenly to the Medicine section, where the regular writer often finds that the symptoms of the disease he writes about cause him to feel too ill to continue.

For the half-dozen people seated in Pete Smithers's office, waiting for the Lifestyles story conference to begin, the bottoms of Smithers's shoes were the only part of him visible, although a clipboard he was holding on his lap occasionally bobbed into view. Fred Becker noticed that Smithers's Bass Weejuns were either new or resoled. Smithers's voice seemed to emerge from somewhere below the desk: "All right, Fred, whatta we got for the folks this week?"

Becker looked over his clipboard—a signal for the others at the meeting to adjust their own clipboards, ready to list the stories Smithers accepted. Sitting with Becker in Smithers's office were Carol Goodenow, the Lifestyles researcher; Keith Johnson, a quiet man from the wire desk; two photo researchers (for reasons unknown to Becker, photo researchers, like FBI men and nuns, traveled in pairs); and Genine McIntyre, Smithers's secretary, a lavishly dressed and carefully made-up young woman known around the office as La Contessa.

"Well, we've got the one from California about people drowning in hot tubs," Becker said.

"Is that a trend?" the voice from behind Smithers's desk said.

"I don't know if you can call it a trend, exactly, Pete," Becker said. "It's not really at the point of being the thing to do in California, or anything like that. More of a phenomenon than a trend. I guess people just get all relaxed in there, and smoke a little something, and chant their mantras, and get in touch with their bodies, or maybe lose touch with their bodies—and they sort of slip beneath the waves."

"Didn't we already do drowning in hot tubs?" Smithers said. "Genine?"

"Scalding in hot tubs," Genine said. "We did a sixty-liner on scalding in hot tubs last year. Some of the people who were scalded did drown, but it was a scalding piece, really, not a drowning piece."

"I thought I remembered a piece we did on drowning in hot tubs," Smithers said.

Becker shrugged. It did seem as if everything to be written about hot tubs had already appeared in the Lifestyles section. He himself had done one story on new hot-tub designs and another story on a study showing that the subject most discussed by people sitting in hot tubs in Marin County, California, without any clothes on was real estate.

"Drowning in water beds," Genine said. "Scalding in hot tubs."

"Put it on the list," Smithers said.

Everyone in the room listed the hot-tubs piece on his or her clipboard. The two photo researchers compared clipboards to make certain they had the same wording. "What else we got, Fred?" Smithers said.

"Well, there's this two-thirds stocking story, also from California."

"Tell me more about that one," Smithers said. "Does that mean they're wearing two-thirds of a stocking? Which two-thirds? What's the point, anyway?"

"Well, I don't know too much about it," Becker said. He was actually hoping that Smithers would decide to drop the two-thirds stocking story. He didn't like doing fashion stories. What he really wanted to say was that it might make sense to wait until Trish Webster, who was sometimes detached from the Show Business section to do fashion pieces for Lifestyles, happened to be available. He knew, though, that suggesting a woman writer for a women's fashion story would upset Carol Goodenow, who was the chairperson of the magazine's women employees committee. When Carol was upset, she often started to cry. That upset her even more, given her belief that women were no more likely to burst into tears than men were, so once she started crying there was almost no stopping her. Becker liked Carol Goodenow, and he tried to avoid doing anything that might upset her. "As I understand it," he went on, "it's not really about wearing two-thirds of a stocking. I don't think. It's more like two-thirds' length. Two-thirds of the way up the leg. Or maybe two-thirds of the way toward the knee."

"Two-thirds stockings! Jesus!" came Smithers's voice from behind and below the desk.

"I guess it really doesn't sound all that interesting," Becker said. He glanced over at Carol Goodenow. He thought he had seen her lower lip start to quiver, but he might have been imagining it. "I mean, I guess we're about due for a stocking story," he went on, trying to make certain Carol didn't think that he was sounding negative simply because the story had to do with women's fashions. "I'm just not sure that this is it."

"Let's scratch it," Smithers said.

Marks were made on clipboards. Nobody said anything for a moment or two. Smithers's desk chair creaked. La Contessa adjusted one of her eyelashes. Keith Johnson, the wire-desk man, looked as if he might fall asleep.

"Then there's this thirty-liner on obscene topiary that was written last week but didn't run," Becker said.

There was another short period of silence. Finally, the voice from behind the desk said, "Obscene topiary?" Smithers, who had scheduled and edited the story the previous week, had apparently forgotten what it was about.

"Dirty bushes," Becker said, working on the theory that the simplest explanation was always best for Smithers.

"In the bushes?"

"No, dirty bushes—bushes made into statues with, well, sexual overtones." Becker looked to see if his careful choice of words had succeeded in refreshing Smithers's memory without embarrassing Carol Goodenow, who was made uncomfortable by talk of sex in public. Carol was blushing slightly.

"Didn't we do dirty bushes?" Smithers said. "Genine?"

"Last week we did dirty bushes, but it didn't run," Genine said. "A thirty-liner. Spaced out by that piece on grown-ups chewing bubble gum."

"Put it on the list," Smithers's voice said.

"Then Cravens, in Indianapolis, suggests a story on this little town in central Indiana that's supposed to be the sex-change capital of the world," Becker said.

"Jesus!" Smithers said. "Dirty bushes. Sex changes. This is getting to be the goddamn Porno section. Isn't that a Medicine story?"

"Well, Cravens slugged it Lifestyles. He thinks the real story is that this little town that used to be a limestone quarrying town was down on its luck because not many buildings made out of limestone are being built these days. And then this doctor there started doing a lot of sex-change operations and it became a sort of cottage industry—renting out rooms for people to live in while they're waiting for their breasts to grow, that sort of thing. Kind of put the town on the map again. Now, apparently, other things are happening with their economic development committee, although I notice Cravens doesn't say exactly what."

"Jesus!" Smithers said again.

"I hear Medicine's going to be all taken up this week with this big wrap-up on the pancreas they're doing," Becker said, beginning to wonder, despite himself, precisely where the pancreas was. "So maybe we can grab this one."

Smithers mumbled something that sounded as if it might have been "goddamned queers," but it was hard to be certain. Carol

Goodenow, her embarrassment over the subject temporarily put aside, leaned forward, apparently at the ready to take down any addition Smithers might provide to a list she kept of remarks he had made that were offensive to one group or another. It was a long list. Many of the remarks sounded rather dated. When stories about homosexuals came up in Lifestyles story conferences, Smithers was likely to become visibly red in the face—visibly, that is, if someone happened to be standing directly in front of his desk, and was thus able to peer down at him through the other end of the gun sight—and mutter something like "pansies" or "goddamned fairies." At a story conference for Show Business, another section Smithers presided over, a proposed story about a gay production of *Romeo and Juliet*—with Romeo as a bartender in a leather bar and Jules as a swish interior decorator—had brought Smithers forward in his desk chair with a crack so sharp that most of those at the conference dropped their clipboards. "The queers are everywhere!" he had shouted, as he arrived abruptly at a more conventional posture—sitting upright behind his desk, as Bob Bingham, the Show Business writer, later put it, "like a normal human being."

"Apparently, he isn't very good at it—the doctor," Becker went on. "From what Cravens says, it sounds like people are always drifting into Indianapolis for repairs. I don't know exactly what the problems are. Cravens says something about 'things not attached as well as they might be.' " As he outlined the story to Smithers, Becker began to think that writing it might be only marginally preferable to dealing in detail with the pancreas. "We could get into legal problems, I guess, mentioning that sort of thing," he added.

Keith Johnson, who had never spoken a word in a story conference, as far as Becker could remember, suddenly blurted out, "I guess that's why they wear their pants tucked inside their boots out that way," and started to cackle. Great grunts of laughter came from behind Smithers's desk. The photo researchers began giggling. Carol Goodenow had turned scarlet. Becker was afraid she might simply bolt from the office, but she seemed to be keeping her chair by an effort of will.

"Pants tucked in!" Smithers yelped from behind the desk. "Put it on the list. Christ knows whether Woody'll let it in the magazine, but at least I'll be able to spend the week reading what Craven files. Is that all?"

"Well, there's this suggestion about disco banks," Becker said.

"That's a Business story," Smithers said abruptly.

"We did disco banks last March," La Contessa said.

"It's still a Business story," Smithers said. "Jesus! Disco banks! The queers are everywhere."

1980

We Could Have Made a Killing

It's time for me to give up on the scheme to launch a 900 number that would tell you who's dead. The person who actually thought of the scheme was my friend James Edmunds—he introduced what he called the National Deadline to the public in a column that appeared in *The Times of Acadiana,* in Lafayette, Louisiana, about ten years ago—but I was in on the ground floor. I think it's fair to say that this was the only time I was in on the ground floor, which is one reason I'm so distressed at indications that the National Deadline is, well, dead.

A real estate shark I know once said to me, as a way of explaining the relative poverty of his friends in the scribbling trades, "The trouble with writers is that you're labor in a labor-intensive industry." Too true. Writing an article or a book is roughly the equivalent of making a chair—or, even worse, making one chair at a time. In the chair industry, the moneymaker is the guy who presides over the manufacture of chairs, or the guy who sells a chair company short, or the guy who buys a chair company and folds it into the hosiery company he's about to spin off or—and here's the richest of them all—the guy who gets in on the ground floor of a chair-selling scheme. That guy doesn't waste his time sanding.

The National Deadline looked like the sort of enterprise that could transform some humble artisans into entrepreneurs. According to

National Deadline lore, the idea for the project had come to James one evening after he and his wife—Susan Hester, who will often pitch in when a scheme of James's shows signs of being a real gem—finished watching a late movie on television and Susan said, "Is Fredric March dead?" The rest is history—or would have been, if things had worked out a little differently.

From Susan's idle question about Fredric March, it was just one step to the name, a telephone number (1-900-WHO-DEAD), and a method of calibrating what you might call certainty of deceasement. Susan works at the public library in New Iberia, so she and James had a leg up on doing the research. It was around that time that I came on board as sort of an informal consultant. Without wanting to claim too much credit for shaping the National Deadline in those early days, I should point out for the record that, on one end of the calibration spectrum, I suggested replacing the phrase "He could be dead, maybe" with the phrase "If he's not dead, he sure is quiet," and, on the other end, I counseled against the terms "extremely dead" and "dead as a doornail." If that isn't being in on the ground floor, I don't know what is.

James and Susan and I talked about the National Deadline for a number of years; you might say that we were tweaking it here and there to make sure that there were no kinks in the operation. Yes, I suppose you could also say that we got so caught up in the fine-tuning that we never got around to the start-up. Writers tend to be better at tweaking than at entrepreneurial pursuits. I suppose we should have been talking about capitalization and stock options and what model private jets we were going to buy.

A month or so ago, James sent me an email that said, "Do you know about this: dpsinfo.com? Dead People Server. Pretty much what the National Deadline was meant to be." A website! We had fallen so far behind that we were no longer even working in the right medium. When I got on to Dead People Server, just about the first thing I saw was a description of how it solved those nagging questions about whether someone who played in an old movie was still alive. I went to the alphabetical listing. Fredric March was there. He died April 4, 1975. Yes, poor Fredric March is in his grave, and the people who provide information of that sort on the Internet are probably receiving so many hits that they're about ready to sell out to Amazon.com,

Inc., for four or five hundred million dollars. Meanwhile, James and I are still sanding.

1999

RSVP

My curiosity about the new *Vanity Fair* has been dominated by one question: Why wasn't I asked to subscribe? Plenty of people were. I happen to know that one J. E. Corr, Jr., who describes himself as the publisher of *Vanity Fair,* sent letters to any number of people informing them by name ("Dear Mr. Upscale") that his magazine wasn't meant for everyone but for "only a handful of bright, literate people." I'm not saying I look forward to a scene a year or so from now in which some high-powered ad-agency man asks J. E. Corr, Jr., about his circulation and Corr, Jr., says, "Oh, well, about a handful." That would be sour grapes. I will say that it's not a lot of fun being among those for whom a new magazine "that captures the sparkle and excitement of our times, our culture" was not meant.

This has happened to me before. A few years ago, a friend of mine phoned and asked, "What are you doing about Robert L. Schwartz's letter on subscribing to *The Newsletter of the Tarrytown Group*?"

"What letter?" I said.

"You know," he said. "The one that says, 'You are cordially invited to join a special, special group of people—the "Creative Minority," as Toynbee called it—who are stimulated, not threatened, by the changes, upheavals, and discontinuities of modern society. It's a group of people who won't settle for the hollow victory of material success—an idealistic, holistic group that seeks totally new perspectives and concepts to bring about a totally new world for everyone.' "

"Well," I said. "Of course the way the mails are these days, you can't—"

"Oh," he said. "Oh, sorry."

"Maybe Schwartz knew how I feel about people who refer to anything but holes as holistic," I said. I shouldn't have said that. It sounded like sour grapes. Also, I don't mean to give the impression that I can't rejoice with my friends when they are among the chosen. I was delighted, for instance, when a woman I know named Millicent Osborn—a woman who lives in one of those rather grand old Park Avenue apartment buildings that must strike people like J. E. Corr, Jr., as the sort of place where the elevator chatter is particularly bright and literate—received an exceedingly complimentary letter from John Fairchild, whose company publishes *Women's Wear Daily* and *W.* Fairchild thought Mrs. Osborn might like to subscribe to *W.* "Our compliments, Mrs. Osborn!" he wrote. "For being one of the best-dressed people in New York! For turning 954 Park Avenue into a home that sizzles with decorating excitement! For giving parties that are the talk of the whole state of New York! For getting the fun out of the fashionable living you do!" Fairchild laying it on makes J. E. Corr, Jr., sound practically curt.

I have always liked to think that Fairchild's letter made Millicent Osborn's day. I realize that there are residents of 954 Park Avenue who would not be particularly gratified to hear that their parties are being talked about in places like Buffalo and Elmira, but Millicent Osborn has never suffered from that sort of insularity. I like to think that she picked up Fairchild's letter in the lobby as she was leaving for the supermarket—at a time in her daily routine when she was not feeling her absolutely most stupefyingly glamorous. She opens the letter. John Fairchild is calling her one of the best-dressed people in New York.

"Oh, it's just a simple little shift I've had for years," she says, causing the doorman to tip his hat. "Do you really like it?"

Then she scurries around to make sure that 954 Park Avenue sizzles with decorating excitement. "The grocery delivery boy told me that the Pearces in 12-D still have that dreadful tapestry of a stag at bay," she tells her husband. "Maybe you could have a word with them."

I also do not want to leave the impression that I have never been selected myself. Just two or three years ago, I got a friendly letter from a Nancy L. Halbert informing me that "the family name Trillin has an exclusive and particularly beautiful Coat of Arms." That was a nice surprise. My grandfather grew up in one of those European towns that used to change countries every week or ten days, and the only claim to distinction I ever heard him make was that he had deserted two separate armies. My Uncle Benny managed to make it from the Ukraine to Missouri early in the century, but I hadn't thought of his passage as the stuff coats of arms are made of. At a family gathering when he was eighty-eight, I happened to remark that I was planning to write something about him in a magazine, and his son said, "Don't mention his name. The Russian army's still looking for him."

I couldn't help but wonder whether these facts were known to the special artist who had, according to Nancy Halbert, already researched and re-created the Trillin Coat of Arms "exactly as the heralds of medieval times did it for the knights and noblemen." I didn't send her $19.95 to find out; I was afraid John Fairchild might not agree with Miss Halbert that a coat of arms adds "warmth and refinement" to any living room, and I was beginning to get the feeling that the decisions I made in these matters were not escaping the notice of John Fairchild and other people whose correspondence I valued. I often imagined a few of the letter writers meeting over martinis and mailing lists to discuss my case. "What about Trillin?" I could imagine J. E. Corr, Jr., of *Vanity Fair* saying.

"Trillin who?" says Robert Schwartz of *The Newsletter of the Tarrytown Group*.

"His family's got an awfully nice coat of arms," Nancy Halbert says. Good old Nancy Halbert. No sour grapes for her just because someone had been forced, through no fault of his own, to stick her with an exclusive coat of arms her special heraldic artists had already researched and re-created. "It's got a lovely border," she continues, "with a bribed immigration officer looking away from it. The center section has crossed steerage tickets rampant on a field of greenhorns."

"Holistically," Schwartz says, "I think he might not interface creatively with your concepts. Also, he's a smart aleck."

"His home doesn't sizzle in the least," John Fairchild says. "I can't imagine who advised him to hang that American Hereford Association poster in the front hall."

The room is silent. "I guess we'll give him a skip," Corr, Jr., finally says. "After all, we're only looking for a handful."

1983

Unpublished Letters to the Ethicist

I was brought up in a Jewish home, but I haven't been observant in years. Last summer, in a rash moment, I said publicly that if Martha Stewart got indicted, I would go back to the synagogue. Now that such an indictment seems likely, I am in a quandary. My older daughter believes that if Ms. Stewart goes to prison my obligations will include attending services regularly, maintaining a kosher home, and refraining from operating a motor vehicle on Shemini Atzereth. My younger daughter thinks that I might at least be able to get a waiver on that business about changing dishes for Passover. I want to keep my word, but I'm wondering whether a Friday-night service or two would do the trick.

C.T., New York City

My husband, who is an antiabortion activist, sincerely believes that life begins at conception. Recently, he learned that he was conceived while his parents were on vacation in Jamaica, and he has come to the conclusion that he is therefore a Jamaican and is in this country illegally. He is now talking about turning himself in and having himself deported. Am I married to a man of principle or a cuckoo bird?

D.F., Tupelo, Miss.

I am an advisor to the President of a very powerful country. In order to divert attention from the economy, which happens to stink, I've advised him to talk about virtually nothing but war against Iraq between now and November, when our country is holding an important election. If the economy still stinks after a war with Iraq, and I advise the President to talk about virtually nothing but war with North Korea until the next election, would I be "playing politics"?

K.R., Washington, D.C.

I am an entrepreneur whose business seriously needs the sort of intervention with the Customs Service only a high-ranking federal officeholder can provide. When I read about the gifts accepted by Senator Torricelli, I bought a home-entertainment center, intending to give it to him at an appropriate time. Now he has dropped out of the race. Would it still be ethical to deduct the home-entertainment center from my taxes? The picture on the television is excellent.

W.S., Short Hills, N.J.

For six years, I was the CEO of a large conglomerate. Then, in 2000, there was a precipitous drop in the company's stock. Fortunately, by complete coincidence, I had sold eighty-seven million dollars' worth of shares the week before. For the final three years of my tenure, I had a compensation package that included one of those Jack Welch riders—I was entitled to any perk that Jack got from General Electric. Now I find that Jack was getting free Yankees tickets and I wasn't. I'm planning to sue my old company for the cost of the tickets, although given the company's current financial situation—it's in Chapter 11—I might get only ten or fifteen cents on the dollar. My wife says that some people might consider the suit unseemly, with so many employees having lost their retirement money and all. But don't you think that fair's fair? The thought of Jack sitting in that box in Yankee Stadium just burns my ass.

B.P., Naples, Fla.

We are advisors to the president of a very powerful country, and we are prominent in a group of so-called hawks urging him to wage war on Iraq. Like every other member of the group, we evaded the war in Vietnam. Some people see an ethical problem in this; they refer to us as chicken hawks. But we figure that if we had gone to Vietnam we could have been killed, and then who would be here to urge the President to wage war on Iraq?

D.C., R.P., P.W., Washington, D.C.

2002

Show and Tell-all

There was a time when I responded to any new memoir about *The New Yorker* the way everyone else on the staff did: I went to a bookstore and, without buying the book, looked in the index for my name. This was before publishers realized that the way to sell more of this sort of book was not to include an index. Finding your name in the index, I should say, was not a cause for joy. Management had neglected to mention in its standard employment agreement that absolutely anything said to anyone connected to the magazine was on the record, so if, in a moment of weakness, you had unburdened yourself to a colleague about an old and completely uncharacteristic shoplifting incident or a marginally kinky sexual predilection or a devastating physical description of the editor who handled your copy, you had to hope that the colleague in question would acquire a crippling case of writer's block before it came time for him to record everything he could recall about life at *The New Yorker.*

Even if your name in the index turned out to be unconnected to an indictable offense, it usually meant that in the author's memory you had said something stupid or embarrassing and he had come back with a wickedly apt rejoinder. When I read about myself in those books, I usually thought I hadn't said exactly what I'd been quoted as saying, but I could never remember the conversation well enough to be sure. I don't know how all of these memoirists held on to such precise memories of casual water-fountain conversations that took place in 1965 or 1973. I'll admit that in those days I never thought of patting them down for wires.

For many years, I didn't give any thought to writing my own book about *The New Yorker.* I couldn't remember many truly mortifying things people had said to me or many clever things I had said back.

Whenever my wife read a *New Yorker* memoir, she'd ask if it was possible that I had actually never uttered a wickedly apt rejoinder.

"I wouldn't say 'never,' " I told her at one point. "When we had that go-around about having a dental plan, someone who thought writers shouldn't concern themselves with such petit bourgeois matters said to me, 'Dostoyevsky didn't have a dental plan,' and I said, 'Yeah, and did you ever get a load of his teeth?' "

"Can you remember any that didn't have to do with the dental plan?" she asked.

"Not offhand," I said. "But it doesn't make any difference, because I don't want to write a book about *The New Yorker* anyway."

Lately, though, I've been getting a little edgy about that policy. It's now clear that I could eventually find myself in the position of being the only person with any connection to the magazine who hasn't discussed his *New Yorker* experience in excruciating detail between hard covers. It has occurred to me that there could come a day, many years from now, when my grandchildren, lacking documentary evidence issued under the imprimatur of a major publisher, refuse to believe that I ever worked for *The New Yorker* at all.

I see us all on the porch of our summerhouse in Nova Scotia. My wife and I, ancient but still quite alert in the middle of the day, are rocking to the best of our capacity in our rocking chairs and these so-far-hypothetical grandchildren are sprawled in hammocks and deck chairs and cushions around us. My wife is saying, "When Gramps was writing those pieces around the country every three weeks for *The New Yorker,* and your mothers were just tiny little . . ."

"Gidoudahere," little Siobhan says. "Gramps never wrote for *The New Yorker.*"

I start to smile, in a way that I think combines fond forbearance of Siobhan's mistake coupled with appropriate modesty, but then I hear the voice of little Deirdre (in this fantasy, for reasons I can't imagine, all of my grandchildren have been given Irish names that I've always had difficulty pronouncing). "My friend Jason's grandfather worked at *The New Yorker,*" little Deirdre says. "He wrote a book all about it." She tells us Jason's grandfather's name, as if intoning the name of some rock star she'd been fortunate to catch a glimpse of in a restaurant.

"To paraphrase what A. J. Liebling once wrote of Hamlin Garland," I say, "Jason's grandfather couldn't write for free seeds."

"Did you know A. J. Liebling, Gramps?" little Seamus says.

"Well," I reply.

"Because my friend Timmy's nana said in her *New Yorker* book that she knew A. J. Liebling!" little Seamus says.

"In her dreams!" I say, not realizing that I've raised my voice a bit. "In her goddamned dreams!"

My wife shoots me one of those not-in-front-of-the-children looks, and then says, brightly, "Gramps once met J. D. Salinger. Tell us what J. D. Salinger said."

"I can't remember exactly," I say, "but it may have been 'Nice to meet you, Calvin.' "

"Was that in a book?" little Siobhan asks.

"Well, no," I say.

Little Siobhan nods, as if her worst suspicions have been confirmed.

Then I hear the voice of little Moira. Until now, we have had no reason to believe that little Moira is paying any attention to the conversation. She is, after all, only three and a half. But she is definitely addressing a question to me.

"Grampy, did you ever have dinner with Mr. Shawn?" little Moira asks sweetly.

"Well, we did have lunch once," I say. "After I'd been at *The New Yorker* only nineteen years. And I have reason to believe that if he hadn't retired before another nineteen years had passed, it would have been quite possible that—"

"My friend Ethan's *bubbe* used to have dinner with Mr. Shawn all the time," little Moira says. "She wrote a book about it. Do you want to hear some of the things Mr. Shawn said to Ethan's *bubbe*?"

"No, I do not want to hear some of the things Mr. Shawn said to Ethan's *bubbe,*" I say. "I think I'd rather hear Al Gore's rendering of *Finnegans Wake* than hear some of the things Mr. Shawn said to Ethan's *bubbe.*"

"Granny," little Moira says to my wife, "why is Grampy talking in his angry voice? Is he mad at Ethan's *bubbe* because she wrote for *The New Yorker* and he didn't?"

"Wrote!" I shout. "Wrote! Is that what you call what Ethan's *bubbe* was doing, Moira? Wrote!"

"Please don't shout at Moira," my wife says. "At least not until you've learned how to pronounce her name."

Little Moira starts to cry. Little Siobhan is looking at me as if I've just nicked her lunch money. As I look around at my grandchildren, I'm starting to wonder whether or not I could come up with enough wickedly apt rejoinders for a book about my life at *The New Yorker.*

2000

TALES OF A CLEAN-PLATE RANGER

"When helicopters were snatching people from the grounds of the American compound during the panic of the final Vietcong push into Saigon, I was sitting in front of my television set shouting, 'Get the chefs! Get the chefs!' "

Alice

Now that it's fashionable to reveal intimate details of married life, I can state publicly that my wife, Alice, has a weird predilection for limiting our family to three meals a day. I also might as well admit that the most serious threat to our marriage came in 1975, when Alice mentioned my weight just as I was about to sit down to dinner at a restaurant named Chez Helène in New Orleans. Chez Helène is one of my favorite restaurants in New Orleans; we do not have the sort of marriage that could come to grief over ordinary food.

Without wanting to be legalistic, I should mention that Alice brought up the weight issue during a long-distance telephone call—breaking whatever federal regulations there are against Interstate Appetite Impairment. Like many people who travel a lot on business, I'm in the habit of calling home every evening to share the little victories and defeats of the day—the triumph, for instance, of happening upon a superior tamale stand in a town I thought had long before been completely carved into spheres of influence by McDonald's and Burger King, or the misery of being escorted by some local booster past the unmistakable aroma of genuine hickory-wood barbecuing into La Maison de la Casa House, whose notion of "Continental cuisine" seems to have been derived in some arcane way from the Continental Trailways bus company. Having found myself on business in New Orleans—or, as it is sometimes expressed around my office, having found it my business to find business in New Orleans—I was about to settle into Chez Helène for a long evening. First, of course, I telephoned Alice in New York. I assumed it would give her great pleasure to hear that her husband was about to have enough sweet potatoes and fried oysters to make him as happy as he could manage to be outside her presence. Scholars of the art have often mentioned Chez Helène as an example of what happens when Creole blends with Soul—so that a bowl of greens comes out tasting of spices that the average greens-maker in Georgia or Alabama probably associates with papists or the Devil himself.

"I'm about to have dinner at Chez Helène," I said.

"Dr. Seligmann just told me today that you weighed a hundred and eighty pounds when you were in his office last week," Alice said. "That's terrible!"

"There must be something wrong with this connection," I said. "I could swear I just told you that I was about to have dinner at Chez Helène."

"You're going to have to go on a diet. This is serious."

It occurred to me that a man telephoning his wife from a soul-food restaurant could, on the excuse of trying to provide some authentic atmosphere, say something like "Watch yo' mouth, woman!" Instead, I said, "I think there might be a better time to talk about this, Alice." Toward the end of the second or third term of the Caroline Kennedy administration was the sort of time I had in mind.

"Well, we can talk about it when you get home," Alice said. "Have a nice dinner."

I did. It is a measure of my devotion to Alice that I forgave her, even though my second order of fried chicken was ruined by the realization that I had forgotten to tell her I had actually weighed only 166. I always allow fourteen pounds for clothes.

1978

What Happened to Brie and Chablis?

What happened to Brie and Chablis?
Both Brie and Chablis used to be
The sort of thing everyone ate
When goat cheese and Napa Merlot
Weren't purchased by those in the know,
And monkfish was thought of as bait.

And why did authorities ban
From restaurants all coq au vin?
And then disappeared sole meunière,
Then banished, with little ado,
Beef Wellington—Stroganoff, too.
Then canceled the chocolate éclair.

Then hollandaise sauce got the boot,
And kiwis stopped being the fruit
That every chef loved to include.

Like quiches, or coquilles St. Jacques,
They turned into something to mock—
The fruit that all chic chefs eschewed.

You miss, let's say, trout amandine?
Take hope from some menus I've seen:
Fondue has been spotted of late
And—yes, to my near disbelief—
Tartare not from tuna but beef.
They all may return. Just you wait.

2003

Chicken à la King

Americans have a strong vision of the Midwest. It includes mother in the kitchen baking bread or putting up vegetables from the garden. As it happens, my own mother for thirty years served her family nothing but leftovers. I was out of college before I begin to think: leftover from what? We have a team of anthropologists in there now looking for the original meal. But in general, mother in the kitchen baking bread or putting up vegetables from the garden. Fields of wheat and corn and soybeans across the prairie, with great storage silos visible on the horizon. The Kiwanis meeting at a café on Main Street every Wednesday at eleven-thirty for lunch—chicken à la king.

At least it used to be chicken à la king. A few years ago, I realized that chicken à la king had disappeared. This country was once awash in chicken à la king. I used to go to a lot of Kiwanis meetings as a reporter—so many, in fact, that I knew all the words to the Kiwanis song, "Oh I'd Rather Be a Kiwanian than in Any Other Club"—and we always had chicken à la king. In fact, I even made up a verse of the song about it: There's nothing can defeat us / whatever life may bring / cause we can go and eat us / some chicken à la king / oh, I'd rather be a Kiwanian than in any other club.

And it wasn't just a Kiwanis dish. Chicken à la king was a multi-regional, multi-class dish. On the north shore of Long Island, old-money society people used to eat chicken à la king at their parties. I know some of you are wondering how I would know what old-money society people ate at their parties. Well, it happened that I went to Yale at a time when old-money society people were thick on the ground. Most of them had three last names. My roommate was named Thatcher Baxter Hatcher. They never actually used those names, of course; they all had nicknames, like Mutt and Pudge and Chip. My roommate was known as Tush—Tush Hatcher.

And Tush took me along to some coming-out parties at some of those fancy clubs. The food was awful. It was at that time, in fact, that I realized that when it comes to food in clubs in this country, the tastiness of the food is in inverse proportion to the exclusivity of the club. If you're someplace and the hors d'oeuvres come around and it's a piece of Velveeta cheese on a slice of day-old Wonder bread, with the crusts cut off, you're in a fancy joint. I finally figured out the reason that these people serve food that tastes like balsa wood: They associate garlic and spices and schmaltz with just the sort of people they're trying to keep out of the club.

Anyway, very late in the evening at these parties, they'd serve what they called supper—although this was a full eight hours after people at home had had their supper. (In Kansas City, we generally try to get everyone fed before dark.) These snotty-looking waiters would come out bearing great silver bowls, and in the bowls: chicken à la king. Not as tasty as Kiwanis Club chicken à la king, but still chicken à la king.

In fact, according to one theory, that's why some people from that background talk without opening up their mouths, in that marvelous way. The theory is that the glop that chicken à la king floats around in—particularly when it's allowed to react chemically with silver, particularly when the silver has been in the family for five or six generations—causes the teeth to bond together.

Of course, they still talk that way, and chicken à la king has disappeared. I think about that a lot, particularly when I'm back in the Midwest and I'm driving through those fields, with the silos miles away on the horizon, and I think, "What do we really know about what's in those silos?" Maybe a lot of things that seemed to be everywhere and suddenly disappeared are stored in there. Maybe there are silos full of Nehru jackets and silos full of CB radios and silos full of beef Stroganoff. And way out there somewhere, dozens and dozens of silos full of chicken à la king.

1985

Missing Links

Of all the things I've eaten in the Cajun parishes of Louisiana—an array of foodstuffs which has been characterized as somewhere between extensive and deplorable—I yearn most often for boudin. When people in Breaux Bridge or Opelousas or Jeanerette talk about boudin (pronounced "boo-DAN"), they mean a soft, spicy mixture of rice and pork and liver and seasoning, which is squeezed hot into the mouth from a sausage casing, usually in the parking lot of a grocery store and preferably while leaning against a pickup. (*Boudin* means blood sausage to the French, most of whom would probably line up for immigration visas if they ever tasted the Cajun version.) I figure that about 80 percent of the boudin purchased in Louisiana is consumed before the purchaser has left the parking lot, and most of the rest of it is polished off in the car. In other words, Cajun boudin not only doesn't get outside the state; it usually doesn't even get home. For Americans who haven't been to South Louisiana, boudin remains as foreign as *gado-gado* or *cheb;* for them, the word "Cajun" on a menu is simply a synonym for burnt fish or too much pepper. When I am daydreaming of boudin, it sometimes occurs to me that of all the indignities the Acadians of Louisiana have had visited upon them—being booted out of Nova Scotia, being ridiculed as rubes and swamp rats by neighboring Anglophones for a couple of centuries, being punished for speaking their own language in the school yard—nothing has been as deeply insulting as what restaurants outside south Louisiana present as Cajun food.

The scarcity of boudin in the rest of the country makes it all the more pleasurable to have a Louisiana friend who likes to travel and occasionally carries along an ice chest full of local ingredients, just in case. I happen to have such a friend in James Edmunds, of New Iberia, Louisiana. Over the past twenty years or so, James's visits to New York have regularly included the ritualistic unpacking of an ice chest on my kitchen table. His custom has been to bring the ice chest if he plans to cook a meal during the visit—crawfish étouffée, for instance, or gumbo, or his signature shrimp stew. On those trips, the ice chest would also hold some boudin. I was so eager to get my hands on the boudin that I often ate it right in the kitchen, as soon as we heated it through, rather than trying to make the experience more authentic by searching for something appropriate to lean against. In Lower Manhattan, after all, it could take a while to find a pickup truck.

Then there came the day when I was sentenced to what I think of as medium-security cholesterol prison. (Once the cholesterol penal system was concessioned out to the manufacturers of statin drugs, medium-security cholesterol prison came to mean that the inmate could eat the occasional bit of bacon from the plate of a generous luncheon companion but could not order his own BLT.) James stopped bringing boudin, the warders having summarily dismissed my argument that the kind I particularly like—Cajun boudin varies greatly from maker to maker—was mostly just rice anyway.

I did not despair. James is inventive, and he's flexible. Several years ago, he decided that an architect friend of his who lives just outside New Iberia made the best crawfish étouffée in the area, and, like one of those research-and-development hot shots who are always interested in ways of improving the product, he took the trouble to look into the recipe, which had been handed down to the architect by forebears of unadulterated Cajunness. James was prepared for the possibility that one of the secret ingredients of the architect's blissful étouffée was, say, some herb available only at certain times of year in the swamps of the Atchafalaya Basin Spillway. As it turned out, one of the secret ingredients was Campbell's Cream of Mushroom soup. (Although crawfish étouffée, which means smothered crawfish, is one of the best-known Cajun dishes, it emerged only in the fifties, when a lot of people assumed that just about any recipe was enhanced by a can of Campbell's Cream of Mushroom soup.) During ensuing étouffée preparations in New York, there would come a moment when James said, in his soft south Louisiana accent, "I think this might be a good time for certain sensitive people to leave the kitchen for just a little while." Then we'd hear the whine of the can opener, followed by an unmistakable *glub-glub-glub*.

A few years after my sentence was imposed, James and I were talking on the telephone about an imminent New York visit that was to include the preparation of one of his dinner specialties, and he told me not to worry about the problem of items rattling around in his ice chest. I told him that I actually hadn't given that problem much thought, what with global warming and nuclear proliferation and all. As if he hadn't heard me, he went on to say that he'd stopped the rattling with what he called packing boudin.

"Packing boudin?"

"That's right," James said.

I thought about that for a moment or two. "Well, it's got bubble wrap beat," I finally said. "And we wouldn't have to worry about adding to this country's solid-waste-disposal problem. Except for the casing." The habit of tossing aside the casing of a spent link of boudin is so ingrained in some parts of Louisiana that there is a bumper sticker reading CAUTION: DRIVER EATING BOUDIN—a way of warning the cars that follow about the possibility of their windshields being splattered with what appear to be odd-looking insects. From that visit on, I took charge of packing boudin disposal whenever James was carrying his ice chest, and I tried not to dwell on my disappointment when he wasn't.

Not long ago, I got a call from James before a business trip to New York that was not scheduled to include the preparation of a Louisiana meal—that is, a trip that would ordinarily not include boudin. He asked if he could store a turducken in my freezer for a couple of days; he was making a delivery for a friend.

I hesitated. A turducken is made by deboning a chicken and a duck and a turkey, stuffing the chicken with stuffing, stuffing the stuffed chicken into a similarly stuffed duck, and stuffing all of that, along with a third kind of stuffing, into the turkey. The result cannot be criticized for lacking complexity, and it presents a challenge to the holiday carver almost precisely as daunting as meat loaf. Or, I wondered, is the duck stuffed into the chicken rather than the chicken stuffed into the duck? While I was trying to remember that, James apparently took my hesitation as an indication that I was reluctant to take on the storage job. I suppose there are people who would rather not have a turducken in their freezer, on the grounds that it goes against the laws of nature.

"There'd be rental boudin involved, of course," James said.

"Fair's fair," I said.

2002

Goldberg as Artifact

I was not surprised to hear that the Smithsonian Institution had expressed an interest in the neon sign on Fats Goldberg's pizza parlor. I have always thought of Fats himself as an American artifact, although he is ordinarily regarded as a medical wonder rather than a piece of Americana. What brings doctors around to the pizza parlor occasionally to have a stare at Fats and poke him around a bit is not merely that he once lost some 160 pounds—no trivial matter in itself, being a weight equivalent to all of Rocky Graziano in his prime—but that he has succeeded for seventeen years in not gaining it back. Apparently, keeping off a large weight loss is a phenomenon about as common in American medicine as an impoverished dermatologist. Convinced that remaining a stick figure is the only alternative to becoming a second mountain of flesh, Fats has sentenced himself to a permanent diet broken only by semiannual eating binges in Kansas City and a system of treats on Mondays and Thursdays that reminds many New Yorkers of alternate-side-of-the-street parking regulations.

Because Fats is now exceptionally skinny, most people call him Larry instead of Fats. (Nobody, as far as I know, has ever called him Mr. Goldberg.) Having known Fats in Kansas City long before he let his Graziano slip away from him, though, I have difficulty thinking of him as anything but a fatty. He has even more difficulty than I do. He is, he cheerfully admits, as obsessed with food now as he ever was. (Fats cheerfully admits everything, which is one reason no one has ever thought of calling him Mr. Goldberg.) One of his doctors has told him that most of the successfully reformed fatties seem to involve themselves in food-related businesses. Still, Fats is restless being a pizza baron. "You can't schlepp pizzas all your life," he often tells me. He is constantly phoning for my reaction to the schemes he thinks up for new lines of work. His schemes are almost invariably concerned with food and are invariably among the worst ideas in the history of commerce. I have reluctantly come to the conclusion that Fats may be like one of those novelists whom publishers speak of as having only one book in them. My usual response to hearing one of his new business ideas—a scheme to produce an edible diet book, for instance—is to say, "Fat Person, there are worse things than schlepping pizzas."

Fats, now that he has had some time to reflect on it, is not surprised that the Smithsonian asked for his sign. "It was a nice piece of neon work," he says. As it happens, one of the regular customers at Goldberg's Pizzeria works for Chermayeff & Geismar Associates, the firm commissioned to design a five-year bicentennial exhibit for the Smithsonian called "A Nation of Nations." When it was suggested that Goldberg's sign might be suitable for a display that would amount to a selection of ethnic neon, Fats said, as he remembers it, "You want me to take it down now or will you come back for it?" (A Smithsonian curator came back for it, Fats having in the meantime ordered a precise replica to take its place.) Fats's cooperation was based partly on an understandable pride ("There I'd be with Lucky Lindy and everybody") and partly on a quick calculation of how many pizza eaters might pass through the exhibit during the next five years.

It is natural for a restaurant proprietor to see publicity as a way of attracting customers, but Fats must be alone among his peers as seeing it also as a way of attracting a wife. Ever since his emaciation, at the age of twenty-five, Fats has thought about finding an appropriate wife almost as much as he has thought about food, and he tends to regard publicity partly as a sort of singles ad. Fats is often mentioned in the press—in articles about pizza or about men's fashions (his views on clothing are as deeply rooted in the fifties as his views on courtship and marriage; sartorially, he is best known for an addiction to saddle shoes) or about what celebrated New Yorkers like to do on Saturdays in the city. ("Larry Goldberg, a bachelor who operates Goldberg's Pizzeria on Fifty-third Street and Second Avenue, said he spent his Saturdays at Bloomingdale's, where he rides the escalators and 'looks for girls.' ") Somehow, though, there are still a few people in town who have not heard of Goldberg's Pizzeria. So wherever he goes, Fats continues to spread the word by handing out small paper Goldberg's menus that list pizzas with names like "Moody Mushrooms" and "Bouncy Meatballs" and "SMOG" (sausage, mushrooms, onions, and green peppers)—the last a house specialty that Fats describes on the menu as "a gourmet tap dance." Extracting a menu from Fats does not require strenuous persuasion. "I don't press them into the hands of accident victims, or anything," Fats once told me. "But I did hand them out to the orchestra at Radio City Music Hall one night as they came out of the pit after the last show."

From the start, Fats was looking forward to the opening of "A Nation of Nations" as his first trip to a museum in the role of a benefactor. He is not one of those New Yorkers who never seem to take advantage of the city's great museums; he long ago decided that museums are ideal places to strike up a conversation with someone who just might turn out to be the future Mrs. Fats Goldberg.

"On Sundays, I schlepp through Central Park and stop for a rest on the steps of the Metropolitan," he once told me. "But I never go inside. The Metropolitan depresses me."

"You mean because of all those Egyptian tombs and everything?" I asked.

"No, it's mostly families," he said. "For girls, the Whitney's the ticket. I usually work the Whitney on Sunday afternoon. I used to go in, but now I just work the lobby and save the buck and a half."

The subject of museums had come up suddenly, as I remember, during a conversation about a business scheme Fats had concocted—a plan to offer a sort of food tour of New York that would take visitors from one ethnic delicacy to another for four or five hours.

"Fats," I said, "I hate to be the agent of your disillusionment once again, but I think you should know that many people do not customarily eat for four or five hours at a stretch. Many people eat breakfast and wait a few hours before eating lunch. Then they go about their business for a while, and then they eat dinner."

Fats looked puzzled. When he is not on a diet—that is, when he is in Kansas City—he does not exactly divide his eating into meals, although I did once hear him say, "Then I stopped at Kresge's for a chili dog on the way to lunch." For several months, he stopped talking about his ethnic-food tour and concentrated on the edible diet book, which many connoisseurs of Goldberg schemes believe to be his worst idea ever. "Don't you see it?" he would say. "The whole thing would be edible. Food coloring for ink. I haven't figured out what we could use for the pages except maybe pressed lettuce, but we'll find something. Each page would have menus for the three meals of the day, but one of the meals would be the page—so, for instance, you'd just eat that page for breakfast."

"If you ate the page for breakfast, Fats, how would you know what to eat for lunch and dinner?"

"It'd sell like crazy," Fats said, ignoring my quibble. "Bloomingdale's, Neiman-Marcus, Marshall Field's. *Goldberg's Edible Diet Book*. I'd autograph them at the cookbook counter at Bloomie's. The cookbook counter is the best place in the store to meet girls."

1976

Inspecting the Cork

This supposedly took place at a particularly fancy restaurant somewhere in the United States. The sommelier arrived at the table with the expensive bottle of wine that had just been ordered. He displayed the label, opened the bottle, placed the cork on the table in front of the customer who had done the ordering, and poured an inch or so of wine to be tasted. The customer ignored the wine in his glass, but he ate the cork.

I came across the story in a recent speech about the trials facing someone trying to serve wine to the sort of untutored clods who frequent American restaurants—a speech that had the tone of those nineteenth-century accounts of the frustrations experienced by someone trying to bring a working knowledge of Latin grammar to the Hottentots.

It was obvious to me that the storyteller didn't understand the story he was telling. He assumed that the cork was eaten out of ignorance. He didn't realize that there are any number of Americans who might want to eat a cork for effect. In other words, we are dealing here with someone who never met my old Army buddy Charlie.

I could easily imagine Charlie eating a cork—although I'll admit that it takes a leap of imagination to envision him in a fancy restaurant, particularly if he happened to be wearing his Jayhawk sweatshirt. It's bright red, and it's designed to look like a jayhawk, beginning with two huge eyes around chest level. Charlie wears it as a symbol of the semester and a half he put in at the University of Kansas before what he always refers to as "the little trouble down at the Tri-Delt house." I don't think cork-eating would present any physical problems that Charlie couldn't handle: He always used to delight in startling convenience-store clerks by finishing off a bag of Fritos in four or five bites without opening it. All in all, I think Charlie would consider cork-eating what he sometimes refers to as "a real hoot."

I can envision any number of ways he might do it. He might swallow the whole thing at once—an alternative available to someone who has always been able to put his gullet on automatic pilot and pour down a couple of cans of Budweiser—or he might put it in his mouth and wash it down with water, as if it were a particularly large anti-cold tablet he had been instructed to take immediately before meals. He might take a small bite, spit it onto the floor, and shout, "You call that cork, my man!" Or he might finish up the cork, turn to the rest of the people at the table, and say, "I'm not a doctor, but I play one on TV, so I know the importance of fiber in your diet . . ."

I think it's more likely, though, that he'd raise the cork to his mouth and chomp off a big bite, as if he were eating a radish. I can just see him chewing the bite slowly, staring very hard at the sommelier the entire time, and doing that trick he does with his stomach to make the beak of the jayhawk seem to open and close. The rest of the people in Charlie's party—the band of galoots Charlie often introduces as "my good friends and accessories"—are playing along, of course. They continue their small talk, occasionally glancing over at Charlie to see if he seems to be satisfied with what he's eating. Maybe a couple of them try to get the sommelier's attention so that they can ask him whether he would recommend a red or a white for chugalugging.

The sommelier is trying to muster the polite and expectant expression he learned in sommelier school, but his face is drained of color and he is emitting some soft beeping sounds that might be sighs or groans. The proprietor, who has come over to see what's going on, at first stands there with a fixed smile. Then he begins to look desperate as he notices other diners following Charlie's example. All over the restaurant, diners are eating their corks. Then Charlie finally swallows what he has been chewing, puts the rest of the cork back on the table, pauses for a moment to give the matter one last bit of consideration, and turns to the sommelier. "Fine," Charlie says. "That's fine. It's not the year I ordered, but it's fine."

1987

The Italian West Indies

I daydream of the Italian West Indies. On bleak winter afternoons in New York, when the wind off the Hudson has driven my wife, Alice, to seek the warmth she always draws from reading the brochures of ruinously expensive Caribbean resorts, I sometimes mumble out loud, "the Italian West Indies." Alice gets cold in the winter; I yearn for fettuccine all year round.

"There is no such thing as the Italian West Indies," Alice always says.

"I know, I know," I say, shaking my head in resignation. "I know."

But why? How did Italy manage to end up with no Caribbean islands at all? The French have islands. The Dutch have islands. Even the Danes had one for a while. The English have so many Caribbean islands that they have been hard put to instill in every single one of them the historic English gifts of parliamentary democracy and overcooked vegetables.

"The English obviously had a lot more islands than they could use," I say. "Aren't they the ones who are always going on about fair play?"

The Italians have none. Christopher Columbus—a Genoan, who taught Ferdinand and Isabella how to twirl spaghetti around their forks—took the trouble to discover the Caribbean personally before the end of the fifteenth century. Try to get a decent plate of spaghetti there now. When I happen into one of those conversations about how easily history might have taken some other course (What if the Pope had allowed Henry VIII's divorce? What if Jefferson had decided that the price being asked for the Louisiana Purchase was ridiculous even considering the inflation in North American real estate?), I find myself with a single speculation: What if the Italians, by trading some part of Ethiopia where it's not safe to eat the lettuce, had emerged from the colonial era with one small Caribbean island?

I dream of that island. I am sitting in one of those simple Italian beach restaurants, and I happen to be eating fettuccine. Not always; sometimes I am eating spaghettini puttanesca. Alice and I are both having salads made with tomatoes and fresh basil and extra virgin olive oil and the local mozzarella. That's right—the local mozzarella. (The residents, descendants of peasants who had managed to coax already-stuffed eggplants from the cruel soil of Calabria, would scoff at the notion of having to import mozzarella.)

The sea below us is a clear blue. The hills above us are green with garlic plants. The chef is singing as he grills our fresh *gamberos*. The waiter has just asked us the question that sums up for me what I treasure about the Italian approach to drinking wine: "You won raid or whyut?" I say "whyut," and lean back to contemplate our good fortune in being together, soaking up sunshine and olive oil, on my favorite Caribbean island, Santo Prosciutto.

Then the proprietor of our hotel stops by our table to inform us that, because of a disastrous drop in the lira, our stay will cost a quarter of what we would have paid for those resorts Alice was reading about in the brochures.

"*Benissimo,*" I say, and ask him if he'd like to join us for a glass of whyut.

1986

Unhealth Food

"Am I the only one worried about how unhealthy the people who work in health food stores look?" I said to my wife, Alice, one day. I described, in some detail, a clerk I had just encountered in a health food store—his sunken chest, his quivering hands, his ominous pallor, the dun-colored tint to his wretched little wispy beard.

"Calm down," Alice said.

"Why isn't there a Whole Grain Defense Committee working to

put some meat on their bones?" I said. "I'm beginning to think those Washington soothsayers are right about how uncaring Americans have become. Dozens of customers a day must walk right by this quasi cadaver, and not one of them is willing to get involved even to the extent of calling 911."

"What were you doing in a health food store anyway?" Alice asked. "You're always saying that health food makes you sick."

"I was on a mission of mercy," I said. "A friend of mine who lives in a place that lacks the shopping resources of this great city had run out of soy waste."

"You know very well there's no such thing as soy waste," she said. "Why do you keep going on about soy waste?"

"Soy waste, granola dust, pure extract of tree stump—what's the difference what they call it?" I said. "Judging from the condition of the clerk, it obviously isn't enough to keep a human being alive."

It happens to be true that health food makes me sick. In fact, health food stores make me feel a bit queasy even if I don't buy anything—partly, I think, because they always smell like capsules that have been in the medicine chest since the Nixon-Humphrey campaign.

"The children said you made a scene in the store," Alice said.

"Not a scene, really," I said. It is true that, as I poked around the aisles looking for the soy waste, I stopped to sniff the air, and suddenly heard myself shout, "Help! I'm trapped in a bottle of multivitamins!" That isn't really a scene though. I think of it as more of an outburst.

"I think you're becoming a crank," Alice said.

"Isn't there some public health law against people who are shopping for food being reminded constantly of the last days of Howard Hughes?"

"A sausage-eating crank at that," Alice said.

"Let me ask you just one question," I said. "If bumblebee leavings and stump paste are so good for you, why can't any of those guys grow full beards?"

1980

HIGH SOCIETY AND JUST PLAIN RICH PEOPLE

"When my freshman-year roommate at Yale, Thatcher Baxter Hatcher, told me that after the war his family no longer dressed for dinner, I thought he meant that they showed up in their undershirts. I said, 'My mom would have never allowed that, Thatcher Baxter Hatcher, and I'm talking here about Kansas City.'"

Errands

I've been back from the summer cottage for a while now, but I still seem to spend most of my time doing the sort of things that the recent biography of William Paley says he never had to do.

These biographies of the mighty stir conflicting emotions in the ordinary reader. For instance, Paley, the founder of CBS, is revealed as a liar, a braggart, a bully, a turncoat, a philanderer, and the sort of parent who in a just world would be tossed in the slammer for dereliction of duty—in other words, the sort of person we're used to reading about lately in biographies of our country's most prominent citizens. On the other hand, he never had to unpack his own car.

This combination is what stirs the conflicting emotions. If you're reading the book on the beach, you might think, "What a thoroughly loathsome human being." But if you're reading it in the license-renewal line at the Motor Vehicle Bureau—the line you're afraid you might wait in for forty minutes only to be told that the form you've filled out with such care is of no use without the birth certificate you keep in the safety deposit box—you might think, a bit wistfully, "I guess Bill Paley would have had somebody to take care of this sort of thing for him."

You would be half right. As I understand it, he would have had two people take care of that sort of thing—one to stand in the line at the Motor Vehicle Bureau and one who was in charge of such matters as sending somebody down to the Motor Vehicle Bureau to stand in line. This, at least, is what I was advised by my wife, who was the person in our family actually reading the book. I wanted to get to it myself, but I was too busy unpacking the car.

"When the Paleys flew from one of their houses to another, they didn't even carry a suitcase," she said. "There were people who went ahead of them to make sure that the closets were in order and the refrigerator was stocked and there were fresh flowers in the house."

Again, if I had been told that while I was lying quietly in the hammock, I might have taken it in as a marginally interesting fact about the habits of the rich. My response had to do with the fact that I was at that moment trying to balance a pile of underwear in one hand while violently pulling on a drawer that seemed to have an old Stroud's Fried Chicken T-shirt ("We Choke Our Own Chickens") stuck in it in a way that prevented it from being opened more than three or four inches.

I let go of the drawer, and paused, still holding the pile of underwear teetering in one hand. "I really shouldn't be doing this," I said to my wife.

"No, you shouldn't," my wife said. "If you threw out that junk you have in the lower drawer and put the underwear in there instead, you wouldn't keep getting that drawer jammed."

"I mean I shouldn't be spending my time unpacking clothes and trying to open drawers that are jammed by Stroud's Fried Chicken T-shirts."

"Not if you're going to get to the cleaners before they close," she said. "I finally got the washing-machine repairman to answer the phone, but I have to leave for my meeting in five minutes if I'm going to stop at the post office. You should probably run over to the cleaners now and finish unpacking later, after you change that one light bulb in the hall."

"What I meant," I said, "is that I really should have people dealing with these things for me. Didn't you tell me that until he went to check the display of some CBS magazine Paley had never been in a supermarket?"

"I don't think you'd be happy having someone else go to the supermarket," my wife said. "You couldn't trust anyone else to come across those weird brands of diet root beer you like."

But it would give me a lot more time. Of course, when Paley had a lot more time, he used it to cheat on his wife and plot against the colleagues who trusted him. Maybe he would have been better off spending a little more time going to the supermarket and standing in Motor Vehicle Bureau lines. I thought about that for a while, and looked at the underwear in my hand. "Is it possible that organizing the underwear drawer is the path to virtue?" I asked my wife.

"Maybe you'd better take a little break," she said. "You're beginning to talk funny. We can pick up the cleaning tomorrow."

1991

Thoughts on Power Neckwear

I like to wear a power tie.
I think it helps identify
With colors that you can't deny

An A-list guy who sits on high
In boxes when the footballs fly.
It shows I've kissed coach seats goodbye.
I've been to Delhi and Shanghai.
I've met the Sultan of Brunei.

My sight is where my problems lie:
I'm color blind, so though I try
To, through my neckties, signify
That normal rules do not apply,
I oftentimes in error buy
A tie that says "This guy is shy
Of influence—a small-fry guy."
The thought that I could mortify
Myself like this just makes me sigh.
Oh, woe is I. Oh, woe is I.

1996

The Tweed Curve

While controversy was raging over *The Bell Curve,* which contends that intelligence among blacks is immutably lower than among whites, there was some speculation that I planned to write a book demonstrating that rich people from Social Register backgrounds are, for the most part, dumb as dirt. I want to make it clear that I have no such plans.

What caused the speculation in the first place? In *Remembering Denny,* a book that dealt partly with the fifties at Yale, I wrote the following about how a high school boy from Kansas City could be permanently affected by prolonged exposure to hordes of old-money boarding school graduates with names like Thatcher Baxter Hatcher: "If I meet someone who is easily identifiable as being from what was once called a St. Grottlesex background, my gut expectation—kicking in fast enough to override my beliefs about judging people as individuals, slipping in well below the level of rational thinking—is that he's probably a bit slow."

Yes, I acknowledge that this is only my gut expectation. When rational thinking exerts itself, a moment later, I understand that intelligent thoughts can be expressed in the accent sometimes called Locust Valley Lockjaw, even if those thoughts are often about sailing or the stock market. Still, you might say that when it comes to being dismissive about the intelligence of an entire class of people, I was ahead of the Curve.

On the other hand, I lacked a political impetus for writing a book. One of *The Bell Curve* co-authors, a political scientist named Charles Murray, manages to come to the same conclusion no matter what he studies—that the government should quit trying to help out poor people. I didn't burn to write *The Tweed Curve* in order to argue that, say, confiscatory inheritance taxes should be applied as a means of keeping some of our more important institutions out of the hands of ditz-brains. To the extent that I considered the project at all, my motive was simply to make a bundle.

I knew I could hire research assistants to run up a few charts for me—distribution of Groton graduates in the academic ranking of the Harvard class of 1959, say, or the average IQ of people who regularly play court tennis compared with the average IQ of people who regularly play handball, or the number of Junior Assemblies debutantes who have submitted winning entries to the Westinghouse Science Talent Search.

The study that I considered particularly elegant in its construction would have compared median SAT scores of students with at least one grandparent in Hobe Sound with the median SAT scores of students with at least one grandparent in North Miami Beach. I called it "The Florida Index." I also tossed around some ideas for quizzes I might use to break up the statistics while furthering my argument. (Name a distinguished American novelist who is a high-caste WASP and not named Louis Auchincloss. Gotcha!)

So what stopped me from cashing in? I'd like to think that some moral qualms were involved—a concern, say, that some oversensitive

Hotchkiss lad who has just been cut from the junior varsity lacrosse team might be crushed by learning that he is probably genetically fated to rise no higher than the Palm Beach office of a white-shoe stockbrokerage.

Also, I have observed the way *The Bell Curve* got taken apart by reviewers who have some background in the field of human intelligence. The unkindest cuts came from people who dismissed Murray as the ideologue who didn't quite understand the theories of his co-author—the late Richard Herrnstein, who was, in fact, a psychologist. Reading those reviews provided some idea of what would have happened in Stalin's time if the mechanical-engineer half of the team assigned to do the book on farm implements had been sent to the gulag just before publication day, leaving the political-commissar half to explain to confused readers precisely how a tractor works.

I was obviously vulnerable to such treatment. I know some would claim that Yale in the fifties presented a flawed sample, partly because the admissions office was fussy about the grades of public high school boys but dipped far enough into the class at certain boarding schools to pick up the slow but socially acceptable father of that Hotchkiss lacrosse player. I know some would dismiss as unscientific my hypothesis on why intelligence deficits seem to accompany old money. ("I guess the blood sort of runs out, or something.") I know someone would discover that my academic background in this field amounts to one year of Human Science, a yard-sale version of biology that was taught at Southwest High School by a man who told us, among other things, that colored people and white people smelled different.

So I decided against publishing *The Tweed Curve*. I realize that this decision could have also been influenced by a lingering feeling, brought on by early association with Thatcher Baxter Hatcher, that there is something crude about suddenly making a bundle. Of course, the intervening decades, with their economic ups and downs, could have changed Hatcher's views on whether the age of one's money is terribly important—compared with, say, the amount of it. He may see my decision as an indication that I've become dumb as dirt.

1995

The 401st

The minute I saw *Forbes* magazine's list of the four hundred richest people in the United States, my heart went out to the person who was four hundred and first.

"He's nothing but some rich creep," Alice said.

"Creeps have feelings, too," I said. The phrase she had used suddenly conjured up a picture of the poor soul I was worrying about: Rich Creep, the Manhattan megadeal cutter and man about town. He lives in the Carlyle. He dates models. He eats breakfast at the Regency, where deals are made so quickly that a careless conglomerateur could find himself swallowing up a middle-sized corporation while under the impression that he was just mopping up his egg yolk with the end of a croissant. He dines every night at places like La Caravelle and Le Cirque. "Bonsoir, Monsieur Cripp," the headwaiter says when Creep walks in with an icily beautiful fashion model who weighs eighty-eight pounds, twelve of which are in cheekbones. "If I may make a suggestion, the overpriced veal is excellent tonight."

On the way to breakfast one morning, Creep happens to see the cover of *Forbes* at the Carlyle newsstand. "The Richest People in America," the headline says. "The *Forbes* Four Hundred." He snatches the magazine from the rack and, standing right in the lobby, he starts going through the list—at first methodically and then desperately. Finally, he turns and slinks back to his room. He can't face the crowd at the Regency. They'd pretend nothing has changed, but then they'd start trying to find some smaller corporation for him to swallow up—the way a nanny might sort through the picnic basket to find the smallest piece of white meat for the least adventurous child. He cancels his dinner date for the evening. He's afraid he might be given a cramped table near the kitchen, where the draft from the swinging doors could blow the fashion model into the dessert cart.

He's afraid that the same French waiters who once hovered over him attentively while he ate ("Is your squab done expensively enough, Monsieur Cripp?") will glance in his direction and whisper to each other, "*Les petites pommes de terre*"—small potatoes.

So who says I have no sympathy for rich people? And this is nothing new. When *Fortune* first published its list of the five hundred largest corporations in America, my heart went out immediately to the corporation that was five hundred and first. Of course, I had no way of knowing its name—that tragic anonymity was the basis for my sympathy—but I always thought of it as Humboldt Bolt & Tube. I felt for the folks at Humboldt Bolt & Tube. I could see them giving their all to build their corporation into one of the largest corporations in America—busting unions, cutting corners on safety specifications, bribing foreign heads of state, slithering out of expensive pollution-control regulations—only to remain unrecognized year after year.

As the Fortune 500 became an institution in American life, I often pictured the scene at the Humboldt Country Club in Humboldt, Ohio, when an important visitor from Wall Street asks casually over drinks, "Do you have any Fortune 500 companies in Humboldt?"

For a moment, no one speaks. The "old man," as everyone in Humboldt calls Harrison H. Humboldt, the son of Bolt & Tube's founder, looks out at the eighteenth green, the hint of a tear in his eye. Finally, someone says, "No, but we've got the third-largest granite pit east of the Mississippi."

1982

Invasion of the Limo-Stretchers

I pinned what Pam Blessinger said about rich people on my bulletin board. For a few months now, it has been in the section I reserve for permanent display, right next to a *Wizard of Oz* quotation that somehow comforts displaced Midwesterners in New York City by stating what should be increasingly obvious: "Toto, I don't think we're in Kansas anymore."

Pam Blessinger spoke as president of the residents' association of New York's Roosevelt Island, which is in the East River in a spot usually described as in the shadow of the Fifty-ninth Street Bridge. Developed ten years ago as a middle-income "new town," Roosevelt Island has become a quiet, family sort of place that one of Blessinger's fellow residents described to *The New York Times* as "an island of Indiana in the middle of Manhattan."

Blessinger was quoted in the *Times* in opposition to a proposed expansion of the development that would include what looked to her suspiciously like luxury apartments. "We're not against white or black or purple," she said. "What we're against is rich people."

There. She said it. The rest of us have been pussyfooting around this for years, afraid of being called prejudiced. Not Mrs. B. She could envision the peaceful lanes of her little island jammed with triple-parked stretch limousines waiting in front of restaurants where a plate of spaghetti costs eighteen dollars and change. She could see the day when respectable citizens who have to get up and go to work the next morning would be awakened in the middle of the night by the braying of rich people being dropped off after charity balls: "It was marvelous, darling!" "Wasn't it marvelous, darling?" "Yes, it was marvelous, darling!"

Mrs. B. said out loud what the rest of us have been thinking: Those people can ruin a neighborhood lickety-split.

No, we are not prejudiced. We wouldn't mind one or two rich people, but these days the supply of them seems inexhaustible. As seems to be true of so many recent developments in American life, this surfeit of richies has come as a surprise to me. When I was growing up, one of the most important things about truly rich people was that there weren't very many of them. Also, my high school teachers told us that people like the Rockefellers had grabbed their piles before the tax laws made it impossible to amass huge personal fortunes.

So why have so many people become as rich as the Rockefellers? Is it possible that these rich people know something about the tax laws that my high school teachers didn't know?

Most of the rich people are in New York. I don't care what *Forbes* says about where they live. They're here. We've got Texas rich people and California rich people and Colorado rich people. We've got rich people with new money and rich people with old money and rich people whose money just needs to sit in the window for a few days and ripen in the sun. There's no variety of rich people we don't have in overstock. New York has more rich people than some cities have people.

For a while, I thought other places might be sending us their rich people. ("Listen, if Frank down at the Savings and Loan doesn't quit talking about how many Jaguars he owns, we're just going to have to put him in the next shipment to New York.") It even occurred to me that whoever is in charge of these other places might have misread the poem on the Statue of Liberty, which definitely says, "Give me you tired, your *poor.*" People make mistakes.

Then I realized that the rich people were coming here on their own hook. They are swarming into New York because they want to be with people who are like they are—rich. There are a lot of places around the country, after all, where someone who is driven around in a stretched-out Cadillac limousine might be made light of ("Will you look at that thing old Albert's got himself? Don't you figure he must think he's always on his way to a funeral?"). For all I know, there are places around the country where someone who is driven around in a stretched-out Cadillac limousine might have rocks thrown at him.

"Send 'em back where they came from," a taxi driver who was hauling me up the East Side Highway one day said as he struggled to get around a gaggle of limos. He had devised a rich-people repatriation plan that sounded very much like Fidel Castro's Mariel boatlift, except that he'd use private jets instead of fishing boats.

"But that would be prejudiced and unfair," I said, although not terribly forcefully.

1986

Dinner at the de la Rentas'

Another week has passed without my being invited to the de la Rentas'. Even that overstates my standing. Until I read in *The New York Times Magazine* a couple of weeks ago about the de la Rentas having become "barometers of what constitutes fashionable society" ("Françoise and Oscar de la Renta have created a latter-day salon for *le nouveau grand monde*—the very rich, very powerful, and very gifted"), I wasn't even aware of what I wasn't being invited to week after week. Once I knew, of course, it hurt.

Every time the phone rang, I thought it might be Mrs. de la Renta with an invitation ("Mr. Trillin? Françoise de la Renta here. We're having a few very rich, very powerful, and/or very gifted people over Sunday evening to celebrate Tisha B'Av, and we thought you and the missus might like to join us."). The phone rang. It was the lady from the Diners Club informing me how quickly a person's credit rating can deteriorate. The phone rang. It was my mother calling from Kansas City to ask if I'm sure I sent a thank-you note to my cousin Edna for the place setting of stainless Edna and six other cousins went in on for our wedding gift in 1965. The phone rang. An invitation! Fats Goldberg, the pizza baron, asked if we'd like to bring the kids to his uptown branch Sunday night to sample the sort of pizza he regularly describes as "a gourmet tap dance."

"Thanks, Fat Person, but I'll have to phone you," I said. "We may have another engagement Sunday."

The phone quit ringing.

"Why aren't I in *le nouveau grand monde*?" I asked my wife, Alice.

"Because you speak French with a Kansas City accent?" she asked in return.

"Not at all," I said. "Sam Spiegel, the Hollywood producer, is a regular at the de la Rentas', and I hear that the last time someone asked him to speak French, he said 'Gucci.' "

"Why would you want to go there anyway?" Alice said. "Didn't you read that the host is so phony, he added his own 'de la' to what had been plain old Oscar Renta?"

"Who can blame a man for not wanting to go through life sounding like a taxi driver?" I said. "Family background's not important in *le nouveau grand monde.* Diana Vreeland says Henry Kissinger is the star. The Vicomtesse de Ribes says 'Françoise worships intelligence.' You get invited by accomplishment—taking over a perfume company, maybe, or invading Cambodia."

"Why don't we just call Fats and tell him we'll be there for a gourmet tap dance?" Alice said.

"Maybe it would help if you started wearing dresses designed by Oscar de la Renta," I said. "Some of his guests say they would feel disloyal downing Mrs. D's chicken fricassee while wearing someone else's merchandise."

Alice shook her head. "Oscar de la Renta designs those ruffly dresses that look like what the fat girl made a bad mistake wearing to the prom," she said.

"Things were a lot easier when fashionable society was limited to old-rich goyim, and all the rest of us didn't have to worry about being individually rejected," I said.

"At least they knew better than to mingle socially with their dressmakers," Alice said.

Would I be ready if the de la Rentas phoned? The novelist Jerzy Kosinski, after all, told the *Times* that evenings with them were "intellectually demanding." Henry Kissinger, the star himself, said that the de la Rentas set "an interesting intellectual standard"—although, come to think of it, that phrase could also be applied to Fats Goldberg.

Alone at the kitchen table, I began to polish my dinner-table chitchat, looking first to the person I imagined being seated on my left (the Vicomtesse de Ribes, who finds it charming that her name reminds me of barbecue joints in Kansas City) and then to the person on my right (Barbara Walters, another regular, who has tried to put me at my ease by confessing that in French she doesn't do her r's terribly well). "I was encouraged when it leaked that the Reagan cabinet was going to be made up of successful managers from the world of business," I say, "but I expected them all to be Japanese."

Barbara and the Vicomtesse smile. Alice, who had just walked into the kitchen, looked concerned.

"Listen," Alice said. "I read in the *Times* that Mrs. de la Renta is very strict about having only one of each sort of person at a dinner party. Maybe they already have someone from Kansas City."

Possible. Jerzy Kosinski mentioned that Mrs. D is so careful about not including more than one stunning achiever from each walk of life ("She understands that every profession generates a few princes or kings") that he and Norman Mailer have never been at the de la Rentas' on the same evening ("When I arrive, I like to think that, as a novelist, I'm unique"). Only one fabulous beauty. Only one world-class clotheshorse.

Then I realized that the one-of-each rule could work to my advantage. As I envisioned it, Henry Kissinger phones Mrs. D only an hour before dinner guests are to arrive. He had been scheduled to pick up a bunch of money that night for explaining SALT II to the Vinyl Manufacturers Association convention in Chicago, but the airports are snowed in. He and Nancy will be able to come to dinner after all. "How marvelous, darling!" Mrs. D says.

She hangs up and suddenly looks stricken. "My God!" she says to Oscar. "What are we going to do? We already have one war criminal coming!"

What to do except to phone the man who conflicts with the star and tell him the dinner had to be called off because Mr. D had come down with a painful skin disease known as the Seventh Avenue Shpilkes. What to do about the one male place at the table now empty—between Vicomtesse de Ribes and Barbara Walters?

The phone rings. "This is Françoise de la Renta," the voice says.

"This is Calvin of the Trillin," I say. "I'll be right over."

1981

CRIMINAL JUSTICE, CRIMINALS, JUSTICES, BUT (PROBABLY) NO CRIMINAL JUSTICES

"I am an absolutist on the First Amendment, except for people who show slides of their trip to Europe. They should be arrested. If they can't be held, they can at least be knocked about a bit at the station house."

Crystal Ball

So far, despite all the attention given to the wannabe terrorist from Nigeria widely known as the Underwear Bomber, nobody has mentioned that I predicted this turn of events. How many dead-on predictions does a person have to make to get a little credit around here? Am I implying that I've been similarly prescient in the past? Well, now that you mention it, yes. In a 1978 column about what was then being called the New Right, I said that I'd had some experience in the early sixties with the previous New Right, a movement most memorable for speeches that reached a level of boredom not witnessed in this country since members of the Communist Party droned their way through the thirties. Given the number of years between the two New Rights, I wrote, another New Right should be coming along around 1994. Sure enough, in 1994, a number of readers (three, if memory serves) wrote to remind me that my prediction had been uncannily correct: Newt Gingrich had led the Republicans in a historic takeover of Congress, and the press was full of stories about the power and vibrancy of the New Right.

A coincidence, you say? A lucky guess that I couldn't repeat? Wrong. In a book I published in 2006 called *A Heckuva Job: More of the Bush Administration in Rhyme,* here is what I said, in one of the nonrhyming passages, about the so-called Shoe Bomber of 2001: "I'm convinced that the whole shoe-bomber business was a prank. What got me onto this theory was reading that the shoe bomber, a Muslim convert named Richard Reid, had been described by someone who knew him well in England as 'very, very impressionable.' I had already decided that the man was a complete bozo. He made such a goofy production of trying to light the fuses hanging off his shoe that he practically asked the flight attendant if she had a match. The way I figure it, the one terrorist in England with a sense of humor, a man known as Khalid the Droll, had said to the cell, 'I bet I can get them all to take off their shoes in airports.' So this prankster set up poor impressionable Reid and won his bet. Now Khalid is back there cackling at the thought of all those Americans exposing the holes in their socks on cold airport floors. If someone is arrested one of these days and is immediately, because of his MO, referred to in the press as the Underwear Bomber, you'll know I was onto something."

That's right: I predicted the Underwear Bomber in 2006. You could look it up. Around the same time, I repeated the prediction in public appearances and, as I remember, a couple of times on television. (I firmly believe that, in this world of ever-diminishing irreplaceable resources, using a line only once represents the sort of wastefulness our society can ill afford.) And what transpired on

Christmas Day three years later? Another bozo tries to blow a hole in an airplane and succeeds only in setting his underpants aflame in a manner that might have rendered him ill equipped for the seventy-two heavenly virgins who were to be his reward if he succeeded. And how is this bozo described by friends and family? Naïve. And where was this bozo educated? University College London, within commuting distance of that diabolical trickster Khalid the Droll.

Has that name—Khalid the Droll—been mentioned even once in the endless press and television interviews with so-called security experts who prattle on about "connecting the dots" and "fostering interagency cooperation" and "eliminating stovepiping"? No, not once. Not once have the people who pontificate from Washington on Sunday morning television shows—the people I refer to as the Sabbath Gasbags—said, "Somebody should have followed up on Trillin's underwear tip." Not once has anybody considered the possibility that, after the shoe-bombing scheme worked to perfection, Khalid the Droll announced to his cell, "When they've had a few years of taking off their shoes, I bet I can make them expose their private parts to full-body scanners." Not once has one of these after-the-fact analyzers considered the possibility that, just as the thirties Communists and the early sixties New Right tried to bore us into submission, Khalid the Droll is engaged in an elaborate scheme to embarrass us to death.

And what will be the next step in this scheme? I'm working on my prediction now. I just hope somebody is paying attention this time.

2010

What Whoopi Goldberg ("Not a Rape-Rape"), Harvey Weinstein ("So-Called Crime"), et al. Are Saying in Their Outrage over the Arrest of Roman Polanski

A youthful error? Yes, perhaps.
But he's been punished for this lapse—
For decades exiled from L.A.
He knows, as he wakes up each day,
He'll miss the movers and the shakers.
He'll never get to see the Lakers.
For just one old and small mischance,
He has to live in Paris, France.
He's suffered slurs and other stuff.
Has he not suffered quite enough?
How can these people get so riled?
He only raped a single child.

Why make him into some Darth Vader
For sodomizing one eighth-grader?
This man is brilliant, that's for sure—
Authentically, a film auteur.
He gets awards that are his due.
He knows important people, too—
Important people just like us.
And we know how to make a fuss.
Celebrities would just be fools
To play by little people's rules.
So Roman's banner we unfurl.
He only raped one little girl.

2009

Marc Rich and Me

As it happens, I went to Boy Scout camp with Marc Rich. That's right. Who's Marc Rich? Is that what you said? The question, if I may say so, reveals an abysmal ignorance of world affairs. Marc Rich happens to be the reclusive, enigmatic, fabulously wealthy commodities trader who was just accused by the government of flimflamming it out of $48 million in taxes and is now believed to be hiding out in Zug, Switzerland, or maybe Spain. That's who. I went to Boy Scout camp with him, in Missouri. In 1949. We lived in the same tent. The name of the camp was Camp Osceola, BSA. It was where Boy Scouts from Kansas City went to camp. I can tell that you don't believe any of this.

One reason you don't believe it is that you think I make things up. The other reason you don't believe me is that all of the stories you've read about Marc Rich talk about how he came to this country with his family from Europe during the war and grew up in Brooklyn with his friend Pincus (Pinky) Green—also a fabulously wealthy commodities trader now, although only marginally enigmatic—and life as a Kansas City Boy Scout doesn't fit your picture of the young Marc trading some Borough Park candy store owner one used Batman comic for enough egg creams to float the entire stickball team. All of the stories you've read, that is, unless you happened to read the story in *The Kansas City Times* on October 5, which revealed that before moving to Brooklyn, Marc Rich's family lived in Kansas City for six years ("Mr. Rich's life-style apparently was nurtured in Kansas City, where he spent his formative years, investigators said") and that for two years Marc went to Southwest High School, which is where I went and where, as long as we're on the subject, the photographer David Douglas Duncan went, and also Charlie Black, who played basketball for the University of Kansas. *The Kansas City Times* did not reveal the

Camp Osceola angle. I'm revealing that now. Marc Rich and I were at Osceola together. Not Pincus Green. I'm not one of those people who can remember every tiny event of their childhood, but I can tell you that there was nobody at Camp Osceola called Pinky.

Still don't believe me? Then do this. Ask someone who attended the second session of Camp Osceola in 1949 about this incident: After lunch one day, Skipper Macy—the director of the camp, and the man who always said "fine and dandy"—got on the subject of languages. Don't ask me why; I already told you that I don't remember every little detail. Skipper tried to find out which camper spoke the most languages—ordinarily, I'll admit, that was not a question that provoked intense competition at Osceola—and which camper do you think was finally called up on stage and slapped on the back by Skipper and told that it was fine and dandy? Right. Marc Rich. You have probably already guessed which Troop 61 Boy Scout—known up to that time mainly for his inability to do knots—said, "And to think . . . we're in the same tent." Right again. Me.

I hope you don't think I'm bringing this up to get a little reflected fame from the fact that my lifestyle was nurtured in the same tent as the lifestyle of the defendant in the single largest tax evasion case in the history of the republic—like those people in Kansas City who say they bought a necktie at Harry Truman's haberdashery at Twelfth and Baltimore. If everyone who says he bought a necktie from Harry Truman really had bought one, the store wouldn't have gone broke, and Harry Truman wouldn't have gone to the Senate, and Roosevelt would have been succeeded by William O. Douglas, and Clifton Daniels would be married to the daughter of a man who was known as "The Cravat King of KC."

The reason I'm telling you this is that the public should hear about Marc Rich from someone who actually knew him—instead of from all of those people who told *The Kansas City Times* that they couldn't quite remember which one he was. We were at Camp Osceola together, in the same tent. We actually sang the same song together at campfires. The song went like this:

Softly falls the light of day,
As our campfire fades away.

Silently, each scout should ask,
"Have I done my daily task?
Have I kept my honor bright?
Can I guiltless rest tonight?
Have I done and have I dared
Everything to be prepared?"

Now do you believe me?

I want you to know that what I am revealing about Marc Rich at Camp Osceola would be of no value to the FBI, which already knows that Marc speaks more languages than most Kansas City Boy Scouts and may even know that I can't do knots. I wouldn't rat on a pal. If I ratted on a pal, I couldn't guiltless rest tonight. I do think, though, that the public has a right to know about the Camp Osceola angle. I can just imagine the questions the reporters from *The Kansas City Times*—not to speak of *The New York Times*—would have asked me had they but known that Marc Rich and I were in the same tent. They would want to know if Marc and I—on campfire nights, as the fire was burning down to embers—talked about crude-oil prices and arbitrage. They would want to know if Marc tried to snooker any campers out of their canteen money. They would want to know whether Marc was elected to the Great Tribe of Mic-o-Say—whose song, sung to the tune of "Oh Come All Ye Faithful," went "O come all ye tribesmen, braves and mighty warriors, oh come ye, oh come ye, to the Great Mic-o-Say"—and, if so, whether the Indian name he adopted (since all tribesmen adopted an Indian name) was something like He Who Buys Cheap and Sells Dear, or maybe Brave Who Cooks the Books. They would want to hear from someone who really knew Marc Rich. That's why I'm revealing all of this.

1983

Rodney King Sings the "Picked Up by the Los Angeles Police Department Blues"

If I done right or I done wrong,
I'd sooner be held by the Vietcong.

1991

The Inside on Insider Trading

"Daddy, what's insider trading?"

"Isn't it customary in most families for the daughter to come down to breakfast and ask the father if she can buy the divine sweater she just saw in the window of some store whose name sounds like a traffic accident?"

"Definitely."

"Then why are you asking about insider trading instead of whether you can buy a new sweater?"

"Can I buy a new sweater?"

"Certainly not."

"That's why."

"What kind of cereal do you want this morning? How about a bowl of this stuff that fulfills your basic daily requirements of niacin, lipides, and riboflavin? That would be a real load off your mind, not having to worry about niacin, lipids, and riboflavin all that time. It would leave you free to worry about whether your breakfast is rich enough in thiacin and pantothenate."

"That kind of cereal is gross, Daddy."

"Now that I think of it, Niacin, Lipides, and Riboflavin sound like some lawyers I used to know. If you think the cereal is gross, you ought to meet Lipides."

"Daddy, you know what Mommy always says: She says if you never give me a straight answer I'm going to grow up to be a smart-aleck like you."

"I thought 'certainly not' was a pretty straight answer to the sweater question."

"Daddy, what's insider trading?"

"Okay. Insider trading is when someone who works on Wall Street gets material information that is not available to the general public and uses that information to make money buying or selling stocks."

"What happens to someone who gets caught at insider trading?"

"He gets arrested."

"But what's his punishment?"

"His punishment is that he has to tell on someone else who's doing the same thing."

"At school, we call that squealing."

"These people call it making a deal."

"Don't they ever have to go to jail?"

"Well, maybe if—"

"I know, Daddy: Maybe if they're represented by Niacin, Lipides, and Riboflavin."

"May I recommend a bowl of this stuff that gives you the same amount of energy the Olympic decathlon champion gets every morning at breakfast? Then if you're only interested in maybe a little shot-putting you'll have a lot of energy left over."

"What I don't understand, Daddy, is what people who work on Wall Street do who aren't doing something you can get arrested for?"

"They try to get material information that is not available to the general public and then they use that information to make money buying and selling stock."

"But if everyone who works on Wall Street does the same thing, why are just some of the people on Wall Street arrested?"

"Those people are arrested for stealing too fast."

"I don't think Mommy would call that a straight answer, Daddy."

"Well, it's a lot like the speed limit on driving. It may be true that everyone drives faster than fifty-five, but that doesn't mean that you can whiz past a state trooper who's doing sixty and not expect to be pulled over to the side. It's the same with those people in the New York Parking Violations Bureau who got indicted for taking bribes from contractors. If they had just waited until they left government and then taken cushy jobs with the contractors, nobody would have said anything. They got indicted for exceeding the speed limit."

"Is that your straightest answer—that business about exceeding the speed limit?"

"Why do you think people are always talking about the risks of life in the fast lane?"

"Could I please have a bowl of that cereal that's chock-full of riboflavin?"

"Sure. Anything else?"

"Yes. I think I need a new sweater."

"No problem."

1986

Four Supreme Court Nominations

DAVID SOUTER ASTONISHES

A character beyond dispute?
No accusations to refute?
Did no one ever institute
A suit that claimed you took some loot?
Not once, did you go on a toot?
Or hit some brute right in the snoot
When he, attempting to be cute,

Insisted that a man named Sout-
er would, of course, be known as Zoot?
Or taste . . . er . . . ah . . . forbidden fruit?
Or once neglect your paper route?

1990

HARRIET MIERS BRINGS TROUBLE ON THE RIGHT

The President, who never tires
Of naming cronies, named Ms. Miers
To be a justice. I'm not kidding.
He said he knows she'll do his bidding.
The social-issues Right went crazy.
They called her record much too hazy.
Though through the code, with some contortion,
Bush signaled that she hates abortion,
They asked, so why is she not willing
To say right out it's baby killing?
Responding to this strong attack, he
Assured the Right she's really wacky.
In phone calls, Rove, in hopes of winning
Support from preachers gave this spinning:
It's by her church that ye shall know her.
Her church is low. No church is lower.
Her church friends (please think Holy Rollers)
Treat embryos like kids in strollers—
Including embryos of rapists.
The Baptists to these folks are papists.
She's not the moderate you deem her.
If you're extreme, then she's extremer.
Her style is not to be dramatic,
But be assured she is fanatic.

2005

SONIA SOTOMAYOR CAUSES SUSPICION

The nominee's Sotomayor,
Whom all good Latinos adore
But right-wingers tend to deplore.
They'd like to show Sonia the door.
Her record, they say, heretofore
Reveals that beliefs at her core
Would favor minorities more:
She'd hand them decisions galore,
Because of the racial rapport.

Whereas white male judges are, as everyone knows, totally neutral.

2009

JOHN ROBERTS ACTS AS UMPIRE

"Judges are like umpires. . . . I have no agenda. . . . And I will remember that it's my job to call balls and strikes and not to pitch or bat."

—John Roberts's opening statement at
his confirmation hearing, 2005

"The Roberts court . . . ruled for business interests 61 percent of the time, compared with 46 percent in the last five years of the court led by Chief Justice William H. Rehnquist."

—*The New York Times,* 2010

Regardless of which law he likes,
He's only calling balls and strikes.
His own beliefs would never trump
Decisions from this simple ump.
Statistics that have just come in
Now show what kind of ump he's been.

Extrapolating from these cases,
Big-business pitchers all are aces.
By chance, the pitchers who are great—
The ones who nick or split the plate,
The ones deserving of ovations—
Just tend to pitch for corporations.

Of balls and strikes that he has eyed,
The union pitches all look wide.
Consumers make for easy calls:
Their pitches simply all are balls.
Environmentalists? It's droll
The way control freaks lack control.

A left-wing lawyer sharp as Darrow
Will find the strike zone much too narrow.
Behind it, crouching, is the Chief,
Quite confident in his belief:
Regardless of which laws he likes,
He's only calling balls and strikes.

2010

Damaged Goods

I heard on the morning news that some kidnappers in the Bronx telephoned the wife of their victim with a demand for $100,000 in ransom money, and she talked them down to $30,000. The newscaster said the story had a happy ending—the victim was returned unharmed, the ransom money was recovered, the kidnappers were arrested—but all I could think of was how the man must have felt when, back in the bosom of his loving family at last, he discovered that his wife had him on discount special.

I suppose a lot of people who heard the story took it as just one more indication that New York City is getting to be one of those places, like Bombay or Tijuana, where the price is always negotiable. They could probably imagine the victim's wife standing in front of some huge counter, poking at her husband the way she might poke at a cantaloupe, and saying, "A hundred grand for that! The way it's going soft around the sides already! You have the nerve to stand here and tell me that you are trying to charge one hundred thousand American dollars for *that*!"

Even a resident of the American Bombay, though, has to be disturbed at the prospect of having a loved one treat him the way she would treat an overripe cantaloupe. "What if I got kidnapped and they called demanding ransom money?" I asked my wife, Alice, after stewing over the Bronx caper for a couple of days. "I don't suppose you'd have any inclination to see if you could talk them into settling for thirty cents on the dollar, would you?"

"You're not going to get kidnapped," Alice said. "Why can't you just worry about high interest rates or acid rain or The Bomb, like normal people?"

As it happens, I didn't use to worry much about being kidnapped. After I heard the kidnapping story from the Bronx, though, it began to occur to me that the days when kidnappers limited their efforts to the better-known names of Manhattan café society may be over. It's possible that the sagging economy has driven kidnappers to the outer boroughs. I had to consider the possibility that some particularly desperate gang was staking out the garage in Brooklyn where I take my car to be repaired. If so, I'm in real danger: If a kidnapper tried to calculate my net worth by simply extrapolating from the amount of money I've poured into that wretched machine, he would figure me for eight or ten million dollars at the least.

All of which meant that I also had to consider the possibility that I might be the cantaloupe being discussed in a scene that flashed across my mind:

KIDNAPPER: Look, lady, even at eighty grand I'd barely come out on the deal myself. I mean, with the price of getaway cars these days and—

ALICE: You mean eighty thousand *before* we knock off the ten for softness around the sides, right?

"Don't get me wrong," I said to Alice. "Nobody could blame you for reminding the perpetrators that it's going to be impossible for this country to get inflation down to some manageable level unless people in every walk of life make some effort toward voluntary control of wages and prices."

"I've never understood why you don't get a hobby," Alice said.

Was it mere chance that she did not directly deny that she might ever consider me cut-rate merchandise? Was it really possible that she might respond to the dread call with a little dickering?

KIDNAPPER: We got him, lady, and we want a hundred grand pronto.

ALICE: (Long tactical silence)

"I suppose there's no reason to assume that just because someone happens to be your husband he's automatically worth the full sticker price," I said.

"Maybe you should get involved in some sort of volunteer work," she said. "Afternoons part-time at one of the thrift shops—something like that."

"Aside from some mileage on the odometer," I said, "I'm sure I have a few little faults that might be mentioned by someone interested in lowering the asking price just a little."

"You mean little faults like going on and on about some particularly silly subject?" Alice said.

"Well, I hadn't actually thought of that, as a matter of fact." Then I did think of it:

KIDNAPPER: Lady, he's driving us batty with all this talk about full sticker price.

ALICE: Why don't we talk again tomorrow, after you've had a chance to get to know him a little better.

1982

The Sociological, Political, and Psychological Implications of the O. J. Simpson Case

O.J.?
Oy vey!

1995

LIFE AMONG THE LITERATI

"The average shelf life of a book is somewhere between milk and yogurt. Books by Dan Brown or Danielle Steel may have a longer shelf life, but they contain preservatives."

T. S. Eliot and Me

For an Authors Guild benefit some years ago, four or five of us were asked to write a rejection letter turning down some classic work of literature. Garrison Keillor rejected *Walden Pond,* by Henry David Thoreau. He said that *Walden Pond* had a lot of good axioms in it, but that the structure was weak. So he suggested turning it into a calendar. I rejected *The Waste Land,* by T. S. Eliot. I rejected it in iambic pentameter, of course. The last couplet of my letter was, "I know this is a blow, Tom, not to worry: / You're still the greatest poet from Missouri." The faintness of praise in calling someone the greatest poet from Missouri can be gauged by the fact that the other poet from Missouri is me. Another way to put it is that T. S. Eliot and I comprise the Missouri school of poetry.

I know you're thinking that there are considerable differences between T. S. Eliot and me. Yes, it's true that he was from St. Louis, which started calling itself the Gateway to the West after Eero Saarinen's Gateway Arch was erected, and I'm from Kansas City, where people think of St. Louis not as the Gateway to the West but as the Exit from the East. But then there are the similarities. For instance, both of us have a penchant for using foreign languages in our poetry. In fact, the rejection letter I wrote to Eliot criticized him for going overboard in that regard:

These many tongues, Tom, into which you lapse
Are foreign tongues—not spoken by our chaps.
Some French, all right, but take a word like "Shantih."
The reader's stumped, no matter how *avant* he
Imagines that he is (Or is that fair?
One might say Sanskrit's truly *derrière*.)

I've never used Sanskrit in a poem myself. I go in more for Yiddish. I think it's fair to say that Eliot was not partial to Yiddish. When the breakup of Yugoslavia provoked a few wars, for instance, I wrote

Croatians are the good guys now,
Although their past is somewhat shady,
So worry not that these same guys
Chased both your *bubbe* and your *zayde*.

Both of us toss in some German now and then. Eliot, of course, includes a passage from *Tristan und Isolde* in the opening stanza of *The Waste Land*, and I, when George W. Bush named an old family retainer as attorney general of the United States, took advantage of the fact that Alberto Gonzales rhymes with "loyal *über alles*." And we both have occasionally written about animals. Eliot famously wrote a series of poems about cats, and I have written, for example, that corgis appear to be a breed of dog assembled from the parts of other breeds of dog—and not the parts that those other breeds were all that sorry about giving up. As a matter of perspective, I should acknowledge that there has never been a long-running Broadway musical called *Corgis*.

Our paths do separate dramatically on the matter of rhyme. It isn't that Eliot shunned rhyme. I still sometimes find myself murmuring couplets from *The Love Song of J. Alfred Prufrock:* "Of restless nights in one-night cheap hotels / And sawdust restaurants with oyster-shells." But in *The Waste Land,* there were so few rhymes that I said in my rejection letter, "So my advice, Tom, 'Hurry up, it's time' / For restoration of some lines that rhyme. / And when that's done, I think it might be neater / If you could sort of tidy up the meter."

I, on the other hand, have stuck stubbornly to rhyme. That might have something to do with the poetic influence of my father. He was a grocer for most of his working life, but he owned a restaurant for a while, and he treated that as an opportunity to put a rhyming couplet on the menu every day at lunch. He was devoted to rhymes, particularly rhymes about pie. He rhymed "pie" with "shy" and "July" and "evening is nigh" and "All right warden, I'm ready to fry. / My last request was Mrs. Trillin's pie."

The result of the separate paths T. S. Eliot and I took is simple: He is thought of as perhaps the greatest literary figure of the twentieth century, and I am a deadline poet, commenting on the events of the day in verse for a hundred dollars a shot.

Deadline poetry is a small subset of rhyming poetry. A very small subset. A few years ago, John Allemang, of the Toronto *Globe and Mail,* and I founded the International Deadline Poets Organization, or IDPO. We were the only members. I hasten to say that IDPO is not the only exclusive literary organization I have ever belonged to. When I was traveling the country to do regular reporting pieces for *The New Yorker,* Jules Loh was doing a similar series for the Associated Press, and we formed the American Association of American Correspondents Covering America. Our meetings were held at O'Hare Airport in Chicago. We were the only members. The American Association of

American Correspondents Covering America had only one rule: You can't quote de Tocqueville. That's how we kept the membership down.

IDPO hasn't needed any rules to keep the membership down. In fact, Allemang's verses no longer appear in *The Globe and Mail,* so I'd say that his membership hangs by a thread, except that saying that would constitute a metaphor and IDPO discourages metaphors. I continue to turn out a deadline poem every week for *The Nation*—or every issue, I should say, since *The Nation* publishes only every other week in the summer, even though the downtrodden are oppressed every day of the year.

It's left to me to speak up for deadline poetry against the implied sneers of people like T. S. Eliot—or what we often refer to at IDPO gatherings as "the Sanskrit crowd." It's left to me to persuade literary critics that in describing deadline poetry, the term "accessible" is preferable to the term "simpleminded." It's left to me to point out that making a deadline almost every week is something never faced by what my family has an unfortunate tendency to call "grown-up poets." Take Eliot, for instance. And I'm not here to knock the competition. But take Eliot, for instance. If he came upon a "patient etherized upon a table" and wasn't quite inspired, he could always wait for the next patient etherized upon a table. If he wasn't turned on by those "half-deserted streets," he could wander around until he found some half-deserted streets more to his liking. Eliot was under no deadline pressure.

And then there's the question of rhyming. "Real poets"—another phrase my family has an unfortunate tendency to use—can choose the words they want to rhyme. Deadline poets are stuck with writing about people in public life, and there are people who persist in going into public life despite the fact that their names are impossible to rhyme. And deadline poets have no truck with the near-rhymes that people in the trade sometimes call slant rhymes—the sort of thing occasionally used by poets like, well, T. S. Eliot, for instance. We are as strict about exact rhyming as my father was when he wrote what was perhaps his best-known menu poem: " 'Eat your food,' gently said mom to her little son, Roddy. / 'If you don't, I will break every bone in your body.' "

For uncompromising rhymers, the presidency has been a particular problem. The nice iambic candidates with strong vowels like Ross Perot and John McCain always seem to lose. For a deadline poet, November has been the cruelest month. Bush is a terrible rhyme. When George H. W. Bush left office, I wanted to write him a poem, and I had to make do with his middle names:

Adieu to you, George Herbert Walker.
Though never treasured as a talker—
Your predicates were often prone
To wander, nounless, off alone—
You did your best in your own way,
The way of Greenwich Country Day.
So just relax, and take your ease,
And never order Japanese.

Clinton was even worse. Clinton is the orange of American presidents. In his second term, right at the beginning of the . . . unpleasantness, it was said that Hillary Clinton was going on the *Today* program to lead the defense. I had to use what in past days we would have called her maiden name—what would now be called maybe her name of origin, her slave name:

And so it's up to our Ms. Rodham
To prove Bill's White House isn't Sodom.
It's left to this adroit señora
To show that it is just Gomorrah.

Oddly enough, Obama, who has often mentioned having a funny name, would have been an improvement on his predecessors if only I hadn't used up all of the relevant rhymes with Osama bin Laden—Yokohama, Cinerama, slap yo' mama.

I'm sometimes asked if I'm ashamed of making a living by making snide and underhanded remarks about respectable public officials, and my only defense has been "It's not much of a living." But sometimes I do think of what might have happened if my path and T. S. Eliot's path hadn't diverged—if, for instance, as a boy in Kansas City I had paid a little more attention in Sanskrit class. Would I have moved to England and started talking funny? Could I have written something obscure enough to be considered profound? Or would I just get rejection letters like the one I wrote to T. S. Eliot about *The Waste Land*—a rejection letter that has as its penultimate couplet, "I've read it, Tom—the lines, the in-betweens. / I don't know what the bloody hell it means."

2010

Paper Trials

For people who make their livings as writers, the routine messages of everyday life have to be put together with some care. You don't want to leave rough drafts lying around. I've known novelists for whom the prospect of composing a note asking that a son or daughter be excused from gym that day can bring on a serious case of writer's block.

Recently, our car had to be left on city streets for a few days, and, attempting to benefit from the experience of a couple of trips in the past to AAAA Aardvark Auto-Glass Repair, I took on the task of composing a sign to inform potential pillagers that it contained nothing of value. Hours later, my wife happened to ask me to do some little chore around the house and I heard myself saying, "I can't right now. I'm on the fourth draft of this car sign."

There was no reason for her to be surprised. She has seen me stuck badly on an RSVP. In fact, a routine piece of social communication can be particularly knotty for writers, since they habitually try to express themselves in ways that are not overly familiar. This is why a biographer who seems capable of producing a twelve-hundred-page Volume One in fairly short order can often be inexcusably late with, say, a simple thank-you note. Reading over what he's put on paper, he'll say to himself, "I can't believe that I wrote anything as lame as 'Thanks for a wonderful weekend.' " Then he'll put aside the entire thank-you-note project until a fresher phrase comes to mind. A few weeks later, while the draft is still marinating on the writer's desk, the weekend's hostess feels confirmed in her impression—an impression that began to surface with the wine-spilling incident on Saturday night—that the biographer is a boor or a yahoo.

What my fourth draft of the car sign said was NO RADIO. I thought that was spare and to the point, without extraneous language. I came to it from NO RADIO OR ANY OTHER VALUABLES, which I decided, after some reflection, protested too much.

"What do you think?" I asked my wife, handing her the sign.

"It's okay," my wife said. "I saw some ready-made signs for car windows at the hardware store, and that's what one of them said, so I guess it's what people think is effective."

"You saw the same sign—worded in just that way?"

"I'm not saying you plagiarized it from the hardware store."

"Actually, I haven't been in there in some time," I said.

"It's really okay," my wife said. "NO RADIO is fine."

It's fine if you're satisfied to be writing at the same level as some gorilla at the sign factory. Thinking I needed fresh ideas, I phoned my older daughter, who lives just around the corner. "What would be a good sign to put in the car to discourage crackheads from smashing the window so they can get at six cents in change on the floor and the spare fan belt and an old pair of pliers?" I asked.

My daughter, a survivor of one of those earnest and progressive nursery schools in the Village, said, "How about USE WORDS NOT HANDS?" This was a reference to what the teachers at her nursery school were constantly saying as the little monsters attacked one another with any weapon available. At one point, we all began to wonder exactly what the words for sneaking up behind another kid and pulling her hair might be.

It wouldn't surprise me at all if that hair puller had turned to a life of petty crime. Much as I enjoyed contemplating the look on his face when he spotted his nursery-school slogan on a car he was about to break into, I decided that the impact of USE WORDS NOT HANDS rested on the sort of allusion that an editor would criticize as "too inside."

The next draft was a complete departure—more of a new approach, really, than just another draft. It said THERE IS NOTHING OF VALUE HERE. Upon reflection, I decided that it sounded too philosophical. I could picture a car thief who came upon it turning to his partner in crime and saying, "Talk about pretentious!" So now I'm sort of stuck. Meanwhile, the car's on the street. It is not completely without protection. An old shirt cardboard taped onto the back window bears the words SIGN IN PREPARATION.

1994

Half an Oaf

There was a discussion at my house recently about whether or not I am an uncultured oaf. This is not the first time the subject has come up. The form these discussions take isn't what you might assume. It's not that somebody accuses me of being an uncultured oaf and I defend myself by talking at length about some movie with subtitles that I've recently seen. That's not the way it happens at all—and I don't just mean that I'd have a different defense, because I haven't seen a subtitled movie in a long time and had trouble following the plot of the last one I did see. These discussions are not accusatory; they're more like dispassionate inquiries. Everyone present seems genuinely curious about whether I can be accurately categorized as an uncultured oaf, and no one is more curious about it than I am.

I think that at this point I should present my credentials. I'm a college graduate. That's not all: I was an English major. There's more: I graduated from a distinguished American research university. All of that makes me wonder whether or not there are a lot of other people with ostensibly respectable academic credentials who have reason to suspect that they may be uncultured oafs.

It's true that I have no advanced degree, a fact my daughters like to remind me of from time to time, as a way to keep me sort of damped down. It's also true that I grew up in the Midwest, in a milieu (a word I've learned since) in which culture did not hang heavily in the air. As was customary in that time and place, my mother took my sister to concerts and road shows of Broadway musicals, while my father took me to the Golden Gloves and the NCAA basketball tournaments. (We all went to the American Royal Livestock Show together.)

Still, this country is way past the days when cultural levels were geographically based. For years, our friend James has been described around our house as the most cultured person we know, and James has lived virtually all of his life in south-central Louisiana, a good two hours from the nearest place showing subtitled movies. He is consulted with particular respect when we have a discussion about whether or not I'm an uncultured oaf.

Not long ago, I read an article about a distinguished literary critic, long deceased, and, as an example of the critic's remarkable writing ability, the article drew particular attention to this sentence: "This intense conviction of the existence of the self apart from culture is, as culture well knows, its noblest and most generous achievement." I had no idea what that could mean.

On the theory that a certified intellectual might be able to enlighten me, I decided to consult someone I know who is an officer of the American Academy of Arts and Letters. There's no substitute for going right to the top. Here's what the certified intellectual had to say about the sentence in question: "I suppose it's meant to imply that culture (whatever that is) has allowed (by encouraging the Romantic ideal) the idea of the self to flourish, indeed triumph, to the extent that we value it more than anything else." Appreciative of his help, I decided not to trouble him further, although what I wanted to ask him was what I would have wanted to ask the literary critic if he had laid that business about the existence of the self on me while, say, we were waiting together in the subway station for a train: "Could you please give me an example?"

Recently, I attended a modern-dance program. I hasten to say that this was not an attempt to amass evidence for any discussion that might come up about who is and who isn't an uncultured oaf. The choreographer had gone to my high school in the Midwest, and I make it a policy to attend any cultural event created by someone who went to my high school—a policy, it may not surprise you to know, that still leaves me with plenty of evenings free for other activities. I loved the modern-dance program. I loved it so much, in fact, that I began to consider the possibility of attending modern-dance programs choreographed by people who had not gone to my high school. A couple of nights later, James, who was visiting from Louisiana, saw the same program, and he loved it, too. Maybe, I allowed myself to think, I am not an uncultured oaf after all.

The only review I saw of the modern-dance program offered testimony to the contrary. It compared the plot to a soap opera. (Actually, I had missed the plot. I don't mean that I failed to follow it: I hadn't been aware that there was one.) Also, the reviewer implied, without using these precise words, that the program had been designed to make modern dance palatable to, well, uncultured oafs.

What did that say about me? What, for that matter, did it say about James? Is it possible that I'm such an uncultured oaf that the person I'd always considered the most cultured person I know is also an uncultured oaf? No one is more curious about that than I am—except maybe James.

2009

Mencken's Mail

My first reaction to reading a letter that requires a letter in return is to wonder whether I can get away with claiming that it got lost in the mail. That is also my second reaction, and it lasts a minimum of six weeks—by which time it's often safe to conclude that the time during which a reply would have been relevant has passed. The replies I do write invariably start with an apology for the delay—an apology that sometimes fills the entire letter with imaginatively concocted tales of broken typewriters or arthritis in the fingers or files destroyed by the arson of embittered office-seekers. Occasionally, I'm pithy. A letter I just sent off began: "Please excuse my tardiness in answering your letter of Sept. 28, 1953. I have been out of the city."

There are disadvantages in not being a letter writer. For instance, when I run across people whose letters I have been meaning to answer for a year or two, they often appear surprised and mildly disappointed to find that I'm alive. But I have also benefited from what might be called the blessings of sloth—the same kind of advantages that come to a man who is too lazy to exercise and can therefore comfort himself with the knowledge of how many muscles he has avoided painfully pulling and how many dreary lectures on proper backswing technique he has been spared. Whenever I'm in danger of feeling guilty about the drawerful of unanswered mail in my desk, I reassure myself with the reminder that answering a letter only brings another letter to be answered. For me, the New York Public Library's announcement that its collection of H. L. Mencken correspondence was available for inspection presented an opportunity not for scholarly research but for proving to myself what enormous problems an intelligent man like H. L. Mencken could cause himself by answering his mail.

My inquiry was rewarded immediately in Mencken's correspondence with Ambrose Bierce, the San Francisco journalist and short-story writer, whom I have always treasured for writing, in a column complaining about slow service on the Southern Pacific railroad, that "the passenger is exposed to the perils of senility." In 1913, Bierce, who had met Mencken in Baltimore, sent him what appeared to be a fairly harmless letter from California. "A few days ago I bought the May number of the rather clever magazine with the unpleasant name *The Smart Set* and was delighted to find in it two things by you," Bierce wrote. "Maybe you write for it all the time. I don't know. Well, I like your work and want to tell you so. I had not known that you could write so devilish well. . . . I hope you prosper in so far as prosperity is compatible with happiness."

If I had been in Mencken's place, I would have resolved to write Bierce back immediately—thanking him, with appropriate modesty, for such a kind letter. Then I would have considered the wisdom of trying to save Bierce future embarrassment by informing him that in certain circles it would be assumed that any literate citizen knew about H. L. Mencken's writing for *The Smart Set* all the time, and devilish well. Then I would have wondered whether I could do that with appropriate modesty. Then I would have wondered if modesty was really appropriate under the circumstances. Then I would have wondered how many drafts would be required to put such complicated thoughts in a form I wouldn't be embarrassed to send to Ambrose Bierce. Then I would have put Bierce's letter in my desk drawer, reminding myself that I should get right to it just as soon as I took care of some other important matters, such as alphabetizing my filing cabinets and giving my baseball mitt its spring application of neat's-foot oil.

Mencken, making one of those quick decisions that are characteristic of the type of people who answer their mail, apparently wrote Bierce a simple note of thanks, because Bierce sounded slightly embarrassed in the next letter he wrote Mencken. "Happening to look you up in *Who's Who,* I've been thinkin' that you can't have been greatly feathered by my 'coming upon' you unexpectedly," Bierce wrote. "The purpose of this note, however, is not apologetic: I'd like to know which of your books you are least ashamed of, so that I may read it." (Most writers I know, including me, would have saved that last line for some revenue-producing effort—perhaps a short story that included a letter from one acerbic literary man to another—but it's possible that Bierce had enough of those lines to toss off two or three at the breakfast table every morning without having to remind himself to write them down. It's also possible that he might have used them in a letter and *then* in a revenue-producing effort.)

From these first letters there followed what letter writers would probably consider a pleasant correspondence—until Bierce went off to Mexico and disappeared. If I had been Mencken at about the time Bierce was presumed dead, the weight of my sorrow would have been lightened a bit by the thought that at least I had one less correspondent to worry about.

As it turned out, though, that thought would have been premature. Bierce had left a daughter. The daughter could read and write English and owned a supply of stationery. In a few years, Mencken found himself locked in correspondence with her about a memoir she proposed writing about life with her father—a memoir to be produced with the literary assistance of Stephen Crane's niece. Not long after that, Mencken found himself composing letters to Stephen

Crane's niece, who had decided, after the Bierce collaboration, that she was ready to write a memoir about life with Stephen Crane. That didn't stop the letters from Bierce's daughter. She asked Mencken's advice about republishing a Bierce anthology and about the possibility of selling movie rights to Bierce's short stories. She asked Mencken's advice about getting the novel of a friend published. After some years of such requests, she, too, died, which would have brought an end to the letters Mencken had to write to the Bierce family except that he was already deeply involved in a correspondence with her cousin, Edward Bierce.

Edward Bierce wanted Mencken's advice on a number of subjects, such as how to get a job on a newspaper. He also enjoyed sending Mencken chatty letters that contained no specific requests but had to be answered fairly quickly in order to avoid another letter asking if anything was wrong. In the thirties, then, Mencken was steadily writing letters not only to Theodore Dreiser and Sinclair Lewis, but also to the last remaining letter-writing heir of Ambrose Bierce.

Edward Bierce's letters seem to have fallen off in the forties. Then, in 1953, Mencken received a letter on the stationery of the Long Beach, California, *Independent-Press-Telegram*. It was signed not by Edward Bierce but by a newspaperwoman who said she knew him—and casually tossed in the information that, two and a half years before, she had covered the trial in which he had been convicted of second-degree murder in the death of his wife. ("He was justified in beating her," the newspaperwoman wrote, "but he should have stopped before he killed her.") The reason for the letter was not to report on Bierce's domestic misfortune but to ask Mencken's help in obtaining a publisher for the newspaperwoman's eighty-thousand-word novel about the Nebraska sand hills and early Wyoming.

That was forty years after the apparently innocent compliment on the *Smart Set* articles. If I had been in Mencken's place during that span of years, I might have begun to feel guilty at some point about having Ambrose Bierce's still unanswered letter in my desk. But, then, nobody would be asking my help in obtaining a publisher for an eighty-thousand-word novel about the Nebraska sand hills and early Wyoming. The blessings of sloth.

1971

Answer Man

In the most recent Great Canadian Literary Quiz, a contest that runs annually in the Toronto *Globe and Mail,* I was the answer to No. 18. Not to boast. Well, to boast just a bit. Being an answer in the literary quiz of an entire country—one that just happens to have the second-largest landmass in the entire world—is not an honor that comes someone's way every day. It's true that at Southwest High School, in Kansas City, I was voted Third Most Likely to Succeed. That was in 1953, though, and a year or so ago I stopped mentioning it if someone happened to ask "Had any honors lately?" I'd decided that my wife was correct in observing that it might have lost a certain freshness.

On the other hand, being the answer to No. 18 in the Great Canadian Literary Quiz was something I considered worth bringing up, in an offhand sort of way, at the office water fountain. The response of one of the office's premier scoffers, I regret to say, was, "I would have thought that every answer in a Canadian literary quiz would be Robertson Davies."

Wrong. Not just wrong, but wrong in a way that reflects the patronizing American attitude that we figures in the Canadian literary world—even those of us who haven't been figures for terribly long—deeply resent. In fact, I can just imagine discussing that very subject with others who are answers to questions on the Great Canadian Literary Quiz. We'd be at a literary soirée at the top of some swanky high-rise in Toronto—Saul Bellow and Robert MacNeil (both answers to No. 34) and Michael Ondaatje (No. 33A) and, even though it crowds the room a bit, British Columbia (No. 49C). We'd all know one another well enough to use the numbers of the questions we're the answers to as sort of in-crowd nicknames:

"You know, Twenty-two, that remark about Robertson Davies

demonstrates just the sort of Yank arrogance you were talking about in your opposition to NAFTA," I'm saying to Margaret Atwood. "Say, isn't that Forty-one coming through the door?" Forty-one is Alice Munro, who has just entered the room chatting with Brian Moore, whom we all call Twenty, of course, or in particularly affectionate moments, Twen.

Just for the record, by the way, I informed the office scoffer that of the fifty answers in the Great Canadian Literary Quiz, many of them multiple answers, Robertson Davies was the answer to only No. 14E. And what was the question whose answer was Robertson Davies? I don't know. Actually, I don't know the question whose answer was me—or as we literary figures tend to say, I. My friend Dusty sent me the *Globe and Mail* that carried the answers to the quiz—she'd circled the answer to No. 18—but not the *Globe and Mail* that carried the questions.

I suspected that question No. 18 had something to do with my longtime contention that I should be recognized as one-sixth Canadian content. For some years, one method Canada has used to avoid being culturally subsumed into the United States is to insist that, say, a film or a broadcasting project include a certain percentage of Canadians—what's called Canadian content. Since I live in Nova Scotia in July and August—one-sixth of the year—I have long maintained that for every six books of Mordecai Richler's on the Canadiana shelf, there should be one of mine.

In making this claim, I've taken the sort of low-key approach that might be expected from a literary figure in Canada. I've simply laid out the simple math at the heart of it and said, in effect, "How about it, guys?" Actually, given the fact that Canada has twice as many official languages as some countries I can think of, I've also said, in effect, "*Alors, qu'est-ce que vous en pensez, les mecs*?"

Maybe No. 18 was an indication that my Canadian content papers have finally come through. ("Which writer has just been certified as fractional Canadian content?")

But what if No. 18 had been something like "Which American writer with vague Canadian connections has made a pest out of himself on the issue of Canadian content?" or "Which Nova Scotia summer resident named Calvin has been observed smiling modestly when complimented on books about the art world that were actually written by Calvin Tomkins?" It occurred to me that, in the world of literature, the pleasures of being an answer are not really dependent on knowing the question.

1998

Publisher's Lunch

For a long time, I've had a lot of ideas for improving the publishing industry, many of them acquired in the course of doing research for a book I have been working on for years—*An Anthology of Authors' Atrocity Stories About Publishers.* (So far, I have failed to find a publisher for the book, despite a friend of mine having improved the original idea considerably by proposing that the anthology be published as an annual.) It has recently occurred to me that there is a way to make my ideas for the industry mandatory through the simple vehicle of New York City ordinances. Because publishers are concentrated in Manhattan, their activities could be regulated in the same way that taxi rates and building permits are regulated. The city council could simply pass a law, for instance, that read "The advance for a book must be larger than the check for the lunch at which it was discussed."

Yes, the publishers would say that such a law was unrealistic. They would threaten a mass move to New Jersey—the way the Wall Street crowd threatened to move to New Jersey when the city hinted about imposing what amounted to a parasite tax on stock-and-bond transactions—but the threat would obviously never be carried out. Where would publishers eat lunch in New Jersey?

Some of the ordinances would be simple consumer protection. Any person furnishing a blurb for a book jacket, for instance, would be required to disclose his connection to the author of the book. A one-sentence parenthetical identification, supported by an affidavit filed in triplicate with the Department of Street Maintenance and Repair, would suffice. If, for example, a new novel by Cushman Jack Hendricks carried a blurb by a famous novelist named Dred Schlotz saying "Hendricks writes like an angel with steel in its guts," the blurb would simply be signed "Dred Schlotz (Drinking buddy at Elaine's)" or "Dred Schlotz (Hopes to be chosen shortstop on the author's team at next East Hampton writers softball game)" or "Dred Schlotz (Just a fellow who likes to keep his name before the reading public between books)."

I suppose the publishers would put up some First Amendment quibble to the Open Blurb Law. But what I propose is really no different from the truth-in-packaging legislation that requires, say, frozen-food manufacturers to list how much MSG and cornstarch the consumer will be eating if he thaws out what purports to be a spinach soufflé. Although there may be writers who believe their books to be different in spirit from a spinach soufflé, spiritual differences are not recognized by the Department of Consumer Affairs.

One ordinance would require any novel containing more than three hundred pages and/or fourteen major characters and/or three generations to provide in its frontis matter a list that includes the name of each character, the page of first mention, nickname or petname, and sexual proclivities. Under another ordinance, passed despite some opposition from an organization called Urban Neurotics United, each publisher would be limited to one Kvetch Novel per month ("A Kvetch Novel," in the language of the ordinance, "will be defined as any novel with a main character to whom any reader might reasonably be expected to say, 'Oh, just pull up your socks!' "). All profits from books published by convicted felons who have held public office would, by law, be turned over to a fund that provides kleptomaniacs with scholarships to Harvard Business School. An author will be legally prohibited from ending a book's Acknowledgments by thanking his wife for her typing. There would be no books by any psychotherapist who has ever appeared on a talk show. Each September, under the joint supervision of the Office of the Borough President of Staten Island and the Department of Marine Resources, the city itself would publish a book called *An Anthology of Authors' Atrocity Stories About Publishers.*

1978

MADLY MAKING MONEY

"My long-term investment strategy has been criticized as being entirely too dependent on Publishers Clearing House sweepstakes."

New Bank Merger

A bank has swallowed up the bank that swallowed up my bank.
It condescends to smaller banks that it will now outrank.
My checkbook must be changed again, I fear.
The branch I was beginning to hold dear
Because it's now familiar, and so near,
Will be well merged, and quickly disappear.
And so again I hardly know which CEO to thank.
A bank has swallowed up the bank that swallowed up my bank.

1995

An Outtake from *Antiques Roadshow*

ROSS LINKARD, LINKARD & SONS ANTIQUES, ALEXANDRIA, VIRGINIA: And what can you tell us, sir, about this bowl you've brought in—ceramic, it appears, with a rustic scene on it that looks to me like . . . Is that a man standing in a hole?

RED-FACED MAN: We've never really been able to determine whether he's in a hole or it's just a very short man. People were a lot smaller in those days, you know.

LINKARD: And may I ask how you come to have this bowl?

RED-FACED MAN: I bought it at a garage sale in New Jersey. From an old woman. Quite old. Blind, actually. Legally blind, that is. A lot of those legally blind people can see, you know. But I remember she never contradicted me when I kept saying how if we bought the bowl we'd probably have to spend a lot more money on it getting the stain out.

LINKARD: I don't see any stain here.

RED-FACED MAN: Well, that's just it. There wasn't any stain. I read in one of those books about how to bargain that you have to take advantage of your adversary's weakness, and I figured that her big weakness was that she couldn't see. So I think I really outsmarted her and picked me up a real bargain.

LINKARD: You cheated a blind person to get this bowl?

RED-FACED MAN: I wouldn't say "cheated." It's what you call a negotiating device. If some ignorant bozo came into your shop to sell you some old picture he'd found in the attic, and you recognized it as a Henry David Thoreau, would you tell him that? No, you'd take advantage of his weakness—ignorance, in this case—and you'd buy it for a pittance. Isn't that what this whole business is about—putting one over on people?

LINKARD: Henry David Thoreau was not a painter.

RED-FACED MAN: Just my point. That would make the picture all the rarer, wouldn't it?

LINKARD: Well, I've gone over this bowl, and I should say first that this type of artifact is relatively common in the Middle Atlantic states.

RED-FACED MAN: Is New Jersey a Middle Atlantic state?

LINKARD: Yes, indeed, it is.

RED-FACED MAN: Right! That checks out exactly! I think we're onto something.

LINKARD: As I was saying, these artifacts are relatively common in the Middle Atlantic states. They tend to be wide, hemispherical vessels, used to hold food or fluids. We see them quite often in kitchens. This one has the classic bowl-like shape. Concave. And then, you see, if you turn it around it becomes convex. That's classic. You'll find that in all of them.

RED-FACED MAN: This is all starting to fall into place. I've obviously got a real find here.

LINKARD: Did the woman tell you anything about how the bowl happened to be in her possession?

RED-FACED MAN: She said it had been in her husband's family for generations. Her husband had recently died and she felt she had to sell it, along with a lot of other items in the garage, to raise money for his headstone. But I wouldn't try going to the bank with that headstone story. You probably hear that a dozen times a day in your line of work, right? I mean, if every helpless-looking old blind woman who said she wanted to sell something to get money to pay for her husband's headstone really did, the countryside would be littered with headstones. We'd be tripping over headstones. The highways would be blocked.

LINKARD: Did she have any idea how the bowl got into the family?

RED-FACED MAN: Her husband had always been told that one of his ancestors got it as a wedding gift in the late eighteenth century from a wealthy flax broker. Since then, a cousin of mine has told me that in the late eighteenth century it was a custom to do pictures of men standing in holes, and that there was also a custom of doing pictures of short men. I understand that when they did both at the same time, you sometimes couldn't see the man at all. So all that checks out.

LINKARD: Well, I don't doubt that it could be of Middle Atlantic origin, but I'd say it's a piece that's quite a bit more recent than the eighteenth century.

RED-FACED MAN: What makes you say that?

LINKARD: Well, for one thing, this inscription on the bottom here that says "microwave safe."

RED-FACED MAN: You don't think that could have been added later?

LINKARD: I think it's highly unlikely. May I ask you, sir, how much you paid for this bowl?

RED-FACED MAN: I paid a hundred dollars. Got her down from a hundred and fifty.

LINKARD: You paid a hundred dollars for a bowl you can get for two or three dollars at Wal-Mart? You've got to be kidding!

RED-FACED MAN: I don't see anything funny about this.

LINKARD: Oh, my, that's rich. Mercy me. A hundred dollars. Lance, Charlie—did you hear that? A hundred dollars. Oh, that's just too good.

RED-FACED MAN: Stop laughing!

LINKARD: Got her down from a hundred and fifty! Got the blind woman down from a hundred and fifty! I can't stand it. I'm going to split a gut. . . . Sir, I don't think you should hold the bowl above your head that way. . . . Argghhh!

[*Brrnng*. Cut to graphic.]

CERAMIC BOWL: $2 TO $3

2001

Dow Plunges on News of Credit Crisis in the United Arab Emirates

Here's something that will make you sigh:
We're all connected to Dubai.

2009

The Alice Tax

The proposal by the House of Representatives to put a 10 percent tax surcharge on income over a million dollars a year—the proposal that so horrified the White House and caused grown senators to shake in their tasseled loafers—is seen by the tax specialists around our house as a considerably watered down version of what we call the Alice Tax.

If George Bush had heard about the original Alice Tax—which has been proposed for years by my wife, Alice—he would have had, to paraphrase the populist philosopher Bart Simpson, a horseshoe. The true Alice Tax would probably inspire what the medical profession sometimes calls "harumph palpitations" in those senators who used the word "confiscatory" to describe a surcharge that would have brought the highest possible tax on incomes over a million dollars a year to 41 percent. To state the provisions of the Alice Tax simply, which is the only way Alice allows them to be stated, it calls for this: After a certain level of income, the government would simply take everything. When Alice says confiscatory, she means confiscatory.

The Alice Tax is not Alice's only venture into economic theory. She also came up with Alice's Law of Compensatory Cashflow, which holds that not buying some luxury item you can't afford is the equivalent of windfall income. So that she might say, "Well, of course we can go to the Caribbean, now that we have the money we saved by not buying that expensive sound system," while I, a befuddled look on my face, start patting various pockets in a desperate effort to find the money she's talking about. But Alice's Law of Compensatory Cashflow is more in the realm of what the experts call Personal Finance. The Alice Tax is meant as Alice's contribution to national economic policy.

The ruling principle of the Alice Tax is the concept of enoughness—a concept so foreign to the current American notions of capitalism that senators are able to see naked confiscation in a tax rate that people who made over a million a year in just about any other industrialized country in the world would consider piddling. Alice believes that at a certain point an annual income is simply more than anybody could possibly need for even a lavish style of living. She is willing to discuss what that point is. In her more flexible moments, she is even willing to listen to arguments about which side of the line a style of living that included, say, a large oceangoing boat should fall on. But she insists that there is such a thing as enough—a point of view that separates her from the United States Senate.

A congressman I saw on television being asked why the surcharge that passed in the House of Representatives was defeated in the Senate pointed out that a tremendous number of senators are millionaires—although, if I may be permitted to be fair for a change, they may not take in that amount each and every year. He was, in other words, arguing for the interpretation that the senators were loath to vote for the millionaire's tax not because their main bankrollers would be affected, but because they themselves would be affected—that rare modern example of absolutely direct democracy.

To be fair once again—actually, I hate being fair twice in a row, but I feel I'm representing Alice to a certain extent here—the senators would argue that they were not protecting their own incomes, but making certain that people vital to the economy were not robbed of their incentive. According to that reasoning, imposing a truly confiscatory tax after, say, an income of ten million dollars a year—a figure we can use for the sake of argument as long as Alice is not in the room—would mean that the entrepreneurial and highly motivated would stop their money grubbing as soon as they reached that level, and thus rob the economy of the expansion and activities their efforts bring.

In the first place, Alice would argue, they wouldn't stop. She would argue that the very fact that they devote their lives to trying to make more money than anybody could possibly use indicates that they behave that way not because they want more money but because they don't know any better. Also, the incentive argument assumes that what most of them do is economically beneficial to the public—an assumption that flies in the face of the past ten years of American history.

Let's take the case of Michael Milken, who made $550 million in 1987. If the Alice Tax kicked in at $10 million, he might have continued trying to rake in the booty anyway, meaning the treasury would be $540 million richer. But let's say he did call off his business dealings for the year when he reached an income of $10 million—which would have been on about January 6, according to my calculations. A lot of people who were laid off because merged or acquired corporations had to divert resources to pay debts might now be working. A lot of companies that went under because of the burden of truly junky junk bonds might have survived. A lot of the felonies committed by Milken after January 6 might have not been committed. A lot of people who were cheated by those felonies might not have been cheated. I rest Alice's case.

1990

Economics, with Power Steering

The Bush economists say folks with gobs
Should not be taxed (the gospel of the eighties)
So they'll invest the money and make jobs.
But that neglects the role of the Mercedes.

That's why this reinvestment talk is cant:
The man who makes a bunch of money lends
No start-up fund to some new widget plant.
Instead, he buys a white Mercedes-Benz.

And if you let him keep more of his pay
He won't finance a new assembly line.
He'll simply buy another one in gray.
The rich stay rich. The Germans like it fine.

1990

Basic Economics

I am faced with the problem of how to discuss the president's new economic plan in a way that does not reveal that I have no understanding of economics whatsoever.

For a while, I used the old method of devising one sentence that made me sound rather knowledgeable. Whenever the subject came up, I repeated the sentence in a confident tone of voice, even though I hadn't the foggiest idea of what it meant. For discussions of the new economic plan, my sentence was "The question is: What's going to happen when the deficit-reduction component begins to bite?"

This is a sentence I cobbled together from a couple of different phrases I heard on the radio in a discussion between two economists who were both unintelligible in an impressive way. One expert said the key would be when something started to bite, although I didn't catch precisely what it was. For all I know, it might have been trout. The other expert mentioned the deficit-reducing component. I stuck the two phrases together. That opening—"The question is"—was my own little contribution.

I liked the result. It had a nice, authoritative ring to it. I've always thought that the word "component" alone could make you sound as if you knew what you were talking about, and this seemed to confirm that theory. For a while, my sentence was very effective. People would say, "What do you think of the economic plan?"

"The question is: What's going to happen when the deficit-reduction component begins to bite?" I would say, in a voice that I hoped sounded like the voice of a tweedy man with a pipe.

"That's a good point," they would say.

"It's just one aspect," I'd say, without bothering to include the fact that I didn't know another. In fact, if you wanted to be absolutely literal about it, I didn't exactly know that one.

"Precisely," they'd say.

How was I able to get away with such blatant fakery? Simple: Most of the people I talk to don't have much more of an understanding of economics than I do. They're faking just as much as I am. They simply used another method: unfocused agreement ("that's a good point . . . precisely").

Actually, that might be overstating it a bit. Almost everyone knows more about economics than I do. I believe that the last time I gave any serious thought to the subject was when I was about eight years old, and I haven't progressed much since then. Listening as an eight-year-old to my parents and their friends talk about how nobody had any money during the Great Depression, I asked my father, "But where did all the money go?"

He couldn't tell me, and nobody since has been able to tell me.

"That's not the point," a businessman I know said many years later, when I asked him where all the money went during the Great Depression. "That's not the way you'd express the economic situation that obtained."

"Just as I thought," I said. "You don't know either."

So a lot of people are faking it. Even so, if you employ the same sentence in four or five straight conversations about the president's new economic plan, they tend to become suspicious. Some smart-aleck might say, "That's what you said last time" or "What's all that 'component' talk about?" or even "Are you faking it again?"

Which means that I'm back to my old problem of how to discuss the president's new economic plan in a way that does not reveal that I have no understanding of economics whatsoever. Sometimes I think of going back and taking all of those economics courses that I avoided so assiduously in college—although I suspect that they are being taught by people who are unintelligible in an impressive way.

Sometimes, I dream of meeting someone who both understands economics and can explain it in simple terms to an oaf like me. I ask him what he thinks of the president's new economic plan. He says that the question is what's going to happen when the deficit-reduction component begins to bite. I agree ("that's a good point"). Then I ask him where all the money went during the Great Depression. He tells me.

1993

Wall Street Smarts

"If you really want to know why the financial system nearly collapsed in the fall of 2008, I can tell you in one simple sentence."

The statement came from a man sitting three or four stools away from me in a sparsely populated Midtown bar, where I was waiting for a friend. "But I have to buy you a drink to hear it?" I asked.

"Absolutely not," he said. "I can buy my own drinks. My 401(k) is intact. I got out of the market eight or ten years ago, when I saw what was happening."

He did indeed look capable of buying his own drinks—one of which, a dry martini, straight up, was on the bar in front of him. He was a well-preserved, gray-haired man of about retirement age, dressed in the same sort of clothes he must have worn on some Ivy League campus in the late fifties or early sixties—a tweed jacket, gray pants, a blue button-down shirt, and a club tie that, seen from a distance, seemed adorned with tiny Brussels sprouts.

"Okay," I said. "Let's hear it."

"The financial system nearly collapsed," he said, "because smart guys had started working on Wall Street." He took a sip of his martini, and stared straight at the row of bottles behind the bar, as if the conversation was now over.

"But weren't there smart guys on Wall Street in the first place?" I asked.

He looked at me the way a mathematics teacher might look at a child who, despite heroic efforts by the teacher, seemed incapable of learning the most rudimentary principles of long division. "You are either a lot younger than you look or you don't have much of a memory," he said. "One of the speakers at my twenty-fifth reunion said that, according to a survey he had done of those attending, income was now precisely in inverse proportion to academic standing in the class, and that was partly because everyone in the lower third of the class had become a Wall Street millionaire."

I reflected on my own college class, of roughly the same era. The top student had been appointed a federal appeals court judge—earning, by Wall Street standards, tip money. A lot of the people with similarly impressive academic records became professors. I could picture the future titans of Wall Street dozing in the back rows of some gut course like Geology 101, popularly known as Rocks for Jocks.

"That actually sounds more or less accurate," I said.

"Of course it's accurate," he said. "Don't get me wrong: The guys from the lower third of the class who went to Wall Street had a lot of nice qualities. Most of them were pleasant enough. They made a good impression. And now we realize that by the standards that came later, they weren't really greedy. They just wanted a nice house in Greenwich and maybe a sailboat. A lot of them were from families that had always been on Wall Street, so they were accustomed to nice houses in Greenwich. They didn't feel the need to leverage the entire business so they could make the sort of money that easily supports the second oceangoing yacht."

"So what happened?"

"I told you what happened. Smart guys started going to Wall Street."

"Why?"

"I thought you'd never ask," he said, making a practiced gesture with his eyebrows that caused the bartender to get started mixing another martini.

"Two things happened. One is that the amount of money that could be made on Wall Street with hedge fund and private equity operations became just mind-blowing. At the same time, college was getting so expensive that people from reasonably prosperous families were graduating with huge debts. So even the smart guys went to Wall Street, maybe telling themselves that in a few years they'd have so much money they could then become professors or legal-services lawyers or whatever they'd wanted to be in the first place. That's when you started reading stories about the percentage of the graduating class of Harvard College who planned to go into the financial industry or go to business school so they could then go into the financial industry. That's when you started reading about these geniuses from MIT and Caltech who, instead of going to graduate school in physics, went to Wall Street to calculate arbitrage odds."

"But you still haven't told me how that brought on the financial crisis."

"Did you ever hear the word 'derivatives'?" he said. "Do you think *our* guys could have invented, say, credit default swaps? Give me a break! They couldn't have done the math."

"Why do I get the feeling that there's one more step in this scenario?" I said.

"Because there is," he said. "When the smart guys started this business of securitizing things that didn't even exist in the first place, who was running the firms they worked for? Our guys! The lower third of the class! Guys who didn't have the foggiest notion of what a credit default swap was. All our guys knew was that they were getting disgustingly rich, and they had gotten to like that. All of that easy money had eaten away at their sense of enoughness."

"So having smart guys there almost caused Wall Street to collapse."

"You got it," he said. "It took you a while, but you got it."

The theory sounded too simple to be true, but right offhand I couldn't find any flaws in it. I found myself contemplating the sort of havoc a horde of smart guys could wreak in other industries. I saw those industries falling one by one, done in by superior intelligence. "I think I need a drink," I said.

He nodded at my glass and made another one of those eyebrow gestures to the bartender. "Please," he said. "Allow me."

2009

Voodoo Economics Up Close

"I don't like the sound of those drums, dear," Edgar said. "I think we should go back to the hotel."

Their guide turned to face them. "You be coming with me, kind mister," he said. "You be seeing real voodoo-economics ritual. No touristy stuff. Plenty supply-side." The guide nudged Edgar in the ribs with his elbow, and said in a softer voice, "You be seeing swollen bureaucracy turned into nude federalism, my mister."

"You mean *New* Federalism," Edgar said.

"Don't quibble, dear," Emily said.

The guide continued down the winding dirt path toward a thick grove of trees—gnarled trees of surpassing weirdness, their limbs heavy with ticker tape.

"I simply don't like those drums," Edgar said. "It sounds like someone's beating the hustings. And listen to that chant!"

In the distance, the sound of voices grew louder and louder. "Voo-doo, voo-doo—trickle, trickle, trickle, trickle," the voices droned in a rhythmic chant. "Voo-doo, voo-doo—trickle, trickle, trickle, trickle."

"Isn't this all simply fascinating?" Emily said, picking her way around a pile of discarded water and sewer grants. "I hope the ceremony's not too bloody, though. Thelma and Harry said that when they went last year, the sorceress just used some leftovers from the hot-lunch program for the gris-gris. Some people at their hotel said they heard that she could change two helpings of broccoli into an aircraft carrier."

"Voo-doo, voo-doo—trickle, trickle, trickle, trickle," the voices chanted. "Voo-doo, voo-doo—trickle, trickle, trickle, trickle."

"I don't like it, I tell you," Edgar said. "It gives me the creeps. And why does our guide look so much like an oil-company lobbyist?"

The guide turned to face them on the path, his eyes darting from side to side, his lips curled in a slight smile. "You be seeing real stuff, my fine sir," he said. "You be seeing too, my kind young lady. Magic! White magic! Lily-white magic! You be seeing less make more, and machine tools depreciate lightning fast before your eyes, quick-quick."

"But what's that awful smell?" Edgar asked.

The guide began to cackle. "We be cooking the books, mister," he said, shaking with mirth and rubbing his hands together. "Heh, heh, heh, heh. We be cooking hell out of the books. Heh, heh, heh, heh, heh."

They had reached a clearing in the grove of trees, and the chant now seemed nearly deafening. "Voo-doo, voo-doo—trickle, trickle, trickle, trickle. Voo-doo, voo-doo—trickle, trickle, trickle, trickle."

"You be seeing now, kind mister," the guide said. "You be seeing now poor folk bounce on safety nets. You be seeing rich folk bounce on poor folk. You be seeing this too, my kind young lady."

The chanters had reached the clearing. They were wearing hooded robes of polyester. As they stood at the edge of the clearing, their chant changed: "Two-four-six-eight—what shall we depreciate?" Then one of the robed figures stepped out from the chorus, slowly walked toward the center of the clearing, violently twisted back in his own tracks at a grotesque angle, and fell, writhing, to the ground—presumably having displaced a vertebra or perhaps even broken his back. Edgar and Emily watched in horror as one chanter after another followed the bizarre ritual.

"They be walking the Laffer curve, kind young lady," the guide said, noticing the look of distress on Emily's face.

"Those poor men!" Emily cried.

"Not for you being worried, kind miss," the guide said. "They be suffering only short-term displacement."

"I'm not so sure I like this," Emily whispered to Edgar. "Maybe we should just go back to that recreation area at the hotel and try to balance the budget on the backs of some American taxpayers. Thelma says it's not that hard once you get the hang of it, except she kept slipping off the rich ones."

Just then, a new group of chanters entered the clearing, moving in a sort of jazz rhythm. Gyrating in a way that made Emily blush, they shouted, "Trickle down, trickle down—let's go to town and trickle down!"

"I'd like to go now, Edgar," Emily said, but at that moment the voodoo sorceress appeared.

"There she is!" Edgar said.

"That be her, nice people," the guide said. "Now you be seeing her stick pins into neo-Keynesian dollies, kind missus."

"Why is she wearing an Adolfo gown?" Emily asked.

"You be watching, good people," the guide said. "She be sacrificing chicken and giving the back and gizzard to poor folk on strictly volunteer basis."

The chorus now began hauling some sort of idol on wheels into the clearing.

"It's a Trojan horse," Edgar said.

"There be the chicken now, kind mister," the guide said.

"That's no chicken; that's a Trojan horse," Emily said, as the sorceress slit open the belly of the horse and tax breaks for the rich began to pour out.

"Nice fat chicken it be," the guide said. "Lucky poor be getting nice fat gizzard."

"Let's get out of here, Edgar!" Emily said.

"Furthermore," the guide continued, "a deregulated oil and natural gas industry assures all Americans a dependable energy supply within the framework of traditional American free enterprise."

"Jesus Christ!" Edgar said. "He *is* an oil-company lobbyist!" Edgar grabbed Emily's hand, and they scrambled toward the path.

"It be nice chicken," the guide shouted after them, having quickly fallen back into his role. "Voodoo be bringing chicken in every pot, two cars in every garage."

1982

All Puffed Up

I haven't quite figured out how cigar smoking got taken over by Wall Street types who wear red suspenders. I haven't figured it out partly because I don't like to think about it. I don't like to think about it because I'm afraid I'll start wallowing in nostalgia for the days back in Kansas City when stogies were smoked by people like my cousin Sam, a man who played in the American Legion drum-and-bugle corps and never heard of a power breakfast.

I hasten to say that I am not bringing this up out of concern for the health of Wall Street types who wear red suspenders. I hasten to say that because they're always quick to respond to such expressions of concern with a lot of hot air about how the New Puritans have tried to rob independent-minded (and maybe even dashing) Americans of their freedoms. If the health of Wall Street types who wear red suspenders was high on my list of worries, I would have long ago devoted some attention to studies indicating that wearing red suspenders, instead of a belt, lowers your sperm count.

My cousin Sam probably had his faults; I'm aware that people with discerning ears for music might have included the American Legion drum-and-bugle corps in this category. But if his wife, Min, ever told him to get that smelly cigar out of the house, I can't imagine that his response would have been to start kvetching about smokers being oppressed. As I understand the customs of American Legion members in Sam's era, the acceptable response to Min's request would have been to go out on the porch with the cigar or to tell Min to shut her trap. The New Puritanism wouldn't have come into it.

One way to figure this, I know, is that cigar smoking follows logically from wine drinking for people who want to demonstrate that they've arrived: one more habit that's expensive and lends itself to pedantry. That view is supported by a recent advertisement for the magazine *Cigar Aficionado,* which lists among the subjects discussed in the current issue "the expensive gamble of owning thoroughbred racehorses, the mystique of a Savile Row suit, and a blind tasting of eighty-three maduros."

In other words, *Cigar Aficionado* can be seen as *Martha Stewart Living* for males, a guidebook for the man who is not quite secure about whether he has truly become what used to be called in my high school a suave dog (with "suave" pronounced, of course, as if it rhymed with "wave").

Someone who is analytically inclined, I realize, would maintain that red suspenders and cigars, one formerly associated with firemen and the other with people like fight managers, have a significant connection. Is it an accident, he'd ask, that people who make their living fiddling with money, an enterprise traditionally considered effete compared with manufacturing a decent American widget, have taken on the symbols of tough guys?

One problem I have with that approach is that the Wall Street types who wear red suspenders and smoke cigars don't necessarily work on Wall Street; some of them just want to look like Michael Douglas in the movie. Another problem I have with it is that my normal response to hearing the analytically inclined ask whether something is an accident is to say, "Yeah, probably."

That attitude makes me equally skeptical about the possibility that this all has to do with sex. After all, even Freud may have said, "Sometimes a cigar is just a cigar." To which Jung may or may not have added, "Sometimes it's an affectation." To which my cousin Sam would have said, "Or a stogie, bozo."

1996

Embarrassment of Riches

The way I see it, some enterprising executive who would be willing to work for, say, $10 or $20 million a year might be able to maneuver himself into a position to become CEO of The Walt Disney Company. Of course he'd have to play his cards right.

The thought that the CEO job at Disney might be available first occurred to me in 1988, during a protracted strike of Hollywood screenwriters. One of the issues in contention was the studios' insistence that, because of the "new, colder realities facing the entertainment industry," the writers accept a rollback of the residual payments they were receiving.

In an article in *The New Yorker,* Joan Didion pointed out that the total received in residual payments by all nine thousand members of the Writers Guild was $58 million, and that the 1987 compensation of The Walt Disney Company's CEO, Michael Eisner, was estimated at $63 million.

The juxtaposition of those two figures cried out for a mathematical adjustment. You could almost hear the readers murmuring, "If the studios simply subtracted fifty-eight million dollars from Eisner's compensation to pay the residuals, the screenwriters would be happy, Eisner would still have five million dollars a year to live on, and everyone could go back to work."

But Disney's board of directors couldn't have simply subtracted $58 million from Eisner's compensation. That would have indicated a lack of confidence in the CEO, and that, in turn, would have weakened the stock—including the stock of the directors.

So, for the good of the stockholders, it would have been better to replace Eisner than ask him to take a $58 million pay cut. That's why I thought some ambitious executive might, while having a round of golf with some members of the Disney board, mention that he would, if given Eisner's job at the same level of compensation, pay screenwriters' residuals for the entire industry out of his own salary, finance his own car and driver, and never put the National Secretaries Day flowers for his secretary on the expense account.

At the time, after all, there were, as there always are, five hundred executives considered capable of running a Fortune 500 company. As I remember the 1988 figures—*Business Week*'s annual issue on executive compensation has always been the one business publication I don't miss—people were running some of the top ten American corporations for as little as a few million dollars annually. Some CEOs may be less capable than others, of course, but $55 million a year less capable?

Disney directors apparently thought so. Eisner remained as the CEO who led the company into Euro Disney, which has now piled up debts of $4 billion despite the insistence of the Disney officials that it is attracting as many people as their projections indicated it would draw.

When I read about those projections being on target, I was reminded of a man in Nova Scotia I'll call Mr. Martin, who used to sell picnic tables for $15 until he discovered, after being urged by a friend to do some calculations, that the materials in each table were costing him $17. So this sort of thing can happen to anyone—although it should be said that nobody ever thought of paying Mr. Martin $63 million a year.

Now Disney wants to build another theme park, called Disney's America, near the Civil War battlefields of northern Virginia, and wants the state to pitch in $132 million for the necessary road improvements. Why should that worry a CEO who makes only half that much annually? Because $60 million is no longer Eisner's salary. The directors, apparently pleased as punch about Euro Disney, last year gave him a compensation package of $202 million.

So Disney, in its public relations battle with opponents of Disney's America, is faced with another tempting juxtaposition of numbers. Virginians can see that if Eisner himself paid for the roads he'd still have a $70 million annual income—$10 million more than the one he lived perfectly comfortably on as late as 1988.

That is not the only embarrassment. A group of distinguished historians oppose Disney's America as a project that will "create synthetic history by destroying real history." The natural way to counterattack is to accuse the historians of being elitists who have lost touch with the common American. And who is the just-folks spokesman for that populist message? A man who pulls down $202 million a year.

Which is why I think this is the time for some wily executive to offer to do Eisner's job for, say, $10 million a year, enabling Disney to pay for the road improvements and have enough money left over to hire fifteen $4 million-a-year CEOs from other corporations.

After working for $10 million for a few years, the wily executive would be in position to go for the real money.

1994

Two Poems on Goldman Sachs

ON CEO LLOYD BLANKFEIN'S STATEMENT THAT GOLDMAN SACHS IS "DOING GOD'S WORK"

On every seventh day the Lord can rest.
He knows that Goldman Sachs will do its best
To work away at that for which He'd hanker:
A pot of dough for each investment banker.

As He looks down at us from high above,
The Lord's not interested in peace and love
And such as that. The Lord has got this itch
To see the Goldman Sachs folks filthy rich.

He wishes they had more than what they've got—
Another house or two, another yacht.
His hopes for these to whom he gave the nod:
More money, as the saying goes, than God.

December 2009

SEC ACCUSES GOLDMAN OF FRAUD IN HOUSING DEAL

—*New York Times* headline

They're doing God's work, their CEO said.
They're kings of the Street. They are regal.
So now we must ask if God ever knew
That some of his work was illegal.

May 2010

THE YEARS WITH NAVASKY

"When I was approached about writing a column for The Nation, *I asked for only one guarantee: Would I be allowed to make fun of the editor? When it comes to civil liberties, we all have our own priorities."*

Ambushed

Looking back, I realize that my first mistake was involving myself with an occasional publication called *Monocle,* a journal of political satire whose editor was the person I came to refer to as the wily and parsimonious Victor S. Navasky. In those days, when we were all young and optimistic, I used to assure Navasky that the lack of a sense of humor was probably not an insurmountable handicap for the editor of a humor magazine. (He always responded with a nervous chuckle.) As an editor, after all, he was exacting. During the New York newspaper strike of 1963, *Monocle* published a parody edition of the *New York Post,* then as predictable in its liberalism as it was later to become in its sleaziness, and I suggested as the front-page headline COLD SNAP HITS OUR TOWN; JEWS, NEGROES SUFFER MOST. Navasky refused to use the headline merely because there was no story inside the paper to go with it—a situation that a less precise thinker might have considered part of the parody.

Even then, I must say, Navasky's hiring policies seemed erratic—particularly his appointing as advertising manager a high-minded young man who found advertising so loathsome and disgusting that, as a matter of principle, he refused to discuss the subject with anyone. What was most memorable about Victor S. Navasky at *Monocle,* though, was his system of payment to contributors—a system derived, according to my research, from a 1938 chart listing county-by-county mean weekly wages for hospital Gray Ladies. My strongest memory of *Monocle* is receiving a bill from Navasky for a piece of mine the magazine had published—along with a note explaining that the office expenses for processing the piece exceeded what he had intended to pay me for it.

In the late sixties, *Monocle* folded. I wasn't surprised. My assurances to Navasky about his not needing a sense of humor had been quite insincere. Also, I had once observed the advertising manager's reaction to being phoned at the *Monocle* office by a prospective advertiser: "Take a message," he hissed at the secretary, as he bolted toward the door. "Tell him I'm in the bathroom. Get rid of him." Then, only about ten years later, Navasky fetched up as the new editor of *The Nation.* It was difficult for me to imagine that he would dare pay Gray Lady rates at a magazine of national reputation—even a money-losing magazine of national reputation. (Historians tell us that *The Nation* was founded many years ago in order to give a long succession of left-wing entrepreneurs the opportunity to lose money in a good cause.) *The Nation,* after all, had always railed against bosses who exploit workers. I thought about Navasky's stewardship of *Monocle* for a while, and then sat down to write him a letter of congratulations on being named editor of *The Nation.* It said, in its entirety, "Does money owed writers from *Monocle* carry over?" I received no reply.

I realize that this history with Navasky is one reason for speculation by scholars in the field about the sort of negotiations that could have led to my agreeing to do a column for *The Nation.* ("If he got caught by Navasky twice, he must be soft in the head.") The entire tale can now be told. The negotiations took place over lunch at a bar in the Village. I picked up the check. I had asked Navasky beforehand if he minded my bringing along my wife, Alice. I figured that she would be a reminder that I was no longer the carefree young bachelor who barely complained about being stiffed regularly by the *Monocle* bookkeepers, but a responsible married man with two daughters and an automatic washer-dryer combination (stack model). Navasky, the cunning beast, said Alice would be most welcome. He knew her to be a sympathetic soul who somehow saw a connection in his saving money on writers and the possibility that he might buy a new suit.

Once we had our food, Navasky made his first wily move. He suggested two very specific ideas for regular columns I might be interested in writing for *The Nation*—both of them of such surpassing dumbness that I long ago forgot precisely what they were. One of them, it seems to me, was on the practical side—a weekly gardening column, maybe, or a column of auto repair hints.

"Those are the silliest ideas I ever heard," I said, with relief. "The only column I might like to do is so far from Wobbly horticulture, or whatever you have in mind, that I don't mind mentioning it because you obviously wouldn't be interested—a thousand words every three weeks for saying whatever's on my mind, particularly if what's on my mind is marginally ignoble." As long as I was safe from an agreement, I thought I might as well take advantage of one of those rare opportunities to say "ignoble" out loud.

"It's a deal," the crafty Navasky said, putting down the hamburger I was destined to pay for and holding out his hand to shake on the agreement. Caught again.

"I hate to bring up a subject that may cause you to break out in hives," I said, "but what were you thinking of paying me for each of these columns?" I reminded him of the responsibilities of fatherhood and the number of service calls necessary to keep a stack-model washer-dryer in working order.

"We were thinking of something in the high two figures," Navasky said.

I remained calm. The sort of money we were discussing, after all, was already a step up from *Monocle* rates. The only check I ever received from *Monocle*—for presiding over a panel discussion in an early issue—was for three dollars. ("Well, it's steady," I said when Navasky later asked if I would run similar discussions as a monthly feature of *Monocle*. "A person would know that he's got his thirty-six dollars coming in every year, rain or shine, and he could build his freelance on that.") Still, I felt a responsibility to do some negotiating.

"What exactly do you mean by the high two figures?" I said.

"Sixty-five dollars," Navasky said.

"Sixty-five dollars! That sounds more like the middle two figures to me. When I hear 'high two figures,' I start thinking eighty-five, maybe ninety."

"You shook on it," Navasky said. "Are you going to go back on your word right in front of your own wife?"

I looked at Alice. She shrugged. "Maybe Victor'll buy a new suit," she said.

I called for the check.

1982

Pinko Problems

For some years, I was worried about the possibility that *The Nation* was getting to be known around the country for being a bit pinko. I was born and brought up in Kansas City, and I wasn't really keen on the folks at home getting the impression that I worked for a left-wing sheet. They knew I did a column for *The Nation,* of course—my mother told them—but most of them did not inquire deeply into *The*

Nation's politics, perhaps because my mother was sort of letting on that it's a tennis magazine. She was able to get away with that because *The Nation* is not circulated widely in Kansas City: In the greater Kansas City area, it goes weekly to three librarians and an unreconstructed old anarcho-syndicalist who moved to town after his release from the federal prison at Leavenworth in 1927 and set up practice as a crank. Still, I was concerned that *The Nation*'s political views could be revealed in the press.

My concern was not based on any notion that the people back home would react to this revelation by ostracizing my mother for having given birth to a Commie rat. Folks in the Midwest try to be nice. What I was worried about was this: People in Kansas City would assume that no one would write a column for a pinko rag if he could write a column for a respectable periodical. They might even assume that payment for a column in a pinko rag would be the sort of money people in Kansas City associate with the summer retainer for the boy who mows the lawn. Realizing that I had struggled for years in New York only to end up writing a column for lawn-mowing wages, they would spend a lot of time comforting my mother whenever they ran into her at the supermarket. ("There, there. Don't you worry one bit. Things have a way of working themselves out.") My mom's pretty tough, but tougher people have broken under the burden of Midwestern comforting.

Without wanting to name names, I blame all of this on Victor S. Navasky. When *The Nation* provoked a public controversy by attacking a book on the Hiss case from a position that might have been described as somewhat left of center, I tried to be understanding. I figured that Navasky was trying to pump up circulation because he lacked some of the financial resources that most people who edit journals of opinion have. Traditionally, people who run such magazines manage financially because they have a wife rich enough to have bought them the magazine in the first place. It's a good arrangement, because an editor who has his own forum for pontificating to the public every week may tend to get a bit pompous around the house, and it helps if his wife is in a position to say, "Get off your high horse, Harry, or I'll take your little magazine away from you and give it to the cook." I haven't made any detailed investigation into the finances of Navasky's wife, but it stands to reason that if she had the wherewithal to acquire entire magazines she would by now have bought him a new suit.

No matter what his motives for running the Hiss piece were, Navasky's cover was obviously blown—and so was mine. I could no longer answer questions about why I wrote for *The Nation* by saying, "It's the closest magazine to my house." Not long after that, while I was doing a promotional tour for a collection of *Nation* columns, a newspaper interviewer in Boston asked me if I could describe the magazine for his readers.

"Pinko," I said, after some reflection.

"Surely you have more to say about it than that," he said.

"Yes," I said. "It's a pinko magazine printed on very cheap paper—the sort of magazine where if you Xerox one of your pieces, the Xerox is a lot better than the original."

1982

The Case of the Purloined Turkey

A secretly Xeroxed manuscript of Richard Nixon's new book has, as they say in the trade, found its way into my possession. For years, I have been waiting for some carefully guarded document to find its way into my possession. In my mind, the phrase has always conjured up the vision of an important document wandering the streets of Lower Manhattan, confused and bewildered, until a kindly policeman on Sixth Avenue provides flawless directions to my house. I figured that a secret document would find its way into my possession if I simply waited around long enough at the same address, looking receptive. That is precisely what happened. I did not ferret out this document. I might as well admit that I hadn't realized Mr. Nixon had produced another volume; it seemed only moments since the last one.

I had assumed, I suppose, that his literary output would have been slowed up by the bustle of moving from San Clemente and by his previous difficulties with trying to buy an apartment in East Side co-ops that persisted in treating him as if he were Jewish or a tap dancer. Ordinarily, complications involving living quarters play havoc with a writer's production; a writer I'll call William Edgett Smith, whose procrastination devices are taught in the senior creative writing seminar at Princeton, once stopped writing for seven weeks in order to see to a leaky radiator. Mr. Nixon apparently suffered no such delays—although in Smith's defense it should be said that he has to manage with no federally funded research or secretarial help to speak of. Despite the interruptions that accompany any move ("The men want to know whether those partly erased tapes in the cellar stay or go, Dick, and what do you want done with the crown jewels of Rumania?"), Mr. Nixon managed to turn out a volume for Warner Books called *The Real War.* I know because a Xerox of the manuscript found its way into my possession.

Although it is customary to refuse to divulge the source of any document that has found its way into one's possession, I should say at the start that the person who gave me this document was Victor S. Navasky, the editor of *The Nation.* If anybody feels the need to prosecute or sue, Navasky's your man. I feel no compunction about shifting the blame to Navasky, because he would obviously be the logical target of any investigation anyway, this being his second caper. At this very moment, *The Nation* is being sued by Harper & Row and *Reader's Digest* for $12,500 for running an article based on a smuggled-out manuscript of Gerald Ford's book, which was somehow published under a title other than *The White House Memories of a Lucky Klutz.* In an era when an unfairly dismissed busboy would never think of suing for less than a million, the purpose of suing *The Nation* for the price of a publisher's lunch is obvious: The plaintiffs want to make Navasky out to be not just a thief but a small-time thief.

My involvement in this started innocently when Navasky said to me, "We've got a copy of Nixon's book."

"I hope you didn't pay full price," I said.

"Not that book. The new one. Smuggled out."

Sticky Fingers Navasky had struck again. I was, of course, astonished. It's no joke to discover that you've been handing in copy to a recidivist. "If you put it back now, maybe they won't notice that it was missing," I said. Warner Books is part of the sort of conglomerate that is often described as "playing hardball," and I figured that they weren't above humiliating Navasky by suing him for something like eighteen dollars and carfare.

"Take it!" Navasky said, thrusting a bulky bundle into my arms. "Reveal something."

I took it, and skulked out the door. The elevator man was reading the sports page of the *Daily News* as we descended. "Just some laundry," I said to him, gesturing at the bundle I was carrying. "Shirts. That sort of thing." He kept reading. So far, so good.

After what seemed like about an hour, I was startled by the jangle of the telephone. It was Navasky.

"Find anything yet?" he said.

I looked down at the manuscript. I was on page 4. "He says, 'The next two decades represent a time of maximum crisis for America and for the West, during which the fate of the world for generations to come may well be determined.' "

There was silence on the phone. Then Navasky said, "Skip ahead."

I skipped ahead to page 105, and started reading. "He says, 'The final chapters have yet to be written on the war in Vietnam,' " I reported.

"Skip some more," Navasky said.

"Well," I said, "on page 287 he says, 'The President has great power in wartime as Commander in Chief of the armed forces. But he also has enormous power to prevent war and preserve peace.' "

There was a pause. "Keep skipping," Navasky said.

I read paragraphs on the advantages of summit conferences and on the difference between totalitarianism and authoritarianism. More silence. Finally, I said, "Shall I keep skipping?"

There was no answer. Navasky had fallen asleep.

What is the purpose of being willing to reveal the contents of a purloined manuscript if there is nothing in it that bears revealing?

"Let's give it back," I said to Navasky.

"Our source does not want it back," Navasky said.

"I can see his point."

"Maybe we should shred it," Navasky said.

"All I have in that line is a Cuisinart," I said. "I have a better idea. I'll put it on Sixth Avenue. Maybe it will find its way into someone else's possession."

1980

I'm Out of Here

When the editor of *The Nation*, the wily and parsimonious Victor S. Navasky, said he was going to double my pay, I did the only honorable thing: I resigned. Maybe I should start at the beginning. Here are some milestones in our relationship since the aforementioned Navasky asked me if I'd be interested in writing a column for *The Nation:*

MARCH 18, 1978. The wily and parsimonious Victor S. Navasky and I have lunch in the Village to talk about his grand vision for transforming *The Nation* from a shabby pinko sheet to a shabby pinko sheet with a humor column and a large office for the editor. I pick up the check. I ask what he plans to pay for each column. He says, "Somewhere in the high two figures."

MARCH 20, 1978. I refer the offer to my high-powered literary agent, Robert (Slowly) Lescher, together with instructions for the ensuing negotiations: "Play hardball."

APRIL 8, 1978. Slowly gets him up to $100.

SEPTEMBER 5, 1978. The W. & P. Victor S. Navasky questions the authenticity of some quotations used in my column. He says, "Did John Foster Dulles really say, 'You can't fool all of the people all of the time, but you might as well give it your best shot'?" I say, "At these rates, you can't expect real quotes."

MAY 14, 1980. Executive editor Richard Lingeman, who would probably be described by one of those hard-nosed post-Watergate reporters as "a longtime Navasky operative," sends me a Table of Organization chart that gives me pause: It lists me under "Casual Labor."

NOVEMBER 10, 1981. The W. & P. Victor S. Navasky says that although he would never try to exert any pressure to influence what I write, he might just point out that columns devoted to ridiculing him are less likely to be sold for republication in newspapers because they are considered "inside" and (although he doesn't say this) perhaps a bit distasteful. I say not to worry: Since *The Nation* never gets around to paying me my share of the republication fees, I feel no pressure at all. To show there are no hard feelings on my part, I write a column revealing him to be a klutz on the basketball court. To show there are no hard feelings on his part, he continues to hold onto my share of the republication fees.

MAY 29, 1982. I receive a letter from a reader who asks, "Is it true that employees of *The Nation* are forced to sell flowers and candy in airports and turn the proceeds over to Victor S. Navasky?" I publish the letter in my column, along with my strongly worded reply ("Not exactly").

OCTOBER 25, 1985. The wily and parsimonious Victor S. Navasky and I have lunch in the Village. He reaches for the check. I am instantly put on my guard. He says he is going to double my pay. I figure he has to be up to something. I resign. He tells me my share of the check is $13.38.

"I've quit," I told my wife when I returned from lunch. "That'll show him."

"Why didn't you just tell him you got a better offer from the newspaper syndication people?" she said.

"Because I prefer to resign on a matter of principle."

"What, exactly, is the principle involved?"

"Worker solidarity."

"Worker solidarity!" she said. "I never heard you talk about worker solidarity before."

"I never got a better offer before," I said.

"I think it's terrible that all you can talk about, even now that you're leaving *The Nation,* is money," she said.

"That's what the owners of the textile mills in Yorkshire in the nineteenth century used to say about the workers who complained that a family couldn't be supported on two and six a day: 'All they ever talk about is money.' "

"Aren't you going to miss *The Nation*?" my wife asked.

Well, of course. It was sort of comforting to know that whenever I'd show up at the office the fellow we call Harold the Committed would ask me if I'd like to see civilization as we know it destroyed in a nuclear holocaust; it's *The Nation*'s equivalent of having an elevator operator who can be counted on to say "Have a nice day." And I do feel solidarity with my fellow workers. I feel kinship with the ancient bookkeepers who have been convinced by Navasky that 10 percent of their salary is going directly into a legal defense fund for the Scottsboro Boys. I feel comradeship with the college interns Navasky has managed to lure into *The Nation*'s slave/study program. I feel brotherhood with Richard Lingeman, who, finding himself in 1956 with a strong hand but no cash during a poker game in New Haven that included Victor S. Navasky, covered a raise by signing a paper for thirty-five years of indentured editorial service, and then failed to fill out his flush. For that matter, I feel a communal bond with all those *Nation* employees selling flowers and candy in airports.

"And how about Victor Navasky?" my wife said.

"Oh, he'll get along without me."

"No doubt," she said. "But will you get along without him? Every time you haven't been able to think of a column idea, you've attacked poor Victor—just the way Ronald Reagan, whenever he was stuck for an answer, used to mention that woman who picked up her Aid for Dependent Children check in a Cadillac."

I hadn't thought of that. Navasky has been, in a manner of speaking, my welfare cheat. Doing the column for the newspapers, I wouldn't have Navasky to kick around anymore. I could imagine editors from Midwestern dailies sending queries back to the syndication people: "Who's this Navasky anyway?" they'd ask, or "What's this mean here—'There's no gonif like a left-wing gonif'?"

"Yes, I will miss the old W. & P.," I said to my wife.

"Well, it would be nice if you did something to show that," she said.

Fine. But what? "I've got it," I said, after a while. "I'll attack him for trying to double my pay."

1986

Inspired by Sununu. Paid by Navasky.

Could there be anyone else who was inspired to write poetry by the presence of John Sununu? It has occurred to me that if I ever get to poets' heaven—as I envision it, it's a place where the accent is on any syllable you want it to be on, and there are plenty of rhymes for "orange"—I might find myself feeling rather awkward during a discussion that turns toward how all of us poets acquired the vital spark of inspiration. William Shakespeare, for instance, might talk passionately, if rather enigmatically, about how inspiring the dark lady of his sonnets was. Sooner or later, the other poets would look my way, and I'd say, "Well, when George H. W. Bush was President of the United States, he had this guy from New Hampshire as chief of staff. . . ."

Sununu surfaced at a time when the small-joke trade was trying to cope with what you might call a serious gray-out. The most prominent members of Bush the First's administration were respectable Ivy League gentlemen whose blandness was not even spiced up by a decent scandal. Political cartoonists had trouble telling them apart.

Only Sununu had all the attributes we look for—arrogance, self-importance, and a management style that he might have picked up intact from the Emperor Caligula. Not since the relatively brief appearance several years before of Robert Bork—who turned out to be more interested in showing himself to be the smartest man in the room than he was in being on the Supreme Court—had Washington served up a character so intent on letting everybody know how intelligent he was.

Was I inspired by all of this? Yes, of course. But to poetry? Not exactly. What led me to poetry was that wondrously euphonious name—Sununu. I couldn't get his name out of my mind. "Sununu," I would murmur to myself while riding the subway or doing some little task around the house. Sooner or later the murmuring became the title of a poem—"If You Knew What Sununu."

After I'd sent "If You Knew What Sununu" to the wily and parsimonious Victor S. Navasky, he phoned me to suggest that I do a poem for every issue of *The Nation*. Steeling myself, I asked how much he intended to pay for each poem.

"How long does it take you to write one of these?" he asked.

"I usually write them on Sunday," I said. "Which is at least time and a half, and in most trades double time. There is also the matter of poetic inspiration—walking on the windswept bluff, and all that. Just to get from here to a windswept bluff that could be considered remotely inspirational . . ."

As I said that, I could hear his calculator clicking away. "How about a hundred?" he said.

What I realized instantly—what I suppose he meant me to realize instantly—was that I would be getting the same money for a poem as I'd gotten from an eleven-hundred-word column.

"What are the conditions?" I asked. With the wily and parsimonious Victor S. Navasky, there is always a condition or two.

"Don't tell any of the real poets you're getting that much," he said.

"Your secret is safe with me," I assured him.

At first, I didn't think a century sounded like much. But then I learned that real poets are normally paid by the line. Three-fifty or four dollars a line is fairly common, I was told, and ten dollars a line is probably tops. Since I was being paid by the poem, I realized, all I needed to become the highest paid poet in the world was pithiness. When I want to get that buzz you get when you know you're working for the absolute top dollar in your field, I write a two-line poem. Fifty dollars a line.

1994

TWENTY YEARS OF POLS— ONE POEM EACH

"I believe in an inclusive political system that prohibits from public office only those whose names have awkward meter or are difficult to rhyme."

JOHN SUNUNU
New Hampshire Governor, White House Chief of Staff

If You Knew What Sununu

If you knew what Sununu
Knows about quantum physics and Greek
And oil explorations and most favored nations
And the secret handshake of Deke,

Maybe you, too, like Sununu,
Would adopt as your principal rule
That you are the brightest, you're lit the lightest,
And everyone else is a fool.

With the IQ that Sununu
Relentlessly tells us is his,
You might think you're paid to devote half your day to
Displaying yourself as a whiz.

But
If it's true that Sununu's
So smart, you'd think that he'd know
What always defines the truly fine minds:
The smartest guys don't let it show.

1990

AL GORE
Vice President of the United States

Observed at a Clinton Press Conference

What's that, behind the President-Elect—
That manlike object stiff from head to toe?
A statue of a noble Southern pol?
A waxen image crafted by Tussaud?
But wait! He breathed. He blinked. He scratched his nose.
This couldn't be an adamantine blob.
This manlike object seems to be alive.
It's Albert Gore. He's there to do his job.

1992

BILL CLINTON
President of the United States

Just Cool It

I liked the way that Reagan simply vanished when he could.
For weeks, we'd hear a single phrase: "He's happy chopping wood."
If we were not aware of him, he didn't seem to care.
When Ronald Reagan wasn't there, he simply wasn't there.
This Clinton's with us day and night—his voice, his plans, his sax.
At times, you want to say, "Hey, Bill, just cool it, guy. Relax."
Yes, Clinton needs a rest, all right, and we need one from him.
We needn't know with whom he golfs, with whom he takes a swim.
We can't absorb so much of him. That's one of our frustrations.
I think that our relationship needs separate vacations.

1993

LLOYD BENTSEN
Texas Senator, Secretary of the Treasury

A Short History of Lloyd Bentsen's Dealings with Special Interests

The man is known for quo pro quidness.
In Texas, that's how folks do bidness.

1993

STEVE FORBES
Contender for the Republican Presidential Nomination

Welcome, Malcolm Forbes, Jr.

And now we have a junior Forbes,
Named Steve, who cheerfully absorbs
The campaign costs. (For he enjoys
What Daddy couldn't spend on toys.)
He longs for tax rates that are flat—
The same for him, a plutocrat,
As for his gardeners and his chars
And all the men who wax his cars.
Economies, he says, can grow
If builders get to keep their dough.
If all of them are forced to share it,
They'll lose incentive to inherit.

1995

RICHARD LUGAR
Indiana Senator, Contender for the
Republican Presidential Nomination

Lugar as Candidate

Poor Lugar's problem's quite specific:
The man is simply soporific.
His speeches, well prepared and deep,
Affect one much like counting sheep.

Although his résumé is great, he
Can really make your eyelids weighty.

His ads now say that he's the guy
We want in charge if bad types try
To do atomic terror here.
He may be right, except it's clear
If Dick is prez—make no mistake—
We'll need the Bomb to stay awake.

1995

PETE WILSON
California Governor, Contender for the Republican Presidential Nomination

On the Withdrawal of Pete Wilson

A month's campaign for Wilson came to naught.
He tried to sell his soul, and no one bought.

1996

ROBERT DOLE
Kansas Senator, Republican Nominee for President

A Deadline Poet's Adieu to Bob Dole

So many folks will miss you when you leave,
And as a poet, Bob, I'm going to grieve.

I'll miss your wit, the darkness of your soul—
But mostly all those words that rhyme with Dole.
Yes, "decontrol" and "poll" and "camisole"
And "goal" and "Old King Cole" and "escarole."
With Clinton staying in the White House it'll
Remain so hard; he rhymes with very little.
You'll be nearby. We say, in voce sotto,
At least the Watergate's not Kansas, Toto.

1996

ALFONSE D'AMATO
New York Senator

Senator D'Amato Says that the Finance Committee May Investigate Clinton Deals

Here's what could drive a man to drink—
To drink until he's wholly blotto:
The thought that he is being judged
On ethics by Alfonse D'Amato.

As this stretch suggests, the senator's name was not easy to rhyme, although I found that it did rhyme with "sleazeball obbligato."

1996

RICHARD NIXON
President of the United States

On the New Surfeit of Presidential Tapes

The tapes are coming thick and fast.
There's JFK, with staff amassed
When war with Russia was so close
We all might have to say *adios*.
And Lyndon Johnson's tapes reveal
The man was keen to make a deal—
And to that end was not averse
To being bullyboy or worse.
Such tapes are bound to be replete
With clay in presidential feet.
(Republicans up on the Hill
Must wish they had such tapes of Bill;
They think that Bill, although he's canny,
Has clay extending to his fanny.)
But when it comes to feet of clay,
New Nixon tapes have won the day.
His quick response to any news
Is break the law or blame the Jews.
We hear him planning to defraud,
Collecting dough for posts abroad,
Discussing B&E techniques.
In Nixon's tapes, the master speaks.

1997

GEORGE W. BUSH

President of the United States

The Effect on His Campaign of the Release of George W. Bush's College Transcript

Obliviously on he sails,
With marks not quite as good as Quayle's.

The fact that those marks got him into Harvard Business School is another confirmation of which class of Americans the original affirmative action system was established to benefit.

1999

JOHN ASHCROFT

Missouri Senator, Attorney General

The Only King We Have Is Jesus

A Newly Unearthed Gospel Song Credited to John Ashcroft

As I told the Bob Jones students,
Seated white and black apart,
This nation is unique, not like the rest.
As I faced those godly youngsters,
I told them from the heart
Just why this land will always be the best:

The only king we have is Jesus,
And I feel blessed to bring that news.
The only king we have is Jesus.
I can't explain why we've got Jews.

So because our king is Jesus,
I'm often heard to say,
Our kids should pray to Him each day in class.
If some kids just stay silent,
That's perfectly okay,
But they'll all be given Jesus tests to pass.

The only king we have is Jesus.
That's the truth we all perceive.
The only king we have is Jesus,
So Hindus may just have to leave.

Now Jesus hates abortion,
'Cause Jesus loves all life.
They call it choice; it's murder all the same.
The killers must be punished—
The doctor, man, and wife.
We'll execute them all in Jesus' name.

The only king we have is Jesus.
It's Jesus who can keep us pure.
The only king we have is Jesus,
And He's Republican for sure.

The homosexual lifestyle
Could make our Jesus weep.
He loathed their jokes about which cheek to turn.
Yes, Jesus came to teach us
With whom we're supposed to sleep.
Ignore that and you'll go to hell to burn.

(FINAL CHORUS SUNG IN TONGUES)
Tron smleck gha dreednus hoke b'loofnok
Frak fag narst fag madoondah greeb.
Tron smleck gha dreednus hoke b'loofnok
Dar popish, flarge dyur darky, hebe.

2001

DICK CHENEY
Wyoming Congressman, Secretary of Defense,
Vice President of the United States

Cheney's Head: An Explanation

One mystery I've tried to disentangle:
Why Cheney's head is always at an angle.
He tries to come on straight, and yet I can't
Help notice that his head is at a slant.
When Cheney's questioned on the Sunday shows,
The Voice of Reason is his favorite pose.
He drones in monotones. He never smiles—
Explaining why some suspects don't need trials,
Or why right now it simply stands to reason
That criticizing Bush amounts to treason,
Or which important precept it would spoil
To know who wrote our policy on oil,
Or why as CEO he wouldn't know
What Halliburton's books were meant to show.
And as he speaks I've kept a careful check
On when his head's held crooked on his neck.
The code is broken, after years of trying:
He only cocks his head when he is lying.

2002

RICHARD PERLE
Chairman of the Defense Policy Board Advisory Committee, Deputy Field Marshal of the Sissy Hawk Brigade (Vietnam War Evaders Lobbying for an Invasion of Iraq)

Richard Perle: Whose Fault Is He?

Consider kids who bullied Richard Perle—
Those kids who said Perle threw just like a girl,
Those kids who poked poor Perle to show how soft
A momma's boy could be, those kids who oft
Times pushed poor Richard down and could be heard
Addressing him as Sissy, Wimp, or Nerd.
Those kids have got a lot to answer for,
'Cause Richard Perle now wants to start a war.
The message his demeanor gets across:
He'll show those playground bullies who's the boss.
He still looks soft, but when he writes or talks
There is no tougher dude among the hawks.
And he's got planes and ships and tanks and guns—
All manned, of course, by other people's sons.

In an uncharacteristically prankish mood, I wrote that poem without knowing anything about Richard Perle's childhood. After it appeared, though, I heard from one of Perle's grade school classmates, who wanted to know how I'd found out that Perle had been bullied. Then another classmate wrote The Nation, *saying that she didn't remember Perle as a wimp but as simply "very serious." After gathering a couple of true details, I answered Perle's defender in* The Nation: *"You were not one of the fourth-grade girls who used to push Richard down the hill on Fuller Street, and you didn't laugh once in sixth grade when Rocco Guntermann, from Mrs. Flynn's class, referred to Richard as 'Perlie Girl'? Fine. Whatever you say. If the United States invades Iraq without provocation, it won't be your fault."*

She wrote again. She remembered Fuller Street and Mrs. Flynn, but she claimed there was no Rocco Guntermann. My final answer in the letters column was, "I suppose Rocco Guntermann, the classmate whose existence you deny, did not say to me just last week, 'We can settle this if Perlie Girl meets me near the swings at five o'clock on Friday, and tell him not to bring two teachers and his mother this time.' Would it surprise you to learn that Rocco is now a psychotherapist in Sherman Oaks?"

2002

COLIN POWELL
Secretary of State

Farewell, Colin Powell

We need to say farewell to Colin Powell,
Who should have long ago tossed in the towel.
Instead he lent his good name to the team
In vouching for its cockamamie scheme.
And now the team has shoved him out the door—
Not needed anymore (they got their war).
He's let himself be used by lesser men.
It's sad to see, as we remember when
Some thought he was the President-Elect to be,
How easily is done a Colinectomy.

2004

TOM DELAY

Texas Congressman, House Majority Leader

I Think I Heard a Liberal Say

I think I heard a liberal say
To this DA, "Hooray! Hooray!
Because you finally made my day
When you indicted Tom DeLay.
They'll never fashion, come what may,
An ethics rule that he'd obey.
Corruption's in his DNA.
It dominates his résumé.
He works the shadowed shades of gray.
The moment that his side held sway,
He made the lobbyists on K
Just hire those who thought his way,
Then pay and pay and pay and pay.
For access, he did pay-to-play.
The Congress of the USA
Became the cages of Bombay.
So here's what I'd like for the Hammer:
A whole bunch of years in the slammer."

2004

CONDOLEEZZA RICE
National Security Advisor

Condoleezza Rice

Sung to the Tune of "March of the Siamese Children" from **The King and I,** ***and Accompanied by the Secretary Herself on the Baby Grand***

Condoleezza Rice, who is cold as ice, is precise with her advice.
Yes, she is quite precise, and, yes, she's cold as ice.
In her can be found talents that abound. She's renowned, though tightly wound. Yes, talents can be found, and, yes, she's tightly wound.

She once avowed we might see a large mushroom cloud if more reign by Hussein were allowed,
Which turned out to be: total bushwa, yes, total bushwa.
When she accused him of buying tubes only used to make nukes the truth was abused.
And she knew she spoke total bushwa, yes, total bushwa.

So to serve her guy, she will testify to a lie she hopes you'll buy—to try to petrify, precisely tell a lie.
Condoleezza Rice, who is cold as ice, is precise with her advice.
Yes, she is quite precise, and, yes, she's cold as ice.

2005

GEORGE ALLEN

Virginia Senator, Presumed Contender for the Republican Presidential Nomination

George Allen Calls a Dark-Skinned American a "Macaca"

Republican insiders once agreed,
When contemplating who'd most likely lead
Their presidential ticket in '08,
George Allen was the perfect candidate.
He fit what's often valued by the Right:
Quite cheerful, Reaganesque, and not too bright.
His '06 Senate race was called a breeze,
But then one comment brought him to his knees.
He said "macaca" in a way that fully
Revealed him simply as a racist bully.
The deed was done that fast; within a beat
This man was set to lose his Senate seat.
One message should have then been learned by all:
That YouTube's always lurking in the hall.

2006

DONALD RUMSFELD
Secretary of Defense

An Opponent of the War Attempts to Say Farewell to Donald Rumsfeld with at Least a Modicum of Courtesy

To be so wrong so often is a curse,
But being arrogantly wrong is worse.
Still, briefings were a hoot. Our favorite feature?
That tone—exactly like a third-grade teacher
Explaining math to those forevermore
Too slow to get promoted to grade four.
So may you find, as down life's road you're wending,
More folks to whom you're always condescending.

2006

DAVID VITTER
Louisiana Senator

On the Latest Washington Scandal

All Washington, D.C., is now atwitter
With talk about some deeds of David Vitter.
With sanctimony, he had always been
Prepared to cast folks out for any sin.
For him, the sanctity of marriage loomed
Above all issues. Gays, of course, were doomed.
And when Bill Clinton misbehaved, Dave's voice

Said resignation was the only choice.
So critics smiled, and backers were appalled,
To learn Dave paid to get his ashes hauled.
Once more, for right-wing folks it really rankles
To see who's caught with pants around his ankles.
Who's next? Who knows? But some would take the view
That sanctimony's often quite a clue.

2007

MIKE HUCKABEE
Arkansas Governor, Contender for the Republican Presidential Nomination

The Nicest Republican

The nice vote goes to Huckabee.
No other is as nice as he.
He leads a decent sort of life.
He's married to his only wife.
His kids, we'd bet, still speak to him.
He's courteous, but isn't prim.
A cheerful fat man who got lean,
He's not vindictive, rude, or mean.
Of course, he thinks our way's been lost:
Abortion is a "holocaust"
And evolution's just a myth
(The apes are not his kin or kith)
And what the Bible says is true.
The Earth's not old. It's rather new—
Six thousand years, from Eve to present.
He's wacko, sure, but he's sure pleasant.

2007

RUDY GIULIANI

New York Mayor, Contender for the Republican Presidential Nomination

An Out-of-Towner Questions a New Yorker About America's Mayor

"So tell me the most charming feature then
Of he who saved the city from collapse."
"It might take me a while to think of that.
Offhand, I'd say vindictiveness, perhaps."

2008

DENNIS KUCINICH

Ohio Congressman, Contender for the Democratic Presidential Nomination

Dark Horse

Revealed, while running hard with perseverance,
A smallish, left-wing man whose frail appearance
Suggested he'd not finished all his spinach.
Voilá: the vegan congressman, Kucinich.

2008

JOHN EDWARDS

North Carolina Senator, Contender for the Democratic Presidential Nomination

Yes, I Know He's a Mill Worker's Son, but There's Hollywood in That Hair

A Country Song About John Edwards

He grew up poor in Carolina, sure.
He's not a fake. He comes from folks like us.
I like the sound of what John Edwards says,
But why's his hair the kind that plain won't muss?
Yes, I know he's a mill worker's son, but there's Hollywood in that hair.

He whacks the corporations where it hurts.
His plan is best for caring for the sick.
His wife's a gem. We're nutty for the kids.
But Lordy that man's pompadour's too slick.

Yes, I know he's a mill worker's son, but there's Hollywood in that hair.
Sure I know he's got substance and grit, and judging by hair is not fair.
Yes, I know he's a genuine guy, and there's plain people's values we share.
Yes, I know he's a mill worker's son, but there's Hollywood in that hair.

2008

MICHAEL BLOOMBERG
Mayor of New York, Moneybags

Will Bloomberg Run?

This Michael Bloomberg is a small, rich smartie
Who isn't comfortable in either party.
From Democrat, in New York's fateful fall,
He switched so he could run for City Hall.
Six years from then, he left the GOP,
Reviving talk among the pols that he
Might try an independent White House go—
Self-financed, in the style of Ross Perot.
Comparing them, Mike's Carville, Kevin Sheekey,
Saw Mike as just as rich and much less squeaky.
A moderate who's rarely overwrought,
Mike seemed nonpartisan, and it was thought
If parties chose extremes, then he could enter
And run successfully right down the center.
His drawbacks? Well, his speeches, some would gripe,
Can mimic Ambien, the CR type.
Perot makes Bloomberg somewhat déjà vu-ish.
And, to be frank, they pointed out, Mike's Jewish.

2008

FRED THOMPSON
Tennessee Senator, Contender for Republican Presidential Nomination

A Short History of Fred Thompson's Quest

I
One candidate the Right still hoped to see
Was big Fred Thompson, since they knew that he
Would always, as he'd done on *Law and Order*,
Protect the unborn and our southern border.

II
Fred Thompson, heir to Reagan, had so far
Just failed to demonstrate he was a star.
He'd started late, and hadn't closed the gap—
Most Reaganesque in that he liked his nap.

III
For Thompson, Carolina was the test
On whither went his presidential quest.
The pros said, "That's a state he has to take,
And he just might, if he can stay awake."

IV
In Carolina, Thompson's finish meant
That it was time for Fred to fold his tent.
Yes, Fred got out, but evidence was thin
That he was there when he said he was in.

2008

MITT ROMNEY
Massachusetts Governor, Contender for the Republican Presidential Nomination

Mitt Romney as Doll

Yes, Mitt's so slick of speech and slick of garb, he
Reminds us all of Ken, of Ken and Barbie—
So quick to shed his moderate regalia,
He may, like Ken, be lacking genitalia.

2008

PHIL GRAMM
Texas Senator, Contender for the Republican Presidential Nomination

A Pep Talk

"We have sort of become a nation of whiners."
—Phil Gramm, *The Washington Times*

As senator, Phil was among the designers
Of laws that helped Enron, which showed no decliners,
Manipulate prices of oil from refiners.
(Its stock can be used in your cat box, for liners.)
His laws helped the mortgage thieves rook naïve signers,
Who then lost their houses and can't afford diners.
So now he decides we're a nation of whiners.
Figures.

2008

JOHN MCCAIN

Arizona Senator, Republican Nominee for President

Sweet Jesus, We Hate Him a Lot

A Hymn of Thanksgiving Sung by Right-Wing Preachers About John McCain

Oh, thank you, Sweet Jesus,
Oh, thank you so much
For any distress John has got.
We hope he continues
This streak of bad luck.
Though Christians, we hate him a lot.

Yes, we hate him a lot, we hate him a lot.
Sweet Jesus, we hate him a lot.

He called us all bigots,
Or something like that.
And just 'cause we slandered his daughter.
We did it for Jesus,
Like all that we do,
And John McCain knows that, or oughter.

Yes, we hate him a lot, we hate him a lot.
Sweet Jesus, we hate him a lot.

He treats us real nice now.
He panders to us.
We know, though, he's not born again.
We hope that he loses.
We'd even prefer
A heathenish Mormon. Amen.

. . . but then . . .

Sweet Jesus, We Like Him Much Better

A Hymn of Forgiveness Sung by Right-Wing Preachers About John McCain

Oh, thank you, Sweet Jesus,
Oh, thank you so much.
At last John has learned he's our debtor.
He chose Sarah Palin,
Who's real born again.
Who cares if his guys didn't vet her?

Yes, we like him much better, we like him much better.
Sweet Jesus, we like him much better.

She wouldn't kill babies,
Which Lieberman's for.
And that's why McCain had to get her.
He listens to us now.
He's up in our laps.
He yelps like a small Irish setter.

Yes, we like him much better, we like him much better.
Sweet Jesus, we like him much better.

2008

MICHELLE OBAMA
First Lady

A Smear Cheer for Michelle Obama

As Performed by the Swiftboat Singers

Who's not a retiring, shy Southern belle?
Whose Harvard degree is the way you can tell
That she's so elite she once ate a morel?
Who doesn't wear flag pins in either lapel?
Michelle.
Rah! Rah! Smear! Rah! Rah!

Who might be a part of a terrorist cell?
Who might have the powers for casting a spell?
Whose fist-knocks may summon the devil from hell?
Who could be, we reckon, a Muslim as well?
Michelle.
Rah! Rah! Smear! Rah! Rah!

2008

SARAH PALIN
Alaska Governor, Republican Nominee for Vice President

On a Clear Day, I See Vladivostok

The Barbra Streisand Standard as Sung by Sarah Palin

On a clear day
I see Vladivostok,
So I know world affairs.
Don't say, "No way."
Though I know elites mock,
It's osmosis that does it—well, that and our prayers.

And Joe Biden sees New Jersey from his shore.
And that's just a state. That doesn't rate. It's me who knows the score.
On a clear day,
On a clear day,
I see Vladivostok . . .
And Novosibirsk . . .
And Krasnoyarsk . . .
And Novokuznetsk . . .
And Omsk . . .
And Tomsk . . .
And more!

2008

ROD BLAGOJEVICH
Illinois Governor

On the Auctioning Off of Barack Obama's Senate Seat

It seemed to Rod Blagojevich
A powerful appointment which
Was his to make should make him rich.
His plan turned out to have a glitch.
Perhaps the feds had flipped a snitch.
So much for Rod Blagojevich.

2008

ARLEN SPECTER
Pennsylvania Senator

The Defection of Arlen Specter

Voilà, a GOP defector!
He's unbeloved Arlen Specter—
As kindly as a rent collector
Or Hannibal, the hungry Lecter.
(Remember when we watched him hector

Anita Hill, so he'd deflect her
From Thomas sniffing her as nectar?)
The Dems say, "Welcome to our sector.
Obama now is your protector."

A vote's a vote.

2009

BARACK OBAMA
President of the United States

Obama's Temper

His calm, say the pundits, is not the right mode.
To look like a leader he'll have to explode.
The man has to demonstrate more of an id.
For that there is nothing like flipping your lid.
That's right: What they say is to get Big Mo back
Obama should contemplate blowing his stack.
According to them, what could help him the most'll
Be some sort of sign that he's finally gone postal.

2010

JOHN BOEHNER
Speaker of the House

An Optimist Greets the New Speaker

It's true for greed this has to be a gainer
(To lobbyists John Boehner's on retainer).
Can anything be said for Speaker Boehner?
Yes. Others in the party are insaner.

2010

CHRIS CHRISTIE
New Jersey Governor, Potential Presidential Candidate

Contemplating the Republican Presidential Field, Late-Night Comics Lament

So Trump is out. We've lost our best buffoon—
We'll surely miss that gaseous air balloon.
Oh sure, there's Newt. Though Newt jokes once were great,
They're getting old. He's past his sell-by date.

Chris Christie was the one we hoped they'd draft.
Yes, in our fondest daydreams people laughed
As we eyed Christie's body, fore and aft,
Comparing him to William Howard Taft.

But Christie has insisted he'll not run.
Is anybody left who's any fun?
Oh Lord, please hear our prayers. We're on our knees.
At least just leave us Sarah Palin—please.

2011

NYC

"The New York term for what others might call a typical American or a real American is out-of-towner."

Curtain Time

Murray Tepper was sitting at the wheel of a dark blue Chevrolet Malibu that was parked on the uptown side of Forty-third Street, between Fifth and Sixth. Behind him, a car was coming slowly down Forty-third Street. As it passed the imposing structure occupied by the Century club, it slowed even more, and, a few yards farther, came to a stop just behind Tepper's Chevrolet. Taking his eyes away from the paper for only an instant, Tepper shot a quick glance toward his side mirror. He could see a Mercury with New Jersey license plates—probably theatergoers from the suburbs who knew that these streets in the forties were legal for long-term metered parking after six. The New Jersey people would be hoping to find a spot, grab a bite in a sushi bar or a deli, and then walk to the theater. Good planners, people from New Jersey, Tepper thought, except for the plan they must have hatched at some point to move to New Jersey. (The possibility that anybody started out in New Jersey—that any number of people had actually been born there—was not a possibility Tepper had ever dwelled on.) He pretended to concentrate on his newspaper, although he was, in fact, still thinking of the state of New Jersey, which he envisioned as a series of vast shopping-mall parking lots, where any fool could find a spot. The Mercury's driver tapped his horn a couple of times, and then, getting no response, moved even with Tepper's Chevy. The woman who was sitting on the passenger side stuck her head out of the window and said, "Going out?"

Tepper said nothing.

"Are you going out?" the woman asked again.

Tepper did not look up, but with his right hand he reached over toward the window and wagged his index finger back and forth, in the gesture some Southern Europeans have perfected as a way of dealing with solicitations from shoeshine boys or beggars. Tepper had been able to wag his finger in the negative with some authority since 1954, when, as a young draftee who regularly reminded himself to be grateful that at least the shooting had stopped, he spent thirteen miserable months as a clerk-typist in a motor pool in Pusan and had to ward off prostitutes and beggars every time he left the base. An acquaintance had once expressed envy for the gesture as something that seemed quite cosmopolitan, but Tepper would have traded it in an instant for the ability to do the legendary New York taxi-hailing whistle that was accomplished by jamming a finger in each corner of the mouth.

He had never been able to master that whistle, despite years of patient coaching by a doorman named Hector, on West Eighty-third. Tepper had encountered Hector while looking for overnight parking spots in his own neighborhood, in the days before his wife managed to persuade him to take space for his car by the month in a multilevel garage a few blocks from their apartment. He hadn't seen anybody use the fingers-in-the-mouth whistle on the street for a long time. He hadn't tried it for a long time himself. Was it something that might simply come to him, after all these years? Now that he wasn't trying it several evenings a week under the pressure of Hector's watchful eye, might it just appear, the way a smooth golf swing sometimes comes inexplicably to duffers once the tension of their expensive lessons has ended? He was about to jam a couple of fingers in the corners of his mouth to see if the gift might have arrived unannounced when he realized that the Mercury was still idling next to him, making it necessary to remain focused on the newspaper.

"He's not going out," the woman shouted to the man at the wheel, loudly enough for Tepper to hear.

"He's not going out?" the driver shouted back, sounding incredulous. "What do you mean he's not going out?"

"He probably parks there just before six and sits there so he can tell people he's not going out," the woman shouted.

The driver gunned the motor in irritation, and the Mercury from New Jersey pulled away. Just past the entrance to the Princeton Club, it briefly stopped again, the occupants apparently having mistaken a no-parking zone in front of the post office for a legal spot. Then the driver slowly made his way toward Sixth Avenue, speeding up suddenly when a spot came open on the left and screeching to a halt a moment later as a sport-utility vehicle two cars in front of him positioned itself to go into the spot. The woman got out of the Mercury and shouted back toward Tepper. "It's your fault!" she said. "That should have been our spot! It's your fault. Making people waste time talking to you! You ought to be ashamed of yourself."

Tepper, pretending not to hear her, went back to his newspaper. He was reading a story about an office betting pool that had been held every week in a commodities-trading firm for as long as anyone in the firm could remember. A committee of the firm's partners met regularly to decide on each week's pool topic, always based on current events. The office pool had been a subject of press interest before. During the Vietnam War, some people objected to the pool's being based for several weeks in a row on casualty figures. One of the firm's partners responded by saying, "People who don't want to play hardball should get out of the game," but the casualty-figure pools were quietly dropped in favor of pools based on how many tons of explosives would be dropped on North Vietnam that week.

The commodity firm's pool was back in the news because it had been based that week on how many people would be cited for hailing a taxicab incorrectly. The mayor, Frank Ducavelli, as part of his never-ending campaign to make the city more orderly, had declared a crackdown on people who stepped out in the street to hail a taxi rather than remaining on the curb, as required by an ordinance that nobody but the mayor and his city attorney had ever heard of. Tabloid headlines didn't have the space for the mayor's entire last name. It was known that when Frank Ducavelli first became a force in the city he had hoped that headline writers might refer to him as the Duke, suggesting not only nobility but the Dodger great Duke Snider. Given the mayor's interest in order and his draconian response to anyone who disagreed with him, though, the tabloids tended to go with Il Duce. The item Tepper was reading about the weekly pool at the commodities-trading firm was headlined IL DUCE EDICT HOT COMMODITY.

The taxi drivers had objected to the enforcement of the ordinance, of course, and the mayor had called them vermin. The senior staff attorney of the New York Civil Liberties Union, Jeremy Thornton, had said that Ducavelli's attempt to enforce the ordinance was "another of the spitballs that our mayor regularly flings at the Constitution of the United States." The mayor had replied that Jeremy Thornton had a constitutional right to demonstrate that he was a reckless and irresponsible fool but that he should probably be disbarred anyway, as a public service. When a city councilman, Norm Plotkin, usually a supporter of City Hall, pointed out that someone flagging a cab from behind a line of parked cars was unlikely to be seen, he had been dismissed by Mayor Ducavelli as "stupid and imbecilic—someone who obviously has no regard whatsoever for public safety and is totally unconcerned about citizens of this city being struck down and killed in the street like dogs."

Years before, in an article about how jokes get created and spread around, Tepper had read that commodities traders were at the heart of the joke-distribution system. The article had inspired him to test a list of licensed commodities brokers for a client who was trying to sell a book of elephant jokes through the mail, and the list had done fairly well—well enough to justify its use again to sell a book of lightbulb jokes and a tape-cassette course on how to be a hit at parties. Tepper had decided that the actual trading of commodities must not require a lot of time if traders could engage in so many extracurricular activities, like organizing betting pools and distributing jokes.

Tepper could hear the drone of another car moving slowly down the street behind him. He decided to use the backhand flick if the car stopped next to him. He had perfected the backhand flick only that week—a speeded-up version of someone clearing away cobwebs while walking through a dimly lit attic. He used only his left hand. Without looking up from his newspaper, he would flick his fingers in the direction of the inquiring parker. It had taken some time to find precisely the right velocity of flicking—a movement that contained authority but lacked aggression.

The first time he had used the backhand flick—it was on Fifty-seventh Street, between Tenth and Eleventh avenues, around the dinner hour—he had obviously flicked too aggressively. The gesture had brought a fat, red-faced man out of a huge sport-utility vehicle—a vehicle so high off the ground that the fat man, before laboriously lowering himself to the pavement, hovered in the doorway like a parachutist who'd taken a moment to reconsider before deciding that he did indeed want to leap out into thin air. Once on terra firma, the fat man had stood a few inches from Tepper's window, which was closed, and shouted, "Ya jerky bastard, ya!" again and again. Tepper was interested to hear the expression "ya jerky bastard, ya"—he hadn't heard it used since the old days at Ebbets Field—but he did recognize the need to flick his hand more subtly. Tepper hadn't replied to the fat man, and not simply because there really didn't seem to be any appropriate reply to "ya jerky bastard, ya." Tepper tried to avoid speaking to the people who wanted to park in his spot.

2001

The Co-op Caper

When Latin American dictators such as Somoza and Trujillo and Stroessner passed from the scene, most Americans got the impression that the exercise of totally capricious tyrannical power was drying up in this hemisphere, but New Yorkers of a certain station understood that the boards of New York co-operative apartment buildings will always be with us. In New York, someone who wants to buy a co-op apartment is also asking to join other residents in a partnership responsible for the entire building, and the board, after examining his references and his tax forms, can reject him without even troubling to give a reason. Supplicants before a co-op board—people whose demeanor in negotiations may ordinarily be contentious or even fearsome—accept this treatment without a peep.

In 1984, John Gregory Dunne, who was then living in Los Angeles, became interested in moving to a co-op in New York, and he asked me to write a letter of recommendation. We had known each other since we worked together at *Time* in the sixties. In fact, when I wrote a novel about working at a newsmagazine, he figured in a claimer that I included at the beginning of the book: "The character of Andy Wolferman is based on John Gregory Dunne, though it tends to flatter. The other characters are fictional." When asked for the co-op recommendation, I sent off a respectful letter, seeded with what I thought of as co-op board phrases like "deeply responsible" and "substantial resources." Then I wrote a second letter, reprinted below, and sent a Xerox copy of it to Dunne. On top of the Xerox I scrawled, "This ought to do it!"

March 16, 1984

Ms. Dominique Richard
Alice F. Mason, Ltd.
30 East 60th Street
New York, NY 10022

Dear Ms. Richard:
This is in answer to your inquiry of March 12 concerning Mr. and Mrs. John Gregory Dunne.

I have known both Mr. and Mrs. Dunne for more than twenty years, and I can say that they would make a splendid addition to any co-operative apartment building. As you may have learned by now from neighbors of Mr. and Mrs. Dunne in Brentwood, the role played by Mr. Dunne's temper in the incidents there was greatly exaggerated in the press.

I have known the Dunne's daughter, Quintana, since her infancy, and I can assure you that she is an attractive and responsible young woman who is working hard day and night on the gruelling practice schedule necessary for anyone who aspires to be a successful punk-rock drummer. The dog that injured the UPS delivery man is hers.

In the event that you have been concerned about the presence of the male nurse who is retained to escort Mr. Dunne home on evenings out, I would like to put your mind at rest. The male nurse in question is remarkably skilled at keeping control without making a fuss. I understand that, by a happy coincidence, he is related to your doorman, Mr. O'Leary, as is Mr. Dunne.

Mrs. Dunne is not Jewish.

Yours sincerely,
Calvin Trillin

1984

An Attack Gecko

The other day, we received a letter that began, "Where but in New York would citizens be buying lizards for protection?" Without reading further, we knew we had heard once again from our angry friend who writes occasionally on the off chance that we have forgotten just how exasperating he finds life in the city. "A few days ago, I dropped in to see some friends of mine, whom I'll call Ralph and Myrna Cole, and discovered they had bought a type of lizard called a gecko," he continued. "When I asked what had driven them to lizardry, Ralph Cole informed me that geckos are to cockroaches what New York bus drivers are to passengers—natural enemies. Once the Coles discovered this characteristic of the gecko (I should probably say of the family Gekkonidae; however many cockroaches there are, this town is always crawling with pedants), they rushed right out and bought one, for three dollars and eighteen cents, the wretched city sales tax (which I have always considered the equivalent of charging admission to a dungeon) included. They have now had their gecko for about a month. At least, they think they have had it; geckos are extremely shy—the only creature in the metropolitan area suffering from that affliction, to judge from the number of people who push ahead of me in line every day—and the Coles haven't seen theirs since they brought it home and uncaged it in their apartment with instructions to gobble up every cockroach in sight. According to the Coles, the kind of gecko they have, which is Brook's gecko (*Hemidactylus brookii*), only two or three inches long, eats three cockroaches a day—or a night, really, since geckos tend to be nocturnal. The Coles, in other words, bought this lizard to act as a kind of mini-predator.

" 'It's nice to go to bed at night knowing that the little fellow is going to down three of them before we get up in the morning,' Ralph told me. 'If he's still here, that is.'

" 'What makes you think he's still here?' I asked, sneaking a glance under the couch.

" 'We may have three fewer cockroaches than usual,' Ralph said. 'Cockroaches multiply very fast, though, and the cockroaches in our apartment were uncountable to begin with, so it's hard to tell.'

" 'We don't have to feed him, of course, because he lives on cockroaches,' Myrna said. 'At least, if he's still here, he does.'

" 'Doesn't it bother you any to have a predatory lizard creeping around your apartment?' I asked.

" 'Well, at first I was worried about waking up one morning and finding the gecko on my pillow,' Myrna said. 'But the pet-shop man told me that I'd be able to tell if a gecko was nearby—it makes a soft noise that sounds like "gecko." '

"Ralph then gave his gecko imitation—'geck-o, geck-o, geck-o'—and I began to worry about the Coles. Frankly, Ralph hasn't been the same since a newsdealer called him a fascist for asking for change for a quarter. Myrna has been acting a bit odd since she boarded a downtown East Side IRT subway and was taken to Philadelphia. Just on a hunch, I called on one of the chief reptile suppliers in the city—a place on Bleecker Street called Exotic Aquatics. (In a civilized city, of course, merchants would be fined for displaying cutesy store names in public; anybody who gave his store a name that included the diminutive of *and*—Knickknacks 'n' Such or Strings 'n' Things—would be put in the stocks.)

"Despite its name, Exotic Aquatics seemed to be run by a sensible tradesman. He was sensible enough, in fact, to inform me that any lizard will indiscriminately eat just about anything it runs across that seems small enough to eat—cockroach, cricket, or Landon button.

" 'Do you mean the gecko doesn't have a special cockroach-eating capacity?' I asked.

" 'Well, I suppose it has been known to eat cockroaches,' he said. 'And some people have always said that geckos are good for cockroach control. But we don't push it. Most of the geckos we sell are for tanks.'

"So there is a picture of urban life for you: Ralph and Myrna Cole, college-educated adults, going to sleep every night feeling slightly more secure because an onomatopoetic lizard is about to put away three of their cockroaches. And, for all they actually know, he may be in Central Park chasing caterpillars."

1971

Testing Grounds

I live in Greenwich Village, where people from the suburbs come on weekends to test their car alarms. "This is a test," I sometimes mutter, when the whine of a car alarm wakes me up late on a Saturday night. I know some of my neighbors must be waking up, too—the two little girls next door, and the man across the street with the funny-looking dog, and the elderly couple who live on the corner. "Don't worry—this is a test," I'd like to assure them. "I'm certain no cars are actually being stolen, because the very same cars will be back next Saturday night for the same test."

Sometimes, as I lie there in bed trying to go back to sleep, I start wondering how the suburbs produce all of these car-alarm testers. I envision a father somewhere in Westchester County sitting in his easy chair, reading his Saturday morning paper. Junior, his teenage son, walks by on his way to revel in his many material possessions.

"Son," Dad says, "have you tested the alarm on that car of yours lately?"

"Oh, Dad," the son whines, "do I have to go all the way to the Village again?"

"Remember what I told you, son," Dad says. "You take care of your car and your car will take care of you."

Meanwhile, in the suburbs of New Jersey, there's a lot of activity at the six-acre parking lot that has become the meeting place of the Bergen County Car Alarm Club. B-Ccac, as it's known, has five hundred members. Most of them spend most Saturdays fine-tuning their car alarms.

They wear identical black and gold coveralls with the club crest on the left breast pocket. The club crest shows an SUV with little marks coming off it, to designate sound, and people next to it holding their hands over their ears. B-Ccac members talk a lot to each other about their HTRs. An HTR is a hair-trigger response. Their goal is an HTR that will set off the alarm if the steps of one normal-sized adult reverberate on the sidewalk within six feet of the car. That's called a single-person HTR. Most of the members have it.

In a country club locker room in Fairfield County, Connecticut, four or five men are arguing. They are businessmen who bet a lot of money on golf games every weekend, except when it's too cold to play golf. When it's too cold to play golf, they bet on which one of their car alarms will go off faster in Greenwich Village.

They spend a lot of Saturday afternoons arguing about odds. The ones who have any car other than a Mercedes believe they should get odds. They believe that a Mercedes alarm is more likely to go off first because a lot of people who live in the Village have a habit of taking a kick at a Mercedes as they walk along the street—and a kick will almost certainly set off the alarm. But Mercedes owners drive a hard bargain. That's how they made enough money to buy a Mercedes in the first place.

Sometimes, as I fall asleep on Saturday night, I think of all the car-alarm testers heading my way. The teenager from Westchester and a bunch of his pals are in his car heading down the Henry Hudson Parkway, practicing some of the songs they're going to sing later in the evening to celebrate the successful testing of his car alarm. The members of the Bergen County Car Alarm Club are driving in caravan toward the George Washington Bridge. The Connecticut golfers have crossed the New York state line, still arguing on their car phones about odds.

I am about to fall asleep. But then an alarm goes off—an early arrival. I begin to wonder how long it would take to locate an alarm and turn it off, once you got inside the car. I can see myself and some neighbors trying to find out. We're holding one of those battering rams they use to knock down doors in drug busts.

The man across the street with the funny-looking dog is there, and so are the two little girls from next door and the elderly couple who live on the corner. (They are remarkably strong for their age.) Rhythmically, we're swinging the battering ram back and then against the driver's window. The window is starting to go, even though we've missed it on a couple of swings and put great dents into the door instead. Somebody in black and gold coveralls shows up and starts shouting something about whose car it is. "Don't worry," I say. "This is only a test."

1988

What's the Good Word?

Not long ago, the people in my neighborhood—Greenwich Village, in Lower Manhattan—were faced with a new problem. Our subway stop was being made beautiful, and we hadn't figured out how to complain about it. The phrases that trip most easily off the tongues of New Yorkers are expressions of complaint. If a linguistic anthropologist camped out in Manhattan for a while, I suspect he'd discover that New Yorkers have fifty or sixty different phrases for expressing irritation and maybe two for expressing enthusiastic approval ("not that bad" and "it could be worse").

The average subway rider would associate expressions of enthusiasm with people he'd describe as being from "Iowa or Idaho or one of them." (True New Yorkers do not distinguish among states that begin with the letter *I*.) For generations—since long before the great cities of this country became associated in the public mind with their problems rather than their wonders—New Yorkers have believed in the old saying that they learn at their mother's knee: "If you can't say something nice, you're never in danger of being taken for an out-of-towner."

This was not the first time the Metropolitan Transportation Authority had presented us with an awkward situation: In recent years, all the old subway trains in New York have been replaced with shiny new silver trains, which are absolutely free of graffiti. They are also air-conditioned.

If you live outside of New York—or if you are one of those thick-headed New Yorkers who prefer traffic jams to subway travel—you are probably thinking that the preceding paragraph was one of my little jokes. It wasn't. The New York subways really do have flashy new cars, but New Yorkers rarely mention that fact. It's a difficult thing to complain about.

Not impossible. I've heard a lot of people complain that the absolutely frigid air-conditioning in the subway cars makes the stations, which are still not air-conditioned, seem even hotter than they are. I've heard people say that they miss the graffiti—which is apparently cleaned off at the end of every run, so that there isn't much reason to put it on in the first place—and resent the censoring of this urban folk art by the philistines who run the MTA. It is also possible to complain about how the decision to acquire new cars was made—or, to put it in the local vernacular, how the MTA unilaterally and high-handedly, without consulting the people who actually use the subways every day, decided to force comfortable and attractive new subway cars on the public.

Improvements in the transportation system rarely meet with the approval of New Yorkers. Some years ago, the then mayor, Edward I. Koch, came back from China smitten with the idea of bicycle transportation. He had protective strips of concrete installed to create a bicycle lane up Sixth Avenue. People complained. Eventually, the concrete strips were removed.

I mentioned at the time that you might have expected the taxi drivers to hate the Mayor's innovation, since it had cost them basically one lane of traffic. ("He likes China so much, he shoulda stood in China.") But who complained most bitterly about the bike lanes? The bicyclers. The true New York bicyclers—particularly the messengers—complained that the bike lane was full of pedestrians and garment-center pushcarts and bike riders who were described as "schlepping around on Raleigh three-speeds."

"Schlepping" is Yiddish, a language that all true New Yorkers—including Irish cops and Dominican grocers and Pakistani newsdealers—speak a little of, partly because its rhythms are famously conducive to complaint. One Yiddish word that all New Yorkers are familiar with is "kvetch"—which actually means "to complain." You often hear them say to each other, "Quit kvetching"—to no apparent effect.

So you can see the sort of problem my neighbors and I faced as workmen in our station replaced worn tiles and restored lovely old mosaics. At first, we made do with complaining about the pace of the work. ("Are they ever going to finish this place?") A couple of people tried to argue that the stunning new floor would be slipperier than the grungy old floor.

At one point, while a neighbor and I waited for an uptown local, I decided that I had to express my approval of the renovations, even at the risk of being taken for somebody from Indiana or Illinois. (I'm from Missouri.) "Not that bad," I said, gesturing toward the shiny tiles and the stunning new floor.

My neighbor looked around. "It could be worse," he admitted. "But where the hell is the train?"

1995

Tourists Trapped

"It's all over," Harry said when I saw him recently in a Lower Manhattan café that we both frequent. "There are no more secrets. We might as well pack it in."

"Are you talking about these guys at the CIA and the FBI selling secrets to the Russians?" I asked.

"No, no," Harry said, "not the CIA and the FBI. The bus-stop signs. I heard on the radio that the city is going to put up three thousand new bus-stop signs. Color-coded. Now any yahoo is going to know just which bus stops where. This is not the city it once was, my friend."

Harry, who was born and brought up not far from the café, is remarkably open about something that few of his neighbors would acknowledge: Native New Yorkers hate the idea of out-of-towners being able to find their way around the city.

Why do they feel that way? Maybe, given the fact that New York moves at a pace that can keep even the savviest city dweller uncertain of his footing, natives have had to find comfort in the thought of some people being totally lost. Maybe native New Yorkers are what English out-of-towners call bloody-minded.

Whatever the cause, Harry puts great store in municipal bafflement. Once, when I was feeling frustrated with the system used to designate subway routes, I mentioned to him that the R and the N trains—which sound from their letters as if they operate two or three boroughs apart—actually stop at more or less the same places.

"Right!" he said, beaming. "But that's not the beauty part. The beauty part is that depending on the time of day, the B train goes to two completely different places. You could get on thinking you're on your way to Roosevelt Island and get off at 168th and Broadway, where nobody's ever *heard* of Roosevelt Island. This is not a town with codes that can be cracked by the first yokel who wanders in, my friend."

I've seen Harry swell with pride like that once or twice since. When occasional intersections in New York—chosen, as far as I could tell, for no particular reason—sprouted signs with an arrow pointing vaguely in the direction of the Javits Convention Center, Harry was ecstatic. "Have you seen those?" he asked me. "There you are, deep in Washington Heights, a hundred one-way streets from nowhere, and you see an arrow saying that if you go down that street you'll get to the Convention Center. And that's the last sign you'll see for miles. I mean, it might as well say 'Omaha' or 'Roanoke.' I love it."

In general, though, things haven't been going well for Harry lately. He suspects that the signs guiding travelers from the airports have been made, as he puts it, "conventionally relevant to the journey." He has always kept a list of unlikely places where visitors have ended up while trying to get to Manhattan from JFK in a rental car, and it's been a year and a half since he heard one he considered worth adding to the list (Fort Lee, New Jersey).

He was in a dark mood for days after the Metropolitan Transportation Authority ended its policy of posting maps of the subway system only inside the trains. When large maps began to appear on subway platforms, Harry just shook his head and sighed at the thought that someone unfamiliar with the route would no longer have to board a train and fight his way over to decipher a map similar in design to spaghetti primavera only to find out that he was going at breakneck speed in the wrong direction.

Harry was also deeply opposed to a decision the Department of Transportation made to add signs saying SIXTH AVENUE to what New Yorkers had never been able to bring themselves to call "Avenue of the Americas." Before then, he could brighten up a gray afternoon by standing on Sixth Avenue waiting to be asked where Sixth Avenue was.

Hearing the bad news about the bus-stop signs, I tried my best to cheer Harry up. "Just about all subway stations that have multiple exits still won't say which street each exit leads to," I said. "There are tourists wandering around in the rain out there, Harry."

"True," Harry acknowledged, "that's true."

"And the announcements over the subway public-address system remain unintelligible, Harry. I met an out-of-towner the other day who thought that for some reason they were being delivered in Turkish."

Harry seemed to brighten a bit. "You know," he said, "I was thinking for a while there of leaving the city."

"What stopped you?" I said.

"I can't find my way around anywhere else."

1997

Social Questions from Aunt Rosie

My Aunt Rosie called from Kansas City to ask me who was at the luncheon that Reinaldo and Carolina Herrera gave at Mortimer's for the Rajmata of Jaipur.

"Is this a bad connection, Aunt Rosie?" I said. "Or have you been trying out the pink Catawba wine again?"

"Don't get smart with me, big shot," Aunt Rosie said. "I knew you when you could have been called the Diaper of Jaipur."

Whenever she calls me "big shot," it's clear that I'm in for trouble. Aunt Rosie takes it for granted that absolutely anybody who lives in New York is clued in about all sorts of sophisticated matters that remain mysterious to what she calls the "meatloaf crowd" at home, and she is horrified anew every time I prove to know less about such things than she does. On one hand, she assumes that I'm personally acquainted with every glitz-hound who has ever been mentioned in the gossip columns; on the other hand, she's constantly complaining that the only one of her nephews who moved to New York is so completely without connections that he can't even get an out-of-town relative tickets to *Cats*.

"Aunt Rosie," I said, "I wasn't even aware that Reinaldo and Carolina Herrera were acquainted with the Rajmata of Jaipur. How in the world would you know that these people had lunch at Snerd's?"

"Not Snerd's, dummy. Mortimer's," Aunt Rosie said. "And I know it because I read it in *Vanity Fair.*"

My heart sank. A couple of years ago, Aunt Rosie and her bridge friends started reading tony magazines like *Architectural Digest* and *House & Garden* and *European Travel & Life*—the sort of magazines that, according to a rather sour friend of mine known as Marty Mean Tongue, are someday going to be made into a composite television show called *Lifestyles of the Rich and Useless*. Aunt Rosie started calling me with questions like, "Listen, how much do you figure the Baroness de Gelt had to fork over for that château they showed in the November issue?" or "Hey, what kind of bucks are we talking about for a yard of that fabric the Countess used on her sunporch in Capri?"

I know how these questions must come about. Aunt Rosie and her bridge pals—the people she always calls the Jell-O Mold Rangers—leaf through these magazines, mainly to speculate on how much everything costs. Then, when the speculation deteriorates into a heated disagreement, Aunt Rosie says, "I'll just call my nephew who lives in New York. He'll be able to tell us, even though he's a little slow."

Now the Jell-O Mold Rangers had obviously taken to reading

Vanity Fair. It was bad enough answering questions about how much I figured some cat-food heiress had to pay a yard for the chintz on her couches. Now I was going to get constant questions about the parties given by dress designers and charity-ball trotters and New Jersey countesses and what Marty Mean Tongue always calls the Von de Von crowd.

Apparently, *Vanity Fair*'s coverage of the Rajmata's luncheon presented a seating chart of the table with first names only, and challenged the reader to guess the full name. "I know who C.Z. is, of course, because I saw her patio in *Architectural Digest* or somewhere," Aunt Rosie said. "And Pat is obvious: She had Oscar's dress on when she was talking to Jerome a couple of issues ago. But who do you think Tom is? I told Myrtle Weber you'd know for sure."

"I don't suppose Tom could be Tom Beasley, Cousin Bernie's partner in the laundromat," I said. "That Tom certainly could be counted on to show up at a free lunch."

"I don't know what made me think you'd know," Aunt Rosie said. "I always told your mother you'd never amount to anything."

There was a long silence. Then Aunt Rosie said, "Myrtle Weber's son in New York said he could get us tickets to *Cats* anytime we wanted them."

"I'm sure he can," I said. "Taxi drivers are surprisingly good at that sort of thing. I read a story about it in *The New York Times*—a publication, I should mention, that you and the Jell-O Mold Rangers might think of reading instead of these glossy gossip sheets you seem to favor."

"I already take the *Times,*" Aunt Rosie said. "For that Evening Hours column they have. That's how I knew who the Lee was that Reinaldo and Carolina seated next to C.Z. and why Estée was put next to Bob."

"Is it because Bob tends to spill things late in the meal?" I said.

"Listen, big shot, I knew you when the only Indian princess you had ever heard of was Pocahontas," Aunt Rosie said. "So save your smart-aleck talk for your fancy New York friends."

1986

Tepper Parked in Front of Russ & Daughters

As Tepper glanced up from the newspaper to make a quick perusal of the Sunday shoppers, he noticed that one of the countermen from Russ & Daughters was standing on the sidewalk, about to tap on the window. Recognizing the counterman from past trips, Tepper slid over toward the passenger door and rolled down the window.

"How you doin'?" the counterman said, bending down to lean on the door.

"Fine," Tepper said. "How are you?"

"I thought I recognized you," the counterman said. "You come in to buy lox sometimes on Sunday."

"Herring salad, usually," Tepper said. "Sometimes a whitefish. Very occasionally, lox."

"I've noticed you out here for a few Sundays now," the counterman said. "I figured maybe you're having trouble getting around, and I could get you something."

"Thanks anyway," Tepper said. "I don't think anything today."

The counterman started to straighten up. Then he said, "Are you waiting for somebody?"

"No," Tepper said.

"Oh. Well . . . ," the counterman said. "Guess I should get back." But he made no move to leave. He smiled, in a friendly way. Finally, he said, "Just here, parking?"

"Exactly," Tepper said. "I'm just here, parking."

The counterman didn't say anything for a while. He was still leaning on the car door, looking in the window. Then he said, "You're just here parking because you feel like it, and if someone wants the spot, it's too bad, because it's your spot, and it's a legal spot—right? Listen, a lot of times, I feel like doing something like this myself. You know, it can get pretty irritating with some of those customers."

"I'll bet," Tepper said.

"They'll say, 'Gimme a nice whitefish.' So I'll say, 'One whitefish, coming right up.' Cheerful. Pleasant. And they'll say, 'A *nice* whitefish.' Can you imagine? This happens every Sunday at least once. I could prevent it, of course. I could head it off. You know how I could prevent it . . ."

"Well," Tepper said. "I suppose—"

"Of course!" the counterman said, "I could just repeat after them exactly: 'A nice whitefish.' But I won't. I won't give them the satisfaction. What I really feel like saying when they correct me—when I say, 'One whitefish, coming up,' and they say, 'A *nice* whitefish'—is, 'Oh? Well, I'm glad you said that, because I wasn't going to get you a *nice* whitefish. If you hadn't said that, I would have looked for a whitefish that's been sitting there since last Tisha B'Av—an old, greasy, *farshtunken* whitefish. Because that's what we serve here mostly. That's our specialty. That's how we've managed to stay in business all these years. That's why the Russ family is synonymous with quality and integrity in this city for maybe seventy-five years—because they sell their steady customers rotten, stinking whitefish. That's why the boss gets up at four in the morning to go to the suppliers, so he can get the *farshtunken* whitefish before his competitors. Otherwise, if he slept until a civilized hour, as maybe he deserves by now, he might get stuck with *nice* whitefish.' "

"There's always something," Tepper said.

The counterman, looking exhausted from his speech, could only nod and sigh. He glanced into the store and then looked back at Tepper. "Listen," he said. "Do you mind if I sit with you for a minute? It looks like it's quiet in there. I could take a little break."

"Why not?" Tepper said. He opened the passenger door and slid over to make room for the counterman.

2001

FAMILY MATTERS

"We got married in that awkward period in the history of domestic relations between dowries and prenuptial agreements."

Naming the Baby Calvin

The English resent the fact that we've never been willing to use the boys' names they favor; they've always suspected us of thinking that their names are for sissies. I once came up with a plan to deal with that. It was a rather utopian plan—a sort of name exchange. For a certain number of years, a lot of Americans would name their boys Cedric and Cyril and Trevor and Evelyn. Well, maybe not Evelyn. I'm not sure an American kid would make it as far as third grade with a name like Evelyn. At the same time, we invite the English to name their boys American names. Then, sooner or later, the United States would have a lot of grown-up men with English-sounding names and there will be a lot of people in England named LeRoy and Sonny.

Think of how proud the English would be on the first year that every single linebacker on the National Football League all-star team is named Nigel. If the plan works perfectly, the Queen's Honors List that same year will have on it a noted musicologist named Sir Bubba Thistlethwaite.

I gave up that scheme. I didn't want to drain any energy away from my campaign to have people name their sons Calvin. It's easy to laugh—you people named Charles and Robert and John. You don't know what it's like walking around with an obsolescent name. Those of us named Calvin sometimes feel like someone named Hepzibah. So we've banded together to get more people to name their kids Calvin. Just for company. I spent a lot of time talking to some good friends in Nova Scotia, where we live in the summer, trying to persuade them to name the baby they were expecting Calvin—so much time, in fact, that they finally said maybe I could think of something else to talk about. After that, I found myself lobbying their five-year-old daughter, Ruthie. I figured she'd be influential when the time came.

I said, "What name were you thinking of as a name for this lovely little addition to your family, Ruthie?"

And Ruthie said, "Static Cling."

"What if it's not a boy?" I asked her.

She said, "Freezer Burn."

When the baby came, it was a boy and they named him Calvin. They *preferred* Calvin to Static Cling. The same week, I got a birth announcement from Rhode Island—another Calvin. Now I think we might be on a roll.

Being named Calvin has not been all negative. During the first term of the Reagan Administration—what I believe historians now refer to as Voodoo I—I was asked by the government to make a cultural-exchange visit to South America. I was surprised to be asked. I had, in my role as jackal of the press, said some unkind things about the Administration. I had speculated, for instance, that for a long time President Reagan had been under the impression that Polaris was a denture cleanser. When the question came up of how close the Reagans were as a family, I had reported the rumor that a trailing photographer on Fifth Avenue had witnessed Ronald Reagan, Jr., wave and yell "Hiya, Dad!" to a man who turned out to be Joel McCrea. "What good sports they are!" I thought. "Sending me to South America anyway on a cultural-exchange visit." Then I got to thinking what the Administration's idea of culture might be, and realized that I had been confused with Calvin Klein.

1990

Merger

Yes, of course I've been thinking about the marriage of Valerie Jane Silverman and Michael Thomas Flaherty—two fine-looking and richly accomplished graduates of Harvard, class of 1987—who tied the knot some weeks ago and adopted as a common family name Flaherman.

I did not need all of those telephone calls asking if I had, by chance, missed the Flahermans' wedding announcement in the Sunday *New York Times*. I stated years ago that the wedding announcements have always been the first news I turn to on Sunday in the *Times*. It has been my custom to do some careful analysis of the family background of each bride and groom, and then to try to envision the tension at the wedding reception.

The names going into the marriage are, of course, helpful to that sort of vision—as is the assumption that every human being has at least one truly dreadful cousin. In an overtly bi-ethnic merger such as the marriage of Valerie Silverman to Michael Flaherty, I would ordinarily have wondered whether Mike Flaherty's dingbat fourth cousin, who has been assuring all of the Silvermans that some of his best friends are Jewish, will actually fall into conversation toward the end of the evening with an equally brash cousin of Valerie Silverman's who has been poking every Flaherty he meets in the ribs and saying, "I guess you've heard the one about Murphy, O'Leary, and the two priests."

In recent years, though, the name taken after the wedding has added to my concerns. Whether or not the bride is going to retain her last name has become an important element in the announcement. You have to wonder whether the Nancy Jones who announces that she will be keeping her surname after marrying a young man named Chomoldsley Rhoenheushch is a committed feminist or a weak speller. And I've been wondering lately whether a wedding someday between, say, the son of Madonna and the daughter of Sting would produce a nice young couple who had to start married life with no last name at all.

The Flaherman nuptials were particularly interesting to me because of the possibility that their approach to merging names as well as lives was the outgrowth of a warning I issued fifteen years ago about the danger of liberated young couples combining surnames by connecting them with hyphens.

At the time, I pointed out that if Penelope Shaughnessy married Nathaniel Underthaler while her best friend, Jennifer Morganwasser, married Jeremiah Christianson, and then the children of those two unions, Jedidiah Shaughnessy-Underthaler and Abigail Morganwasser-Christianson, themselves got married, these offsprings would end up as a couple named Jedidiah and Abigail Shaughnessy-Underthaler-Morganwasser-Christianson. Which means that they could never expect to get their name into a newspaper headline unless it was a headline announcing, say, World War III.

I think what the Flahermans—and, presumably, others by now—have done is a resourceful solution to the problem of how modern women can retain their names without creating monikers that make the signature run off the line every single time. One of the people I talked to about this situation—those of us who are devoted to the wedding section of the *Times* are likely to be sharing impressions of this or that announcement late on a Sunday morning, when people in other households are discussing the trouble in the Balkans or thinking about turning to the breakfast dishes—said that Flaherman struck him as a less euphonious name than, for instance, Silverty, but I consider that a quibble.

So congratulations to the Flahermans. And what if they have a son who wins the hand of Daphne Shaughnessy-Underthaler-Morganwasser-Christianson? We'll deal with that problem when we get to it.

1992

Incompatible, with One *L*

I married Alice under the assumption that she could spell "occurred." She now insists that nothing specific was mentioned about "occurred." It seems to me, though, that implicit in someone's making a living as a college English teacher is the representation that she is a speller with a repertoire adequate to any occasion. She certainly knew that the only person in her line of work I had any experience being related to, my cousin Keith from Salina, reached the finals of the Kansas state spelling bee. She now says Cousin Keith's spelling triumph was never spoken of between us. I distinctly remember, though, that I listed for Alice the highlights of our family's history, as any prospective bridegroom might for his future wife, and Cousin Keith has always been part of my standard Family History recitation—along with my cousin Neil, who was once the head drum major of the University of Nebraska marching band, and my Uncle Benny Daynofsky, who in his early eighties was knocked down by a car while planting tomatoes in his own backyard in St. Joseph, Missouri. It is significant that she does not deny knowing about Uncle Benny.

Is spelling the sort of thing that modern young couples get straightened out beforehand in marriage contracts? I wouldn't bring this up after all of these years, except that, as it happens, I can't spell "occurred" either. I was forced to look it up twice in order to write the first paragraph, and once more to get this far in the second. Somehow, I had expected to marry someone whose spelling would be, if not perfect, at least complementary to mine. We would face the future with heads held high, and maybe a short song on our lips—confident that together we could spell anything they dished out. Before we had been married a month, the real world started to eat away at that fantasy: It turned out that Alice was not very good on "commitment." I don't mean she didn't have any; she couldn't spell it. I have never been able to spell "commitment" myself.

I know how to spell "embarrass"—usually considered by double-letter specialists to be a much more difficult word. I have been able to spell it for years. I planted "embarrass" in my mind at an early age through a rather brilliant mnemonic device having to do with bar stools. In fact, not to make a lot out of it, I had always thought of my ability to spell "embarrass" as a nice little facility to bring to a marriage—the sort of minor bonus that is sometimes found in a husband's ability to rewire lamps. (I can't rewire a lamp, but I can change the bulb, usually. That qualifies as what I believe is called an "allied skill.") We have now been married thirteen years, and Alice still has not asked me how to spell "embarrass." Apparently, she has a mnemonic device of her own. I have never inquired. That sort of thing doesn't interest me.

For a while, our reformist friends used to urge us to make a list of the words that troubled both of us—their theory being that some wretched consistency in the American educational system would be further documented by the fact that a husband and wife who went to public schools thirteen hundred miles apart were left without the ability to spell precisely the same words. Converts to the new politics of lowered expectations have told me that I should simply accept Alice's spelling limitations and comfort myself with thoughts of the many splendid qualities she does have—the way Americans are now supposed to settle for only two gigantic automobiles, reminding themselves that some people in Chad have none at all. I have tried that. I have reminded myself that Alice can explain foreign movies and decipher road maps. I suspect that in a pinch she might be able to rewire a lamp. But, having come of drinking age in the 1950s, I may be culturally immune to the politics of lowered expectations. I can't get over the suspicion that a politician who preaches that doctrine is really arguing that we ought to settle for him.

I still find myself thinking back on the old-fashioned scenes I had envisioned for our marriage: We are sitting peacefully in the parlor—after having kissed the little ones good night—and I glance up from the desk, where I have been polishing off a letter to the *Times* on our policy in the Far East, and say, "Alice, how do you spell 'referred'?" Alice tells me. Or, on another evening, Alice looks over from her side of the desk (in this version of our marriage, the custodian of an abandoned courthouse in Pennsylvania had sold us an eighteenth-century double desk for eighty-five dollars including delivery to New York in his brother's pickup), where she has been composing a letter to her parents saying how sublimely happy she is. She asks me how to spell "embarrass." I tell her.

1978

Naming the German Baby

It's been more than two months since I read in *The Washington Post* that in Germany the government has to approve the name of your child. I think my response to the *Post* item has paralleled the stages people sometimes move through in response to a family catastrophe, beginning with denial and going on to anger. I now remember specifically that the first words I uttered upon reading the item were "Get serious!"

But the story I'd just read was obviously real. In Germany, if the clerk in charge of such matters at your city hall doesn't approve of the name you propose to give your newborn baby, you have to name the baby something else. That's right: the clerk. The government says it's a question of the clerk protecting the child. If they tried that in this country, the question would be who's going to protect the clerk.

In Germany, on the other hand, there are all sorts of regulations like this that the citizenry docilely accepts—although the *Post* piece did report that a doctor in Dusseldorf recently went to court to challenge a law that makes it a crime to take a shower after ten in the evening. (I know what you're saying now. You're saying, "Get serious!" That means you're in the denial stage. I suggest that you go to your public library, look up *The Washington Post* for March 25, 1991, and turn to page A14. Then you can move on to anger.) Next time you're assured that we have a strong cultural unity with the countries of Western Europe, keep in mind that Germany has laws against taking a shower after 10 P.M.

In Germany, name-clerks routinely turn down names that don't make it clear whether the child is a girl or a boy, for instance, or names that might sound unfamiliar to the other children at school or names that mean something odd in the language of a foreign country that the child in question will almost certainly never visit.

Let's say that you want to name your new son Leslie because you have reason to believe that your rich and essentially vicious Uncle Leslie would be so touched by such a gesture that he would leave you a bundle to see little Leslie through college. (I'm using American names because I don't want to irritate you with unfamiliar German names at a time when this thing has already put you in a bad mood.)

The clerk says absolutely not: Little Leslie could be mistaken for a female. You say that if enough of Uncle Leslie's boodle is involved, you don't care if little Leslie could be mistaken for a parking meter. The clerk says no. You appeal to a court. The judge upholds the clerk. You get so mad that you take a shower at ten-fifteen. You get arrested. Now this kid of yours has real problems: He doesn't have a name and one of his parents is in the slammer.

I don't mean that I approve of parents giving their children silly names. My views on this matter are on the record. I have stated publicly that naming a child after a store—Tiffany, for instance, or K Mart—is probably unwise. Twenty years ago, I counseled that Sunshine was not a good name for a child, although perhaps perfect for a detergent. I disapproved of the slogan-names favored by Chinese Communists in the fifties because, let's face it, Assist Korea is no name to have on the playground.

But if Sunshine feels more like a Norbert when he grows up—maybe he thinks Norbert is more appropriate for someone keen on regular promotions in the actuarial department—he can simply change his name. His mother, who changed her name from Maxine to

Starglow when she dropped out of college in 1971 to become an apprentice goatherd, can still picture that sweetly dirty little toddler as Sunshine. Should any of this have anything to do with government clerks? Get serious.

1991

Father's Day Is Gone

Father's day is gone. It's over.
Dad was briefly in the clover—
Feeling wise, a valued leader
Who deserved that power weeder.
Cracking wry, a bit like Cos, he
Now reverts—it's back to Ozzie.

1991

Stage Father

By now, my wife's policy on attending school plays (a policy that also covers pageants, talent shows, revues, recitals, and spring assemblies) is pretty well known: She believes that if your child is in a school play and you don't go to every performance, including the special Thursday matinée for the fourth grade, the county will come and take the child. Anyone who has lived for some years in a house where that policy is strictly observed may have fleeting moments of envy toward people who have seen only one or two productions of *Our Town*.

One evening this spring, though, as we walked into an auditorium and were handed a program filled with the usual jokey résumés of the participants and cheerful ads from well-wishers, it occurred to me that this would be the last opportunity to see one of our children perform in a school theatrical event. That view was based partly on the fact that the child in question is twenty-six years old. She was about to graduate from law school. I was assuming that the JDs slogging through the bar-exam cram course would not decide to break the tedium with, say, a production of *Anything Goes*.

As I waited for the curtain to go up on the 1995 New York University Law Revue, entitled *The Law Rank Redemption,* I found myself thinking back on our life as parental playgoers. I realized that I couldn't recall seeing either of our daughters in one of those classic nursery-school-pageant roles—as an angel or a rabbit or an eggplant. I thought I might be experiencing a failure of memory—another occasion for one of my daughters to say, as gently as possible, "Pop, you're losing it"—but they have confirmed that their nursery school was undramatic, except on those occasions when a particularly flamboyant hair puller was on one of his rampages.

I do recall seeing one or the other of them as an Indian in *Peter Pan* and as the judge in *Trial by Jury* and as Nancy in *Oliver!* and as the narrator (unpersuasively costumed as a motorcycle tough) in *Joseph and the Amazing Technicolor Dreamcoat* and as a gondolier in *The Gondoliers*. We heard their voices in a lot of songs, even if a number of other kids were sometimes singing at the same time. We heard "Dites-moi, pourquoi" sung sweetly and "Don't Tell Mama" belted out. All in all, we had a pretty good run.

I don't want to appear to be one of those parents who dozed through the show unless his own kid was in the spotlight. To this day, when I hear "One Singular Sensation," from *A Chorus Line,* I can see Julia Greenberg's little brother, Daniel, doing a slow, almost stately tap-dance interpretation in high-topped, quite tapless sneakers. I'm not even certain what my own girls did in the grade-school talent show at PS 3 that I remember mainly for the performance of the three Korn brothers. One of them worked furiously on a Rubik's Cube while his older brother accompanied him on the piano. The youngest brother, who must have been six or seven, occasionally held up signs that said something like TWO SIDES TO GO or ONE SIDE TO GO. I have always had a weakness for family acts.

I won't pretend that all school performances were unalloyed joy. We used to go every year to watch our girls tap-dance in a recital that also included gymnastics, and the gymnastics instructor was an earnest man who seemed intent on guarding against the possibility of anyone's getting through the evening without a thorough understanding of what goes into a simple somersault. He described each demonstration in such excruciating detail that I used to pass the time trying to imagine him helplessly tangled in his own limbs as the result of a simple somersault that had gone wrong:

"Untie me," he is saying.

"Not until you take an oath of silence," I reply.

Even so, I came to believe over the years that my wife's policy on school plays, which sounds extreme, actually makes sense. It used to be that whenever young couples asked me if I had any advice about rearing children—that happens regularly to anyone whose children grow up without doing any serious jail time—I'd say, "Try to get one that doesn't spit up. Otherwise you're on your own." I finally decided, though, that it was okay to remind them that a school play was more important than anything else they might have had scheduled for that evening. School plays were invented partly to give parents an easy opportunity to demonstrate their priorities. If they can get off work for the Thursday matinée, I tell them, all the better.

1995

Just How Do You Suppose that Alice Knows?

Just how do you suppose that Alice knows
So much about what's au courant in clothes?

You wouldn't really think that she's the sort
To know much more than whether skirts are short
Or long again, or somewhere in between.
She's surely not the sort who would be seen
In front-row seats at Paris fashion shows.
In fact, she looks at that sort down her nose.
For her to read a fashion mag would seem
As out of synch as reading *Field & Stream*.
Biographies are what she reads instead.
And yet she has, in detail, in her head
Whose indigos are drawing "ooh"s and "oh"s.
Just how do you suppose that Alice knows?

We're leaving, and I'll ask her, once we've gone,
"What *was* that thing that whatzername had on?
It lacked a back. The front was sort of lined
With gauzy stuff. It seemed to be the kind
Of frock that might be worn by Uncle Meyer
If he played Blanche in *Streetcar Named Desire.*"
And Alice knows. She knows just who designed
The rag and why some folks are of a mind
To buy this *schmattameister*'s frilly things
For what a small Brancusi usually brings.
She mentions something newly chic this year.
To me it looked like antique fishing gear.
I'm stunned, as if she'd talked in Urdu prose.
Just how do you suppose that Alice knows?

She gets no email info on design.
(She's au courant but, so far, not online.)
No fashion maven tells her what is kitsch.
She goes to no symposium at which
She learns why some designer's models pose
As Navajos or folks from UFOs.
I know that women have no special gene
Providing knowledge of the fashion scene,
The way that men all have, without a doubt,

The chromosome for garbage-taking-out.
And yet she's fashion-conscious to her toes.
Does she divine these things? Does she osmose
What's in the air concerning hose and bows?
Just how do you suppose that Alice knows?

1994

Turning the Tables

I'm afraid the fact that I was in a men's room at the time is germane. This was just off Interstate 84, east of Hartford. Driving through New England, my wife and I had stopped at a franchise restaurant. As I was about to leave the men's room, I glanced at an unfamiliar object on the wall and suddenly realized that it was a pull-down diaper-changing table. In the men's room.

My first thought was that the presence of a diaper-changing table in the men's room might have been a fluke. It might have reflected a gesture by a single corporation, made because the vice president of customer services happens to be a modern woman or happens to be what my daughters used to call a SNAG—a college acronym for a "sensitive new-age guy." (He goes to a lot of pro-choice demonstrations and tends to cry a lot in movies.) Evidence against the fluke theory presented itself that very day in a men's room a few hours down the road and, not long after that, in a men's room on a car ferry. At that point, I heard myself mumbling, "It's here, guys. It's here."

The next time I spotted a changing table, it had a logo on it that showed a picture of a koala below the words Koala Bear Kare. My friend Pierre had been visiting us, and I'd driven him to the airport to get a plane home. We walked into the men's room at the airport together. He saw Koala Bear Kare at the same time I did. He didn't seem alarmed. Pierre's children, like my children, are grown. For both of us, grandchildren remain hypothetical.

I nodded toward Koala Bear Kare. "I assume you're checked out," I said. That was the phrase we always used in our house for anyone who had some experience in diapering. It made being a practiced nappie-swapper sound sort of like having a security clearance.

"Oh, sure," he said. "And I know you're checked out."

"Yes, of course," I said. Even when Pierre and I were young fathers, a forward-looking male knew that if he didn't participate in that elementary aspect of baby raising, he might be robbing himself of the opportunity to say, during a stressful family conversation fifteen or twenty years down the road, "I changed your *diapers*!"

"I'm checked out on changing diapers," Pierre said. "But I might have a little trouble figuring out how to get that gizmo down out of the wall."

"On the other hand," I said, "it seems to me that there was a time when you were concerned about your ability to master a dishwashing machine. And now you're noted for glassware that twinkles with that sparkling shine."

I would think that most modern fathers are checked out. But I would also think that a lot of modern fathers—some SNAGs among them—have considered themselves more or less off duty when the family's eating out. In fact, it wouldn't surprise me if some of them had polished the gesture they use in public when the baby is in obvious need of changing—a sort of apologetic shrug, communicating both regret at not being able to shoulder the burden this time and helplessness in the face of a world organized to assign changing tables only to women's rooms.

If my recent experience is any guide, the world is no longer organized that way. I can't help wondering how this will affect families. I can't help wondering how it will affect men's rooms. Traditionally, the atmosphere in men's rooms is a little—well, edgy. Will the presence of a cooing baby being powdered loosen things up? Will strangers now stop by the Koala Bear Kare table, say something like "Cute little booger," and fall into a conversation about diaper-rash remedies?

I also can't help wondering why I hadn't heard about this before. I try to keep up. Is it possible that men—presumably the only people who use the men's room—have consciously kept mum about the availability of changing tables? If so, I hope they are not laboring under the misapprehension that there is a realistic possibility of keeping this secret. What they ought to be doing is polishing a new gesture—a cheerful smile that goes along with saying, "Let me get this one, honey. You finish your chicken fajita while it's still hot." It's here, guys. It's here.

1995

Slipcovers Just Bloom in the Spring, Tra La

I know I'm going to get in trouble for this. I'm supposed to believe that the reason men tend to have more interest in, say, carburetors than women do is because little boys are given trucks at Christmas instead of dolls. I do believe that. Really. I've believed it for years. I continued to believe it even after my friend Bernie Mohler, the feminist, gave his five-year-old daughter a catcher's mitt for Christmas only to have her plant a marigold in it.

I believe all that stuff. I've even cooperated to the extent of maintaining total ignorance when it comes to carburetors. I'm not absolutely sure what a carburetor looks like, but, given the choice, I'm certain I'd rather have a doll. I'm just fine on this issue. Except for this: I believe that in the spring, female human beings get a deep biological urge to replace the living room slipcovers.

I'm not talking about something imposed by society—something that has to do with getting dollhouses for Christmas. I'm talking about something buried way down there in the chromosomes somewhere. And I'm talking about all women. I believe that in the spring Margaret Thatcher, on her way out of 10 Downing Street to deliver a stiff lecture to a group of poor people, will stop as she strides through the living room, turn to the Chancellor of the Exchequer, and say, "Doesn't it seem to you that the chintz on that armchair by the window is getting a bit tatty?" I believe that Sandra Day O'Connor's thoughts turn to slipcovers in the spring. So do the thoughts of female automobile mechanics and female physicists and female mud-wrestlers. So, as it happens, do the thoughts of my wife.

Come springtime, I find her in the living room, staring hard at the couch. "How long have we had that couch?" she asks. That's an indication that her plans for the couch go beyond new slipcovers. When it comes to furniture, I try not to get into a discussion with my wife about length of service, because on that subject our figures tend to differ. She'll fix her glance on some innocent armchair that I think of as brand-new, and say, "Well, we've had almost forty years of good wear out of that armchair now . . ."

She thinks the resistance I have every spring to replacing the couch is caused by stinginess. She's wrong. Only part of it is caused by stinginess. I've never denied that I'm troubled by how much redecoration costs these days. I hear stories. A friend of ours I'll call Mark Singer had a bathroom wallpapered not long ago, and when I asked him how it worked out, he said, "Fine, although I think that, all in all, we'd rather have had a car." That's the sort of story that can give a stingy person pause.

But there's also a factor that has nothing to do with stinginess. Take the conversation we had just last week:

"What do you think of that couch?" my wife asked.

"Couch?" I said. "What about the couch?" This is an answer that is preselected by a biological code.

"What do you see when you look at that couch?" my wife asked.

"See?" I said. "Couch? Which couch are we talking about?"

"There's only one couch," she said.

"Oh, that one," I said. "Well, I see a piece of furniture with a back and cushions and four stubby little legs. I see a sitting instrument. I see a device designed to hold human beings, once they've folded themselves in two places."

"You don't see how threadbare it's getting on the arms?"

"Arms?" I said. "Threadbare?" (You can tell that these answers are biologically mandated: Nobody would sound that dumb if he had a choice in the matter.)

"I don't think you do see it," she said. "I honestly don't think you can see it."

"Making fun of someone's physical handicaps is the last thing I would have expected from you," I said. I wasn't talking about my eyesight. I was talking about my biologically imposed inability to see the need for a new piece of furniture as soon as my wife saw it.

"Maybe we can just make do with new slipcovers instead of getting a whole new couch," she said.

"Well, I agree that this is probably not the best time to buy a new couch," I said, jumping at the opportunity to encourage the less damaging of two serious hits. "Particularly considering the money we're probably going to have to spend on the car."

"The car?" she asked. "What's wrong with the car?"

"Well, I haven't had it looked at yet," I said. "But I don't like the way the carburetor's sounding."

1987

Hate Thy Neighbor

My wife keeps telling me that I don't really hate the neighbor of ours who talks a lot about the importance of trim and gutter maintenance. I've had this problem with my wife before.

She is the person who insisted that I was only joking when I said several years ago that people who sell macramé ought to be dyed a natural color and hung out to dry. She is the person who tried to shush me when I told a man who pushed ahead of me in an airport line that only certified dorks wear designer blue jeans.

It is my wife who argued that I had no legal standing for making a citizen's arrest of someone for performing mime in public. It's clearer than ever that she is to blame for the children's excessive tolerance.

I haven't done any trim and gutter maintenance in so long that I'm no longer quite certain what there is about them that needs to be maintained. I also feel that way about the points and plugs on the car. I know they're important, but I can't quite remember just why. The same neighbor—he can be called Elwood here, although around the house I always refer to him as Old Glittering Gutters—cannot see my car without patting it on the hood as if it were an exceedingly large Airedale and saying, "When was the last time you had a good look at the points and plugs?"

"I'd rather not say," I always reply.

It's none of his business. His points and plugs are, I'm sure, sharply pointed and firmly plugged in, or whatever they're supposed to be. His trim and gutters are, it goes without saying, carefully maintained. You could probably eat out of Elwood's gutters if that's the kind of person you were. I hate him.

"You don't really hate him," my wife said. "You may think he's a little too well organized for your tastes, and you may not want him over for dinner all the time. But you don't hate him."

Wrong. Elwood has a list of what's in his basement. He says that the list is invaluable. He wonders why I don't have a list of what's in my basement. He doesn't seem to understand that if I made such a list, it would have to be a list of what might be in my basement, and it would have to include the possibility of crocodiles. Elwood's list is cross-indexed. A man who has a cross-indexed list of what's in his basement is not a little too well organized, he's hateful.

The other day, Elwood asked me what sort of system I used to label my circuit breakers. I tried to remain calm. I made every effort to analyze his question in a manner detached enough to prevent physical violence. I tried to think of reasons why Elwood would assume that someone who had already confessed ignorance as to the whereabouts of his 1984 gasoline credit card receipts ("There might be some stuffed in the glove compartment there with the spare points and plugs, Elwood, but I hate to open that thing unless it's a real emergency") would have his circuit breakers labeled at all, let alone have them labeled according to some system.

I calculated, as precisely as I could, what chance there was that a jury, learning of the question that preceded the crime, would bring in a verdict of not guilty on the grounds that the strangling of Elwood had clearly been a crime of passion.

"The system I'm using now," I finally said, "is to label them Sleepy, Grumpy, Sneezy, Happy, Dopey, Doc, and Bashful. However,

I've given a lot of thought to switching to a system under which I would label them Dasher, Dancer, Prancer, Vixen, Comet, Cupid, Donder, and Bruce. I'm holding up my final decision until a friend of mine who has access to a large computer runs some probability studies."

"Probability of what?" Elwood said. I noticed that as he asked the question he retreated a step or two toward his own house.

"Just probability," I said.

When I got back inside my house, I told my wife about the conversation and about the possibility that Elwood now believed me to be not simply slovenly in the extreme but completely bonkers.

"Poor man," she said. "He probably thinks you're dangerous."

"He may be right," I said.

"You have to try to think of Elwood as a human being," my wife said, "someone with feelings, and a wife and children who love him."

"I suspect his children perform mime or sell macramé in public," I said.

"Also," she said, "it really wouldn't be such a bad idea to label the circuit breakers."

I looked at her for a while. "You're right, of course," I finally said. I got a felt-tipped pen, went to the circuit-breaker box, and started right in: "Sleepy, Grumpy, Sneezy . . ."

1986

Long-Term Marriage

I figured the big question about our twentieth wedding anniversary might be whether the local newspaper would send a reporter out to interview us, the way reporters always used to interview those old codgers who managed to hit one hundred. ("Mr. Scroggins offers no formula for longevity, although he acknowledged that he has polished off a quart of Jim Beam whiskey every day of his adult life.") I figured that might be the big question even though the local newspaper is *The Village Voice.* Or maybe I figured that might be the big question *because* the local newspaper is *The Village Voice.* In Greenwich Village, after all, we are known rather widely for being married. We enjoy a mild collateral renown for having children. Several years ago, in fact, I expressed concern that we might be put on the Gray Line tour of Greenwich Village as a nuclear family.

We got married in 1965. In those days, a lot of people seemed to be getting married. In recent years, though, it has become common to hear people all over the country speak of long-term marriage in a tone of voice that assumes it to be inextricably intertwined with the music of Lawrence Welk. In the presence of someone who has been married a long time to the same person, a lot of people seem to feel the way they might feel in the presence of a Methodist clergyman or an IRS examiner. When I asked a friend of mine recently how his twenty-fifth college reunion had gone—he had attended with the very same attractive and pleasant woman he married shortly after graduation—he said, "Well, after the first day, I decided to start introducing Marge as my second wife, and that seemed to make everyone a lot more comfortable."

This awkwardness in the presence of marriage has, of course, been particularly in the Village, a neighborhood so hip that it is no longer unusual to see people wearing their entire supply of earrings on one ear. ("I don't hold with jewelry or none of them geegaws," Mr. Scroggins said, "although over the long haul I've found that a single gold stud in one ear can set off a spring ensemble to good advantage.") In the Village, a lot of people don't get married, and a lot of those who do seem to get unmarried pretty much on the way back from the ceremony. When our older daughter was in first grade at PS 3, one of the romantically named grade schools in the Village, I happened to be among the parents escorting the class on a lizard-buying expedition to a local purveyor called Exotic Aquatics; as we crossed Seventh Avenue, the little boy I had by the hand looked up at me and said, "Are you divorced yet?" When I said that I wasn't, he didn't make fun of me or anything like that—they teach tolerance at PS 3, along with a smattering of spelling—but I could sense his discomfort in having to cross a major artery in the company of someone who was a little bit behind.

Reaching a twentieth anniversary might just intensify such discomfort among our neighbors. I could imagine what would be said if that little boy's parents happened to meet by chance now and our names came up. (As I envision the sort of lives they lead, she has just quit living with her psychotherapist in New Jersey to join a radical feminist woodcutting collective; her former husband is in the process of breaking up with a waitress who has decided that what she really wants to do is direct.) "Oh, them!" the woodcutter would say. "Why, they've been married for *decades*!" The more I considered it, the more I thought that if a reporter in our neighborhood came out to interview people on the twentieth anniversary of their marriage, the questions might be less like the ones he'd ask a citizen who had reached the age of one hundred than the ones he'd ask someone who has chosen to construct a replica of the 1939 World's Fair out of multicolored toothpicks in his recreation room. ("Tell me, Mr. McVeeter, is this some sort of nutso fixation, or what?")

Then I happened to run into the old college classmate I call Martin G. Cashflow. In both investments and social trends, Cashflow prides himself on just having got out of what other people are about to get into and just having got in on the ground floor of what other people haven't yet heard about. After Cashflow had filled me in on his recent activities—he had just got out of whelk-farming tax shelters and into chewing of hallucinogenic kudzu—he asked what I'd been up to.

"Twentieth anniversary," I mumbled.

"Terrific!" Cashflow said. He looked at me as if I had just revealed that I was in on the ground floor of a hot electronics issue. At least, I think that's the way he looked at me; I really don't have much experience at being looked at as if I had just revealed that I was in on the ground floor of a hot electronics issue.

Cashflow told me that among people in their twenties, marriage has come back into fashion. As he explained, the way things have been going, marriage is part of a sort of fifties-revival package that's back in vogue, along with neckties and naked ambition. "Best thing you ever did," Cashflow said. "They're all doing it now, but look at the equity you've got built up."

I shrugged modestly. You don't brag about that sort of thing. Then I went home and told my wife that we were in fashion.

"Not while you're wearing that jacket we're not," she said.

I told her about the fifties package that people in their twenties were bringing back into vogue. She said that if the alternative was to be identified with those little strivers, she would prefer to be thought of as inextricably intertwined with the music of Lawrence Welk.

I could see her point, but I still looked forward to an interview with the local paper. I would be modest, almost to a fault. I would not mention Jim Beam whiskey. The reporter would try to be objective, but he wouldn't be able to hide his admiration for my equity.

1985

BEASTS OF THE FIELD, FISH OF THE SEA, AND CHIGGERS IN THE TALL GRASS

"No, Daddy does not hate cats. That would be prejudice, and you girls have been brought up to abhor prejudice. Daddy has never met a cat that he liked."

Loaded for Raccoons

When the raccoons started getting at the garbage cans this summer, I naturally consulted the man in our town we call the Old Timer. He's the one who told me that we could assure ourselves clear water by keeping a trout in the well, although, as it turned out, I couldn't find a trout except for a smoked trout that some guests from the city brought as a sort of house gift, and I didn't think it would be terribly gracious of me to toss that down the well, even assuming a smoked trout would do the trick. He's also the one who's always saying things like "A porcupine that looks kinda cross-eyed will attack a house cat lickety-split."

"You already tried red onions, have you?" the Old Timer said when I told him about my raccoon problem. I really hate it when the Old Timer asks questions like that. The only acceptable answer is something like "Well, naturally, that's the first thing I did, but for some reason it didn't work; must be the wet spring we had for onions is all I can think of." If, instead, you say, "Well, no . . . ," the Old Timer is going to shake his head for a while without saying anything, as if he's determined not to allow wholesale galloping ignorance to upset him.

"Well, no . . . ," I said when the Old Timer asked me about red onions. He shook his head slowly for so long that I thought he might be having some sort of attack.

Naturally, I hadn't tried red onions. I didn't even know what trying red onions meant. Did you festoon each garbage can with red onions, as if you were decorating a squat plastic Christmas tree? Did you plant a semicircle of red onions around the garbage can area the way infantrymen set up a defense perimeter of concertina barbed wire? Did you sit at a darkened window until the patter of little paws indicated that the time had come to fling red onions at approaching raccoons?

What I had tried was tying down the garbage-can lids—until, on the morning of the weekly garbage pickup, I found myself unable to get the knots undone, and stood there helplessly while the garbage collectors, with a cheerful wave, continued down the road. Then I secured the lids by means of those stretchable cords with hooks on the end of them—I have some for lashing things to the roof rack of the car—but it turned out that the raccoons could pull the lids up far enough to get their tiny paws in there and pull out eighty or ninety square yards of crab shells and melon rinds and milk cartons.

"A raccoon gets ten yards from half a red onion, he'll turn tail and run, sure as shootin'," the Old Timer said.

I hate it when he says "sure as shootin'." I tried red onions anyway, though—cut in half, as the Old Timer had instructed, and placed on top of the lid with the cut side up. The raccoons ate them, except for the skins, which they mixed into some coffee grounds and spread on the rosebush.

I wasn't surprised. The Old Timer is usually wrong. He never admits it, of course. One time, he told us that a scarecrow with a red hat would keep deer out of the garden, sure as shootin'. So we put a scarecrow out there, and put a red hat on it, and the deer came the next night and treated our garden like a salad bar. A neighbor who happened to be awake in the early dawn hours (maybe he was sitting at a darkened window waiting to fling red onions at raccoons) noticed that one of the big bucks was wearing a red hat when it left. I told the Old Timer that the deer had demolished our entire lettuce crop, and he said, "Yup, I suppose they did." When it comes to tempting a normally peaceful person to violence, that Old Timer ranks right up there with raccoons.

In fact, while I was testing my next plan, my wife and daughters told me that I was forbidden to use violence on the raccoons.

"This will only startle them," I said, secretly hoping that it would do a lot more. My plan was to set mousetraps just under the garbage can lids. The raccoons pull up the lids as much as my stretch-cords allow. They stick their little paws in there and feel around, hoping to find some chicken bones with peanut butter on them to spread on the porch. *Powee!* I should have known that the gang of raccoon apologists I live with would object. A few days before, they had objected when I talked about putting the fish heads I use as crab bait into a bait bag—a heavy mesh bag that keeps the crabs already in the trap from eating up the bait while still more crabs are being attracted. They said it would be cruel and deceitful.

I tried to tell them that there is no way you can be deceitful to a crab. Crabs don't think. ("Hey, this smells like a good fish head. I'll just crawl into this place, even though it seems a little like the place that Uncle Manny crawled into just before he disappeared forever. Hey . . . Hey, wait a minute! I've been deceived!") No bait bags, they said, and no mousetraps.

So I gave it to them straight about raccoons. I told them that raccoons are about the meanest animal around. I happened to know from reading Albert Payson Terhune's books about collies that raccoons drown puppy dogs, just for sport.

"Don't be silly," my wife said. "Raccoons are so cute."

"That's what the puppy dogs think," I said. And puppy dogs do think, all the time. ("Hey, these cute little guys want to play in the water. This is fun! Hey . . . Hey, I've been de—*glub, glub, glub.*")

It was no use. They wouldn't give in. That's why I finally used a padlock on my garbage cans. I wanted to use a key lock, but the Old Timer said that a raccoon could pick a key lock nine times out of ten.

"He's probably wrong," I said to my wife.

"Maybe not," she said. "He didn't say 'sure as shootin'.' "

So I put on a combination lock, on the advice of the Old Timer. He said, "A raccoon's cunning, but he's got no head for figures."

1985

True Love

The newest research shows
(So says the *Times,* in Section C)
That birds and bees and beasts
Are more promiscuous than we.

The birds we always thought
Were faithful till the day they died
Are almost sure to have
A little something on the side.

The California mouse
So far's the only thing they've found
That's married, you might say:
This mouse just doesn't play around.

Yes, California mice
Have just one lifelong love to give.
It's odd they stay so true,
Especially living where they live.

1990

Talk About Ugly!

So there I was, butchering a monkfish. As everyone knows, a monkfish is the ugliest creature God ever made.

I realize that those are fighting words among connoisseurs of the drastically unattractive. There are, for instance, people who sincerely believe that a catfish has got all other fish beat for ugliness. I'm here to tell you that compared to a monkfish the average catfish looks like Robert Redford.

In the Pacific Northwest there are people who think that the ugliest creature around is the giant clam they have out there called the geoduck. It's pronounced as if it were spelled gooeyduck, which adds to its unpleasant impression—although, as it happens, gooeyness is one of the few unattractive characteristics it doesn't possess. I won't try to tell you a geoduck is handsome. Its most striking feature is a clam neck that seems to be about the size of a baby elephant's trunk. Still, if I had to describe the appearance of a geoduck in a couple of words, I'd say "moderately disgusting." That's a long way from ugliness at the monkfish level.

The monkfish is also known by such names as goosefish, angler, and bellyfish. Calling it something else doesn't help. Its appearance still brings to mind that fine old American phrase, too little heard these days: "Hit upside the head with an ugly stick."

The head, as it happens, is the ugliest part of a monkfish. It is huge—a lot bigger than the body. It is shaped sort of like a football that has been sideswiped by a Ford pickup. It has, in the words of a fisherman I know, "all kinds of doodads hanging off it." In Nova Scotia, which is where I come in contact with monkfish, fishermen cut the heads off while still at sea. The stated reason for disposing of the head is that the fish plant won't buy it, since nobody has ever figured out a use for a monkfish head. (It doesn't keep long enough to be employed as a device you can threaten to show children if they don't quit fighting over the Nintendo.) I've never been able to escape the feeling, though, that fishermen cut off the head because they don't want anything that ugly on their boat. It makes them shiver.

If you were thinking that without the head a monkfish compares in pure natural beauty to, say, a snow leopard, forget it. The rest of a monkfish is plenty ugly. There is a skin that, by rights, ought to be on a geoduck or something that sounds equally gooey. Instead of the sort of bone structure a respectable fish has, the monkfish has something that reminds most people of a beef bone—although not in a way that makes them long for the open range. Covering the meat on either side of the bone there is a sort of membrane. Is the membrane disgusting? Try hard to think of a membrane you've really liked.

So there I was, butchering a monkfish. Why? Because in our part of Nova Scotia, buying an unbutchered monkfish off a fishing boat is the only way you can get a monkfish, and monkfish, like catfish and geoducks, are absolutely delicious. Also, because I have always harbored a secret desire to have people say of me, "He's the sort of guy who can butcher a monkfish." If they did say that, of course, it might be misleading; I don't actually do many other things that are like butchering a monkfish. On the other hand, let's face it: How many things are there that are like butchering a monkfish? Don't forget the membrane.

Removing the membrane is my least favorite part of butchering a monkfish, although, as a veterinarian I know always says about ministering to a cow that has a badly upset stomach, "There's nothing about it that reminds me a whole lot of opening presents on Christmas morning." I keep thinking that there's some sort of membrane-removal shortcut I don't know about. I always listen to the noon radio show they have for farmers and fishermen in the hope that someday I'll hear some home economist say something like "To get the pesky membrane off a monkfish, simply bury the fish in cornflakes for fifteen or twenty minutes, then wipe briskly with a dry cloth." So far, nobody on the show has discussed monkfish. Probably too ugly.

So there I am, with the membrane and the gooey skin and the beef bone. What am I thinking? Sometimes I'm thinking, "Well, at least it doesn't have the head on." Sometimes I'm thinking, "Don't forget how good this is going to taste." When none of that does any good, I'm thinking, "You're the sort of guy who can butcher a monkfish."

1990

Animal Wrongs

I'm relieved that the talk about bringing back dinosaurs through some sort of DNA fiddling faded away over the summer. It came at a time when I was failing to cope successfully with squirrels. I don't think of myself as having any greater than normal fear or loathing of animals. When I was a boy, I had a dog. When I kick at a cat, it's nearly always for good reason. Still, when I look back on what I've written about my daily life over the years, I'm struck by how many different animals I'm already trying to deal with, almost always unsuccessfully.

I have discussed my doubts about whether Ivory soap will really keep deer out of a garden (or merely leave them feeling fresher) and whether deer whistles will really keep them away from a speeding car; this was at a time when you might say that I was being threatened by deer on two fronts.

Any number of times, I have dealt with the issue of chiggers, the microscopic itch machines whose prevalence on the plains is the real reason so many Midwesterners over the years have chosen to move to New York, a chigger-free jurisdiction. I have described the duration of a chigger bite's itch (just short of eternal) and what can stop it (amputation, sometimes). To gauge the itching intensity of the bite, I even invented a unit of measurement, called the milamos—the itching strength of a thousand mosquito bites. (The average chigger bite has an eight-milamos itch.) I have revealed to those who don't come from the chigger region that a tourist from, say, Joplin, Missouri, who is standing on the top of the Eiffel Tower and gazing down at Paris is not contemplating the beauty of the City of Lights; he is thinking, "Even if they're over here, they couldn't get up this high."

I have had run-ins with animals that I have failed to share with the reading public. Many years ago, for instance, I was attacked by a red-winged blackbird. This was not long after the release of Alfred Hitchcock's *The Birds,* and I think the problem was that the movie had got around to the drive-ins: Birds were seeing it, and getting ideas. Bearing no grudges, I have tried to maintain a bird feeder, only to see it turned into a squirrel feeder. I was once chased by a goose, although—to distinguish that episode from Jimmy Carter's encounter with a killer rabbit—there was never any indication that I had been singled out for attack.

So I was understandably unenthusiastic about concerning myself with dinosaurs. There was no question of staving off a Tyrannosaurus rex with a bar of Ivory. Forty years ago, E. B. White wrote about descending from his office, on the nineteenth floor, to an assembling point on the tenth floor for an atomic-bomb drill—a drop of not nine but eight floors, he noted, since a floor numbered 13 did not exist. "It occurred to us, gliding by the thirteenth floor and seeing the numeral fourteen painted on it, that our atom-splitting scientists had committed the error of impatience and had run on ahead of the rest of the human race," he wrote. "They had dared to look into the core of the sun, and had fiddled with it; but it might have been a good idea if they had waited to do that until the rest of us could look the number thirteen square in the face."

I offer a smaller version of White's point—offering smaller versions of White's points being what most of us scribblers have to settle for. I'm not suggesting that scientists should abandon their DNA research and concentrate on an effective chigger repellent, although any effort they could put toward that end in their spare time would be greatly appreciated where I come from. I do find myself thinking, though, that it might be nice if the largest herbivores in the history of the world did not return until we had at least figured out how to keep the deer away from the begonias.

1993

Horse Movie, Updated

When you can't get to sleep—either because you still have the cares of the world too much with you or because you went a little heavy on the jalapeño peppers—there's often a forties movie to watch on TV. The one I had on was one of those heartwarming stories about a plucky little girl whose pony grew up to be a great trotter, or something along those lines. The little girl was played by a well-known child star like Margaret O'Brien. The trotter was just played by some regular horse.

There was a love interest, of course, provided by the plucky little girl's older sister—Teresa Wright, maybe, or someone with that look—and the older sister's boyfriend, who was somebody like John Agar. They spent a lot of time spooning on the front porch. Some crooked gamblers didn't want the little girl's horse to win. They never do. They never seem to realize that in a heartwarming movie the smart move is to put your money on any horse owned by Margaret O'Brien. So they had sent some big mug like Slapsie Maxie Rosenbloom to scare the little girl into withdrawing her horse from the big race. This is another thing that crooked gamblers never seem to learn: Plucky little girls don't scare easily.

There was also a nice priest named O'Reilly in the movie—a friend of the little girl's who was always there for her after her parents died and her older sister started spending so much time on the front porch. He was either a big priest played by a Ward Bond–type or an elfin little priest played by Barry Fitzgerald. I'm not absolutely clear on that point, because the print of this movie was not in perfect condition, and my television set tends to get snowy unless a warm body is right next to it. I was too tired to get out of bed and go stand next to the television set, and after a rather unpleasant scene the week before, I had promised my daughters that I would no longer attempt to keep the reception clear by strapping their cat to the antenna.

So it's true that I wasn't getting a perfect picture. Also, I wasn't paying as much attention as I might have. That was partly because of the jalapeño peppers: Reaching over regularly to grab a handful of them from a bowl I had next to the bed may have caused me to lose the thread of the plot now and then. Still, I was pretty sure I heard this odd bit of dialogue between the plucky little girl and the priest. At the time, the priest and the little girl were at the rail of the track, watching the trotter do a trial run. The priest had a stopwatch in his hand. As the horse crossed the finish line, the priest flicked down his thumb, read the watch, and turned to the little girl with a jubilant expression on his face. Before he could say a word, though, the little girl asked him, "I suppose your personal position on abortion is identical to the position of the church?"

Well, the priest was taken aback, of course. He pretended he hadn't heard—unless he really hadn't heard, or unless I had only imagined that *I* had heard. He just went right on and said that Bold Ben—that was the horse's name, unless it was Old Len or Gold Ken—had come in under the track record.

Then, suddenly, Slapsie Maxie Rosenbloom loomed up from behind a pillar and told the little girl that if her horse didn't have a strong interest in being turned into dog food it had better slow down in the stretch. I expected the little girl to say something plucky, but what she said was, "The fault is really not yours. So many people who exhibit antisocial behavior are products of impoverished homes, of mothers and fathers who have never shown any interest in their children, of—"

"Hey, watch how you talk about my mom," Slapsie Maxie said. He didn't seem threatening, though. In fact, as he walked away, he looked as if he might cry. "Nicest old dame there ever was," he was mumbling.

The priest seemed undecided about whether it was appropriate to offer comfort to a hireling of the crooked gamblers, but before he could make up his mind he found himself confronted by the little girl. "Well," she said, "do you think a woman should have control over her own body or don't you?"

The priest tried to remain calm and friendly, although I could see that he was upset to learn that the little girl even knew about such things. He told her that this was a subject she might want to wait to discuss until she was older and in a different kind of movie. I thought he had a pretty good point. It had been a long day for me—one of those days when the cares of the world seem to be with you every second, as if you're plugged into an all-news radio station. I figured that about all I could handle at that hour was having my heart warmed a little bit, by a combination of the movie and the jalapeño peppers, so I could be lulled into dreamland.

But the little girl wouldn't stop. "I suppose you think I'm also too young to talk about whether the church is playing ball with some of the most repressive dictators in the world," she said.

The priest just looked sort of uncomfortable at that, and I found that I was mumbling, "C'mon, little girl. Give us a break."

Just then, the older sister and John Agar walked up—all excited because they had just found out that Cold Glenn was at twenty-to-one, meaning that if he repeated his practice performance they'd all win a packet and save the farm. I was greatly relieved. I figured we were back to the horse movie. But then the plucky little girl said to Agar, "Don't you think that in the final analysis pari-mutuel betting is just another terribly regressive tax, aimed at those in our society who can least afford it?"

Well, that's not really the sort of thing that John Agar had ever had to think about in a horse movie, so I couldn't blame him for looking dumbfounded. Actually, he looked worse than dumbfounded. He looked as if he had just caught a horseshoe upside the head.

The priest, who had been looking troubled all this time, turned to the older sister and said, "My dear, if there's ever a time when you need someone to talk to, I hope . . ."

I couldn't imagine what he was talking about. Then I realized that he thought the little girl's question about abortion had to do with her older sister. Being a forties-movie priest, he thought that you could get pregnant from spooning on the porch.

"... for the church teaches that all life is sacred," the priest was saying, "and that life begins the moment ..."

Here's a priest who has been in fifty movies without uttering a sentence of doctrine—I hadn't even known that he was Catholic—and this kid's got him started on the sacredness of life.

"Now look what you've done, kid!" I said. "It wasn't enough that you made poor Maxie cry!"

She turned to me. "Although an informed citizenry is the cornerstone of democracy, the average American watches six hours of escapist television programming a day," she said, "most of it no better than this movie."

"You're the one who ruined the movie, you rotten little prig!" I shouted. "I hope Moldy Wen pulls up lame!"

I jumped out of bed and turned off the television, but I was too upset to fall asleep. I thought I could still hear a little girl's voice from the direction of the darkened set ("It's not surprising that a cat torturer would shout at a child. Studies show that most child abusers ..."). Finally, I got up and switched the set back on—to another channel. The program was a debate between two experts in Washington about whether our society will be destroyed by a nuclear holocaust or by the economic disasters stemming from ever-increasing budget deficits. What they were saying was pretty familiar stuff for someone who had spent the day plugged into the cares of the world—global warming, widespread bank failures, that sort of thing. It was so familiar, in fact, that I found it rather soothing. After a while, as my eyes began to close, I thought I heard one of the experts say, "But golly, everything would be all right everywhere if only Holding Pen wins the big race." And it lulled me off, finally, into dreamland.

1985

Weighing Hummingbirds: A Primer

A hummingbird weighs as much as a quarter. I learned that early this summer, while I was listening to a radio interview with a hummingbird expert on the Canadian Broadcasting Corporation. The CBC interviews interesting people just about all day long, at the same time that American stations are playing the sort of music that makes middle-aged people snap at their children.

I live in Canada in the summer, so by around Labor Day I know a lot of things like how a hummingbird compares in weight to small change. People who live in Canada year-round know even more than I do. What I know tends to drain away over the winter.

The other day, somebody called me in Canada from New York to ask what I thought about the fact that the number one and number two bestsellers in the United States are books about how dumb Americans are. I said, "Hey, wait a minute! I know how much a hummingbird weighs. What's so dumb about that?" I did admit that I'd probably be forgetting whatever I knew about hummingbird weight by around February ("Let me see, was it thirty-five cents, or maybe half a buck?"). The person on the phone said that one of the books included a list of things that Americans ought to be familiar with but aren't, and that hummingbird weight wasn't on it. Apparently the list runs more toward things like Planck's constant and the Edict of Nantes.

If the people who put together that list came up to Canada and asked a Canadian to identify the Edict of Nantes, the Canadian would just ask if he could answer at the end of the week, figuring that by then the CBC would be interviewing a Nantes specialist from the University of Western Ontario or somebody who just came back from a relief mission to Nantes or maybe the ambassador from Nantes to the United Nations, and the Edict would obviously come up during the conversation. Then the Canadian would say to the list gatherers, "By the way, did you fellows know that a hummingbird weighs as much as a quarter?"

A Canadian quarter. As far as I know, bird weights mentioned on the CBC are always given in Canadian currency. For an American living in Canada, that was, of course, a question that came to mind right away. I find that facts learned from the CBC can start an entire chain of questions. For instance, the first thing I asked my wife about the hummingbird fact was this: Do you think a hummingbird also weighs the same as two dimes and a nickel?

Now that I think of it, that particular question didn't start a chain, because she said it was a stupid question and left it at that. But then she asked a question of her own: How do they weigh a hummingbird? Hummingbirds move around a lot, and my wife was concerned that someone who was intent on weighing one would have to dispatch it first.

"Not at all," I said, happy to be able to put her mind at rest on this question. "You've seen those TV documentaries where they shoot a dart into a wildebeest to put him asleep long enough to outfit him with a radio transmitter. Well, this is the same sort of thing, except that the dart is exceedingly small, about half the size of a common straight pin. It's surprisingly easy to hit a hummingbird with the tiny dart. The difficult part is slapping him gently on the cheeks to bring him around after the weighing. That takes a delicate touch indeed." I hadn't actually heard that on CBC, but it sounded like something you might hear on CBC, which is almost as good.

1987

All the Lovely Pigeons

I suppose it's still faintly possible that those who engineered the mysterious snatching of four thousand pigeons from Trafalgar Square had only the best interests of the pigeons at heart. There is that ray of hope to cling to.

I can imagine many people in England trying to reassure one another with such thoughts as they read increasingly grim speculation about the pigeons in the morning papers. "Don't look so glum, Alfie," Alfie's wife says, as she puts the eggs and grilled tomato and thick-cut bacon in front of him. "Maybe this was some nice gentleman who has a home for older pigeons in a lovely part of Sussex where they don't have to be around those nasty foreigners."

It may be, of course, that Alfie was looking glum because, breakfast traditionally being the only edible meal in England, he knew his day had already peaked well before nine in the morning. But he was probably thinking of those pigeons. The English are known for having almost unlimited sympathy for animals that are unromantic or even animals that Americans might describe as having a bad case of the uglies. The United Kingdom is a country in which the monarch harbors corgis.

Apparently, there was, at first, hope that the pigeons had been taken by some poor lad who desperately wanted to race pigeons but lacked the wherewithal to buy his own flock. Alfie was able to imagine the Trafalgar Square pigeons soaring gracefully over the Somerset moors or being pampered by a kindly pigeon fancier like that nice detective on *NYPD Blue*.

But I heard on the radio that the pigeon-racing authorities dismissed that theory, explaining that Trafalgar Square pigeons are too old and out of shape to be competitive racers.

"I was thinking they might have special races for older birds," Alfie may have said when that news came out. "Like the over-50 division in tennis."

I have to say that I was pessimistic from the start. Any sensible analysis of the case has to start with a brutal but undeniable fact: People eat pigeons.

When the New American Cuisine began to take hold in northern California, I remember beginning each visit to San Francisco by checking to make certain there were still pigeons in the parks. My fear was that between my trips to the city, all the poor birds might have been snatched up by what I think of as sleepytime restaurants (everything is on a bed of something), smoked, and served on a bed of radicchio.

I don't think the Trafalgar Square caper indicates that smoked pigeon on radicchio has replaced bangers and mash in the hearts of the English. The pigeons could be served as anything. As Escoffier, or one of them, may have said, "Chopping up is the great leveler."

In fact, a young man, who told *The Sun* that he had taken fifteen hundred of the pigeons and sold them to a middleman, said, "As far as I know, they go to curry houses all over Britain."

We all hope he's wrong. People who would snatch Trafalgar Square pigeons for restaurant stewpots would snatch almost any animal, no matter how repulsive—although the Queen will be relieved to hear they'd probably draw the line at corgis.

1996

The Playing Fields of Mott Street

For years, whenever I took an out-of-town guest on a walking tour of Lower Manhattan, I always included the opportunity to play tic-tac-toe against a chicken in Chinatown. I try to hit the highlights. The chicken was in a Mott Street amusement arcade otherwise known for the decibel level attained by its electronic games. Next to a game with a name like *Humanoid Avenger,* there was a glass cage that held an ordinary-looking live chicken. The player pressed buttons on the scoreboard to indicate his own choices, then waited with trepidation as the chicken, pecking at a board in a private area of his cage behind some opaque glass, registered his invariably brilliant countermoves. Backlit letters came on to keep track of the *X*'s and *O*'s and to announce "Your Turn" or "Bird's Turn." Anyone who beat the chicken got a huge bag of fortune cookies that must have been worth at least thirty-five or forty cents, and it only cost fifty cents to play.

Years ago, the writer Roy Blount, Jr., told me he'd heard that the chicken had been trained by a former student of B. F. Skinner, the legendary Harvard behaviorist. I used to tell my guests that. It was a way of refuting the false teaching that graduate work is of no value in the workaday world. Blount, as it turned out, was absolutely correct. I later spoke to that former graduate student and to a few other animal trainers in Hot Springs, Arkansas, which had become the small-animal training capital of the world. (It is also Bill Clinton's hometown, but I like to think there's no connection.) Mark Duncan, who ran a place called Educated Animals, told me that he offered—in addition to a parrot that rides a scooter, a macaw that plays dead, a raccoon that shoots baskets in answer to mathematical problems (you ask what two and two equals, he shoots four baskets), a rabbit that shoots off a cannon, a Vietnamese pig that drives a Cadillac, and a rooster that walks a tightrope—a chicken that dances while a rabbit plays the piano and a duck plays the guitar.

"What tune do they play?" I asked.

"Their choice," he said.

If you were my guest, of course, playing the chicken in Chinatown didn't even cost fifty cents. As the host, I put up the money. Invariably, the guest would take stock of the situation and then say, "But the chicken gets to go first."

"But he's a chicken," I would say. "You're a human being. Surely there should be some advantage in that."

Then, I have to admit, a large number of my guests would say, "But the chicken plays every day. I haven't played in years."

I suppose you can't blame people for getting the excuses out of the way before the game begins, and in that arcade it proved necessary. I never saw any of my guests do better than a draw against the chicken.

Then, in the early nineties, the chicken died. In *The New York Times,* Michael Kaufman wrote a nice send-off. I said at the time that there have been congressmen laid to rest with less effusive obituaries. I was sad, of course, but I comforted myself with the certainty that those geniuses in Hot Springs could train another chicken to play tic-tac-toe quicker than a rooster can walk a tightrope.

That was not to be. Apparently, the arcade was getting pressure from the animal people (by "animal people," I don't mean people who were abandoned in the woods as children and raised by a pack of wolves; I mean people who are intensely concerned about the welfare of animals). The animal people said that playing tic-tac-toe on Mott Street was demeaning to the chicken. Demeaning? I never saw the chicken lose a game. It might interest the animal people to know that I eventually saw a film clip of B. F. Skinner himself playing the chicken in tic-tac-toe. Skinner is smiling, but it looks to me like a whistle-past-the-graveyard sort of smile. The chicken looks confident, as well he might.

1993

ENGLISH AND SOME LANGUAGES I DON'T SPEAK

"As far as I'm concerned, 'whom' is a word that was invented to make everyone sound like a butler."

Short Bursts

Short bursts of language attract me. I'm keen on slogans. I also like mottos—license plate mottos, for instance, like New York's "The Empire State," or New Hampshire's "Live Free or Die." Not long ago, some residents of Wisconsin started a campaign to change the state license plate motto—they didn't feel they were truly captured by the motto "America's Dairyland"—and someone suggested "Eat Cheese or Die." At one point, I got interested enough in license plate mottos to offer suggestions for states that don't have any mottos at all. The motto I suggested for the Nebraska license plate, for instance, was "A Long Way Across." I'm still working on a motto for Arkansas. The one I have so far seems a little verbose: "Not as Bad as You Might Have Imagined."

Midwesterners have to avoid boastful mottos. Oklahoma's license plate motto, for instance, is "Oklahoma's OK." If the Midwest had a regional license plate motto, it would be "No Big Deal." Although the hamburger restaurant I was addicted to when I was growing up in Kansas City happened to have what connoisseurs agreed were the best hamburgers in the world, its motto was not "The Best Hamburgers in the World" but "Your Drinks Are Served in Sanitized Glasses." I have to say, parenthetically, that restaurant mottos are generally weak, although I admired the motto of a barbecue restaurant in western Kentucky that specialized in barbecued mutton: "Mary Had a Little Lamb. Why Don't You Have Some, Too."

I've also been active in political mottos and campaign slogans. I suppose my most successful slogan was one I made up for a candidate who was running for mayor of Buffalo: "Never Been Indicted." Politicians love mottos, and ever since the New Deal there have been attempts to attach motto-like names to administrations. There was a brief attempt in the Carter administration to use the motto "A New Foundation." Every time I heard it, I could see some beady-eyed contractor standing in front of my house, shaking his head back and forth, and saying, "I'm afraid what you need, my friend, is a whole new foundation."

By chance, this was during a period when I was imagining mottos for families in our neighborhood. The Bartletts, down the street, had the motto "A Triumph in Group Therapy." The Bernsteins would be calling themselves "The Best Mixed Marriage Yet." Our family tried a number of mottos, and then we settled on the one my family had used when I was a child: "Zip Up Your Jacket."

The Reagan administration, the administration of the Great Communicator, naturally coined some lasting phrases. One of them was "the truly needy"—the people who weren't just malingering. I wasn't certain what they meant by "truly needy" until a lawyer from Greenwich who'd been appointed chairman of the Federal Synfuels Corporation said, in 1981, that the salary of $150,000 was so far below a living wage that he'd have to move out of Greenwich if he accepted the job. I envisioned everyone who made less than $150,000 having to move out of Greenwich. I could imagine them packing up their station wagons and heading west in a caravan, like a preppy *Grapes of Wrath*. I could see them in their little camps outside Lake Forest and Sewickley, making their suppers of cold breast of chicken and white wine on the tailgates. The local people, referring to the Greenwich refugees contemptuously as "Greenies," would greatly resent them, of course, as people willing to be bank executives for $135,000 a year. Whenever the greenies would go into town for supplies—a decent piece of brie, for instance—people would say, "G'wan, we don't need your kind here."

Political columnists have pet phrases, mostly to hide ignorance. "Too soon to tell" is the rare phrase that permits you to sound more informed by saying you don't know. I use it myself. If I'm asked what long-term effect on the economy the deficit is going to have, I say, "It's too soon to tell." The other night, one of my daughters asked me how to find the area of an isosceles triangle, and I said, "Too soon to tell."

A few months ago, I was talking to a friend of mine named Nick, who's sixteen, about what we always call Rule #6. When Nick was a little boy, he was a handful, and his mother got a little desperate. So she posted some rules on the refrigerator door. The only one of the rules Nick and I have been able to remember was Rule #6: "Enough's enough." Just after we had our chat about life under Rule #6, I read in the *Times* about an attempted robbery at a branch bank in Brooklyn by a sort of amateur robber. He got away with some money, but the assistant bank manager, a woman in her middle years, chased him out the door, pursued him down the street, tackled him, and had to be restrained by some passing sanitation workers from doing him serious physical damage. When she was asked why she had done all of this, she said that the bank had been robbed just six months before and "enough's enough."

Well, of course, the robber had no way of knowing this. I think the bank should have been required to post a warning sign, like those signs that warn you that a microwave is in use: WARNING. RULE #6 STRICTLY ENFORCED AT THIS BRANCH.

1990

Like a Scholar of Teenspeak

Things have finally returned to normal among the teenagers I know, after a spring filled with vocabulary tension brought on by the Scholastic Aptitude Tests.

"Relax," I kept saying to S., the teenager I know best, as the pressure in her crowd mounted. "I read that a lot of colleges don't pay much attention to SAT scores anyway. Also, you can always go to work in the dime store."

"Relaxing would be a Herculean task—meaning a task very difficult to perform," S. said. "Because among my friends there's no dearth of anxieties. A dearth is like a paucity—a scarcity or scanty supply. In fact, most of the people I know have a plethora of anxieties—a surfeit, an overabundance."

All of S.'s friends were talking that way. One evening, when we were giving S.'s friend D. a ride uptown, D. said, "I'll be on the corner of Thirteenth and Sixth Avenue, in proximity to the mailbox."

"In proximity?" I said.

"Kind of in juxtaposition to the mailbox," D. said. "That's a placing close together, or side by side. If I get tired while I'm waiting, you'll find me contiguous to the mailbox."

"What if someone wants to mail a letter?" I asked.

"If that eventuality—that contingent event, that possible occurrence or circumstance—occurs," D. said, "I'll move."

This is not the way teenagers normally speak. Ordinarily, they don't need many long words—or, for that matter, many words of any size. Some of them can make do for days on end with hardly any words at all beyond the word "like"—as in the sentence "Like, I said 'Like, what?' and he was like, 'Like, okay.' "

As it happens, listening to someone who says "like" every second or third word can get irritating. When S.'s father brings that fact to her attention, in an appropriately courteous and dignified manner ("If you say 'like' once more at this dinner table, you're going to be put in a foster home!"), S. can explain why each use of the word "like" is absolutely logical.

She explains that "like" in some cases is used the way a non-teenager would use "more or less" or "sort of." She explains that "he was like" means not exactly "he said," but something more in the order of "his speech and his manner indicated." Her explanations sound persuasive—which is almost as irritating as listening to some-one who says "like" every second or third word.

In fact, S. has logical explanations for a lot of teenage talk. She can explain why it's okay to use "stupid" or "crazy" as adverbs meaning "very" or "truly," so that you could say both, "that guy is stupid crazy" or, if he happens to be stupider than he is crazy, "that guy is crazy stupid." She can explain the difference between "snapping" and "ranking"—both words for harassing or insulting—well enough to correct her parents at the dinner table, so that if her father says, "S., stop ranking on A.," she might say, "That wasn't a rank. It was more of a harsh snap." S. is, like, a scholar of teenspeak.

When I thought about that fact this spring, it occurred to me that the teenagers I know wouldn't have been under any tension at all if only the SATs were given in their own language: "Like is to like as a) like is to like, or b) like is to like." The problem emerged from the Educational Testing Service's stubborn insistence on giving the test in English. That hardly seems fair.

Think of how difficult it would be for nonteenagers to bone up on vocabulary if they were required to take a test in teenspeak. I can imagine, say, two golfers of middle years and competitive tempera-ments ready to hit their drives on the first green. Al swats his drive right down the center of the fairway and says, "Super-fly fresh! That, as you may know, is an exclamation indicating approval or delight."

"The vocabulary test is not for another month," Jack says irritably, as he tees up. He hits a dribbler, and starts pounding a nearby bush with his driver.

"Chill, money," Al says. "Which is to say: Relax."

"Speak English!" Jack shouts.

"Like, take a chill," Al says.

Jack turns toward Al, waving his driver in the air menacingly. Suddenly, S. emerges from behind the bush.

"It's understandable that you have a plethora of anxieties," she tells Jack. "But you have to make a Herculean effort to control them."

Jack, seeing the logic in that, puts the driver in his golf bag and apologizes for the outburst. "It was stupid crazy of me," he says.

1988

Literally

My problem with country living began innocently enough when our well ran dry and a neighbor said some pump priming would be necessary.

"I didn't come up here to discuss economics," I said. Actually, I don't discuss economics in the city either. As it happens, I don't understand economics. There's no use revealing that, though, to every Tom, Dick, and Harry who interrupts his dinner to try to get your water running, so I said, "I come up here to get away from that sort of thing." My neighbor gave me a puzzled look.

"He's talking about the water pump," Alice told me. "It needs priming."

I thought that experience might have been just a fluke—until, on a fishing trip with the same neighbor, I proudly pulled in a fish with what I thought was a major display of deep-sea angling skill, only to hear a voice behind me say, "It's just a fluke."

"This is dangerous," I said to Alice, while helping her weed the vegetable garden the next day. That morning at the post office I had overheard somebody say that since we seemed to be in for a few days of good weather, he intended to make his hay while the sun was shining. "These people are robbing me of aphorisms," I said, pausing to rest for a while on my hoe. "How can I encourage the children to take advantage of opportunities by telling them to make hay while the sun shines if they think that means making hay while the sun shines?"

"Could you please keep weeding those peas while you talk," she said. "You've got a long row to hoe."

I began to look at Alice with new eyes. By that, of course, I don't mean that I actually went to a discount eye outlet, acquired two new eyes (20/20 this time), replaced my old eyes with the new ones, and looked at Alice. Having to make that explanation is just the sort of thing I found troubling. What I mean is that I was worried about the possibility of Alice's falling into the habit of rural literalism herself. My concern was deepened a few days later by a conversation that took place while I was up in one of our apple trees, looking for an apple that was not used as a *dacha* by the local worms. "I just talked to the Murrays, and they say that the secret is picking up windfalls," Alice said.

"Windfalls?" I asked. "Could it be that Jim Murray has taken over Exxon since last time I saw him? Or do the Murrays have a natural gas operation in the back forty I didn't know about?"

"Not those kinds of windfalls. The apples that fall from the tree because of the wind. They're a breeding place for worms."

"There's nothing wrong with our apples," I said, reaching for a particularly plump one.

"Be careful," Alice said. "You may be getting yourself too far out on a limb."

At breakfast the next morning I said to Alice, "You may be getting yourself too far out on a limb yourself."

She looked around the room. "I'm sitting at the kitchen table," she said.

"I meant it symbolically," I said. "The way it was meant to be meant. This has got to stop. I won't have you coming in from the garden with small potatoes in your basket and saying that what you found was just small potatoes. 'Small potatoes' doesn't mean small potatoes."

"Small potatoes doesn't mean small potatoes?"

"I refuse to discuss it," I said. "The tide's in, so I'm going fishing, and I don't want to hear any encouraging talk about that fluke not being the only fish in the sea."

"I was just going to ask why you have to leave before you finish your breakfast," she said.

"Because time and tide wait for no man," I said. "And I mean it."

As I dropped in my line, I wondered if she'd trapped me into saying that. Or was it possible that I was falling into the habit myself? Then I had a bite—then another. I forgot about the problem until after I had returned to the dock and done my most skillful job of filleting.

"Look!" I said, holding up the carcass of one fish proudly, as Alice approached the dock. "It's nothing but skin and bones."

The shock of realizing what I had said caused me to stumble against my fish-cleaning table and knock the fillets off the dock. "Now we won't have anything for dinner," I said.

"Don't worry about it," Alice said. "I have other fish to fry."

"That's not right!" I shouted. "That's not what that means. It means you have something better to do."

"It can also mean that I have other fish to fry. And I do. I'll just get that other fish you caught out of the freezer. Even though it was just a fluke."

I tried to calm myself. I apologized to Alice for shouting and offered to help her pick vegetables from the garden for dinner.

"I'll try to watch my language," she said, as we stood among the peas.

"It's all right, really," I replied.

"I was just going to say that tonight it seems rather slim pickings," she said. "Just about everything has gone to seed."

"Perfectly all right," I said, wandering over toward the garden shed, where some mud seemed to be caked in the eaves. I pushed at the mud with a rake, and a swarm of hornets burst out at me. I ran for the house, swatting at hornets with my hat. Inside, I suddenly had the feeling that some of them had managed to crawl up the legs of my jeans, and I tore the jeans off. Alice found me there in the kitchen, standing quietly in what the English call their smalls.

"That does it," I said. "We're going back to the city."

"Just because you stirred up a hornet's nest?"

"Can't you see what happened?" I said. "They scared the pants off me."

1981

Roland Magruder, Freelance Writer

During the first week of summer, at a beach party in East Hampton, a portly man wearing tan Levi's and a blue-and-white gondolier's shirt told Marlene Nopkiss that he was a "socioeconomic observer" currently working on a study entitled "The Appeal of Chinese Food to Jewish Intellectuals." Marlene had already suggested that the rejection of one dietary ritual might lead inevitably to the adoption of another when it occurred to her that he might not be telling the truth. Later in the evening, she was informed that the man was in fact the assistant accountant of a trade magazine catering to the pulp-and-paper industry. She was more cautious a few days later, nodding without commitment when a man she met at a grocery store in Amagansett said he spent almost all of his time "banging away at the old novel." A few days later, she saw his picture in an advertisement that a life-insurance company had taken in *The New York Times* to honor its leading salesmen in the New York–New Jersey–Connecticut area. She eventually decided that men automatically misrepresent their occupations in the summer on the eastern end of Long Island, as if some compulsion to lie were hanging in the air just east of Riverhead. The previous summer, in another Long Island town, everybody had said he was an artist of one kind or another; the year before that, in a town not ten miles away, men had claimed to be mystical wizards of the New York Stock Exchange. Around East Hampton, she seemed to meet nobody who did not claim to be a writer. When Marlene drove past the Sunday-morning softball game in East Hampton, she was fond of saying—

even though she was invariably alone—"There stand eighteen freelance writers, unless they're using short-fielders today, in which case there stand twenty freelance writers." Marlene was beginning to pride herself on her cynicism.

So she was understandably skeptical when, at a party at Bernie and Greta Mohler's summer place near East Hampton, a young man named Roland Magruder answered her question about his occupation in the usual way. "What *kind* of writer?" she said suspiciously. She could not believe that he had not heard how difficult she was to impress with this approach.

"A freelance writer," said Magruder, who was quite aware of how difficult she was to impress with this approach, and had even heard odds quoted on the matter.

"What kind of freelance writer?" asked Marlene.

"A sign writer."

"A sign painter?"

"No," said Magruder. "I write signs. Cities retain me to write signs on a freelance basis. I specialize in traffic work. YIELD RIGHT OF WAY is a good example."

"Somebody *wrote* YIELD RIGHT OF WAY?" asked Marlene.

"*I* wrote YIELD RIGHT OF WAY," said Magruder, permitting a tone of pride to creep into his voice. "Do you think something like YIELD RIGHT OF WAY writes itself? Do you think it was written by the gorilla who installed the signs on the expressway? He would have probably written LET THE OTHER GUY KEEP IN FRONT OF YA. Have you been going under the impression that VEHICLES WEIGHING OVER FIVE TONS KEEP RIGHT was composed by John V. Lindsay?"

"But these messages are obvious," argued Marlene.

"You would have probably said that it was obvious for Brigham Young to say 'This is the place' when the Mormons reached Utah, or for Pétain to say 'They shall not pass,' or for MacArthur to say 'I shall return.' I suppose you think those lines just happened to come out of their mouths, without any previous thought or professional consultation. I think, by the way, if I may say so, that my NO PASSING says everything 'They shall not pass' says, and without succumbing to prolixity."

"You mean to say you're being paid for writing STOP and ONE WAY and SLOW?" asked Marlene. She tried to include as much sarcasm as possible in her voice, but Magruder seemed to take no notice.

"A certain economy of style has never been a handicap to a writer," he said. "On the other hand, while it's true that traffic signs are a vehicle that permits a pithiness impossible in most forms, I do longer pieces. NEXT TRAIN FOR GRAND CENTRAL ON TRACK FOUR is one of mine—at the Times Square subway station. There's another one at the Times Square station that you certainly haven't seen yourself but that I think has a certain flair: THIS IS YOUR MEN'S ROOM; KEEP IT CLEAN. I've heard several people talk of that one as the ultimate expression of man's inability to identify with his group in an urban society."

That was almost too much for Marlene. She had found herself beginning to believe Magruder—his self-confidence was awesome, and after all, who would have the gall to take credit for ONE WAY if he hadn't written it?—but bringing in sociological criticism was a challenge to credulity. Just then, Bernie Mohler passed by on his way to the patio and said, "Nice job on SHEA STADIUM PARKING, Roland."

"What did you have to do with Shea Stadium parking?" asked Marlene.

"That's it," said Magruder. "SHEA STADIUM PARKING. It's on the expressway. Do you like it?"

Before Marlene could answer, a blond girl joined them and asked, "Was that your THIS IS WATER MILL—SLOW DOWN AND ENJOY IT I saw on Highway 27, Roland?"

Magruder frowned. "I'm not going to get involved in that cutesy stuff just to satisfy the Chamber of Commerce types," he said. "I told the town board that SLOW DOWN says it all, and they could take it or leave it."

"I thought your NO PARKING ANY TIME said it all," remarked a tall young man with a neat beard. "I've heard a lot of people say so."

"Thanks very much," Magruder said, looking down at the floor modestly.

"Oh, did you do that?" Marlene found herself asking.

"It wasn't much," said Magruder, still looking at the floor.

"You don't happen to know who did the big NO sign at Coney Island?" Marlene asked. "The one that has one NO in huge letters and then lists all the things you can't do in smaller letters next to it?" Marlene realized she had always been interested in the big NO sign.

"I introduced the Big No concept at the city parks several years ago," said Magruder. "Some people say it's a remarkable insight into modern American urban life, but I think that kind of talk makes too big a thing of it."

"Oh, I don't," said Marlene. "I think it's a marvelous expression of the negativism of our situation."

"Well, that's enough talking about me," said Magruder. "Can I get you another drink?"

"I'm really tired of this party anyway," said Marlene.

"I'll drive you home," said Magruder. "We can cruise by a KEEP RIGHT EXCEPT TO PASS sign, if you like. It's on the highway just in front of my beach house."

"Well, okay," said Marlene, "but no stopping."

"I wrote that," Magruder said, and they walked out the door together.

1965

Nerds, Dorks, and Weenies

The reason so many Hollywood movies are made about nerds in high school who triumph in some improbable way over the jocks is this: Nearly everybody who makes movies in Hollywood was himself a nerd in high school.

They weren't called that, of course. The word changes all the time. But they know who they are. So do I. I keep track of these things. I even keep track of the current word for "nerd." I'm that sort of person.

I wouldn't ordinarily refer to anyone as a nerd myself, of course. I prefer the term "dork." It means the same thing, and to me it has always sounded worse. I think there's a special ring to the phrase "What a dork!" I'm flexible, though. I'll use any word, as long as it has a dorky sound to it. In fact, "dork" wasn't the word we used when I was in college. Our word was "weenie." Now that I think of it, "What a weenie!" has a nice ring to it, too, but that may just be nostalgia on my part.

A few years ago, I was told that the new word for weenie was "dweeb," as in "he's a total dweeb." Apparently, a total dweeb is the only kind of dweeb you can be. There's no dweeb spectrum. You can't be "just a little bit dweebish" any more than you can be "a tad dorky." In these matters, it's ordinarily all or nothing. Although I have to say that once, many years ago, I did hear someone described as having "weenielike tendencies."

Last summer, I went to England to see what they were calling nerds these days over there. That's not what I told the immigration officer when he asked the purpose of my visit, of course. I said, "Tourism."

My main consultant was a young man I'll call Danny Jowell. When I asked Danny what the English called a nerd, he didn't hesitate for a moment. He told me that an English nerd is a wally.

I was stunned. Wally is a perfectly respectable first name. Then I decided that it just shows you how strange the English are: If they were going to use a word that's precisely the same as a first name, they have plenty of names over there that sound more nerdlike than Wally. Nigel, for instance. In fact, I rather like "nigel" as the word for nerd. It trips off the tongue: What a nigel!

Meanwhile, I've tried out "wally" over here, and everyone seems to think it sounds pretty dumb. Of course, the people I went to college with think anything but "weenie" sounds dumb. They're kind of set in their ways. In the early seventies, I revisited the campus, and naturally I was interested in what the new word for "weenie" was. I knew it was a period of uncharacteristic tolerance among undergraduates, so I expected them to use whatever word it was in a tolerant way, as in "I ran into a rather interesting dweeb today." What I found instead was that they had become so tolerant they didn't have a word for "weenie."

When I returned from my visit, the first question I was asked by a classmate of mine was, "What's their word for 'weenie'?"

"That's just it," I said. "They don't seem to have a word for 'weenie.' "

"In that case," he said. "They're *all* weenies."

1990

Holistic Heuristics

I've decided to skip "holistic." I don't know what it means, and I don't want to know. That may seen extreme, but I followed the same policy toward "gestalt" and the twist, and lived to tell the tale.

"Aren't you even curious about what it means?" my wife, Alice, the family intellectual, asked me one day.

"No, I think I'll just give it a skip," I said. "Thanks, anyway."

Alice had just finished comparing the East and West Coast definitions of "holistic" with a friend of ours who was visiting from California. Our friend—I'll call him Tab, although his name is, in fact, Bernard—had mentioned meeting the woman he now lives with in a hot tub that belonged to someone who practiced holistic psychology. (Now that I think of it, Tab may have said that the host practiced organic orthodontia; I only remember that it was one of the healing arts.) I should probably explain that a hot tub is a huge wooden vat in someone's backyard—back where the barbecue set used to be a long time ago. In California, I gathered from Tab, people who are only casually acquainted take off all of their clothes, climb into a hot tub together, and make up new words.

"How about 'heuristics'?" Alice asked.

"Is that the same word?" I said, thinking she might have hit me with a Boston pronunciation, just for laughs.

"Different word," Alice said. "But also very big these days."

"I think I'll give that one a skip, too," I said. "Fair's fair."

I'm quick to acknowledge that, through no efforts of my own, I'm in a better position than most citizens to be cavalier about these matters. Having a family intellectual available, I can always arrange to have words like "holistic" or "heuristics" translated if it should prove absolutely necessary—if they turn up on a road sign, for instance, or on a menu or on a visa application.

I should make it clear that I have no objection to new words. I am, for instance, a regular user of the word "yucky"—which, as far as I can tell, was invented out of whole cloth by Oscar the Grouch. I have even invented a new word myself now and then—on long evenings, when there's nothing much on the tube. I was particularly proud of finding a new word to replace awkward phrases like "the woman he now lives with"—"CeeCee" was my word, from the old newsmagazine euphemism "constant companion"—but then Alice told me that "CeeCee" sounded like a breath mint.

What I have a resistance to is not new words but words that come into a vogue that may not last as long as the one for the twist—disappearing from the vocabulary of the sophisticates just about the time that a slow reactor like me has learned the difference between the East Coast and the West Coast definitions. I realize that passing up words like "holistic" may strike some people as laziness or even philistinism, but I have always liked to think of it as a sort of negative act of character. The speed of trends being what it is these days, after all, about the only way a citizen can exhibit an independent spirit is to remain totally inert.

When I'm trying to impress Alice, for instance, I remind her that I have resolutely ignored drinking fashions for twenty-five years, steadily knocking back Scotch whisky the entire time. They turned to wine; I drank Scotch. They smoked pot; I drank Scotch. They ordered Perrier water; I drank Scotch. They snorted cocaine while naked in a hot tub; I drank Scotch. I like to think that late on some Saturday nights Alice can point to me—slumped in the corner, sodden with Scotch—and say, "There sits a man of principle."

1978

I Say!

According to *The New York Times,* a survey taken recently in Western Europe indicates that Europeans don't much like the English. No news there. The organization responsible for the survey—the European Economic Community—says that the hostility toward Great Britain is the result of a dispute now going on over the EEC's spending practices and agricultural program, but I don't think that's it at all. I think that Europeans are hostile toward the English because the English have some irritating habits—the habit, for instance, of ending sentences with questions that sound like reprimands. You say it's difficult for you to tell because you haven't read the survey? Well, you'll have to read it then, won't you. See how snotty that sounds? It sounds as if the person who said it expects you to say, "Well, yes, I suppose I will have to read it, and it was terribly stupid of me not to have realized that before." Think how snotty it would sound in an English accent. Think how snotty it would sound to a Frenchman whose understanding of English may be imperfect and who might have thought that the Englishman was saying, "Quit standing on my foot—would you?" It sounds snotty, but the English actually don't mean anything by it. They don't know any other way to talk.

Why do the English talk so funny? For one thing, they're all hard of hearing. All Englishmen are hard of hearing. That's why they end a lot of sentences with questions—just to check and make sure the other fellow heard what they were saying. (When you think about it that way, it's not snotty; it's actually rather thoughtful.) That's why they're always saying "I say!" It gives the other fellow a warning that they're about to say something, and then he knows to tune in. This used to be a secret—that all Englishmen are hard of hearing. All the English knew, of course, but they wouldn't let it out to foreigners. I'm the one who found out about it. I found out watching Harold Pinter plays.

The people in Harold Pinter plays are very hard of hearing. That is what professors of drama mean, I suppose, when they talk about how a dramatist has a heightened sense of reality: He takes people who are just hard of hearing and he makes them very hard of hearing. People in Pinter plays are always repeating themselves because the other character didn't hear them the first time:

"Hello."

"What?"

"Hello."

"I thought you said goodbye."

"No. Hello."

"What?"

"Goodbye."

Even after I uncovered the secret of Harold Pinter, I tried to keep it to myself. I had learned my lesson several years before, when I revealed that the Italian movies everybody considered so profound would seem silly to anyone who understood Italian. I wasn't claiming that I understood Italian; in fact, Italian often sounds to me as if the speaker is telling a lot of other people to quit standing on his foot. I was just saying that Americans who went to see an Italian movie that had been called profound concentrated hard on getting the subtitles read before the scene changed, figured that a lot of nuances must have been lost in reducing great hunks of dialogue into one line of type, and didn't stop to consider the possibility that the movie was simply silly. Then a couple of the profound Italian directors made their first movies in English, and all the critics said the movies were silly. I thought the critics would then realize that all the movies they had said were profound would also have seemed silly if only they had understood the dialogue, but instead they said that even a profound director can't hit every time at bat. I also thought a lot of people would come up to me and apologize for having called me a philistine and a hopeless lout, but nobody did. So when people asked what I thought of Harold Pinter plays—even after I knew the secret—I just said, "Very English. His plays are very English."

Of course, the dispute at the headquarters of the European Economic Community must have been exacerbated by the special way that people who go into the British diplomatic service talk—

particularly their habit of putting together packages of adverbs and adjectives that don't match, like "perfectly awful" and "frightfully nice." I know they don't mean anything by it, but it can't be much fun to listen to all the time. The French representative to the EEC must get the feeling that he's constantly being served a chocolate parfait with béarnaise sauce.

"I say!" the representative of the United Kingdom says, although the warning is quite unnecessary, since the French hear better than anyone (that's why they talk so fast).

"Please don't," the French representative says. "At least not so soon before lunch."

At this point, I assume, the Italian representative has the wit to speak only in subtitles.

It can't help that what the English want to discuss in the EEC is the agricultural program. While the French or Belgian or Italian representative is politely negotiating an agreement for exporting vegetables to the United Kingdom, he is secretly seething with the knowledge that the English are going to overcook them. This must be the sort of thing diplomats are referring to when they talk about hidden agendas. The French representative is supposedly talking in purely economic terms about the exportation of asparagus, but the memory of what the British had done to a French asparagus he once encountered in Brighton is causing him to negotiate through clenched teeth. The British representative sails along without noticing.

"I say! That would be terribly good," he says, as the agreement is reached.

"But is it the green asparagus or the white asparagus that you want, monsieur?" the French representative says.

"Well, that's up to you," the Englishman says. "Isn't it."

1984

Pardon My French

According to the newspapers, people in France are worried that the French language may be losing out to English. I'm not worried about that at all. As it happens, I don't speak the French language. So as far as I'm concerned, the faster the French language loses out to English the better. It doesn't even have to be very good English that French loses out to. I look forward to the day when I get in a Paris taxi and the taxi driver says to me, "To where does it be that we're coming to, buster?"

I would tell him to take me to the Pasteur Institute, which recently horrified even the president of France by changing the names of its scientific journals from French to English. Once I got there, I would say, in the manner of a British headmaster congratulating the winning rugby team, "Good on you, Pasteur Institute! Good on you!" Then I would tell them, in American, "Atta way to chuck, Pasteur Institute, baby. You're the kid, Pasteur Institute." Then I would give everyone at the Pasteur Institute a high five—what used to be called an *haute cinq* over there before the French language started losing out to English.

Then I would get back in my cab and go to the nearest bar, where I would say, in my best English, "Gimme a beer, mac, and step on it." When the bartender answered, in English, I would refrain from criticizing his accent, despite all the times that French taxi drivers pretended not to understand my directions in the days when the French still spoke French. I'm above that sort of thing, although just barely.

Understand my directions? Yes, I'll admit it: I use a little French whenever I'm over there. Not verbs. I don't do verbs. I used to do a few. In fact, I knew some pretty complicated verbs—what I believe the French intellectuals call Sunday-go-to-meeting verbs. For instance, if I wanted to know where the beach was, which I often did, I could say "*Ou se trouve la plage?*"—which, literally translated, is "Where does it find itself the beach?" But that seemed silly to me. A beach knows where it is.

The head of the Pasteur Institute said that the institute simply had to face up to the fact that the international language of science is now English. He said that in 1988 the institute received 249 manuscripts, half of them from French-speaking countries, and only 6 percent were written in French. Good. I think if we really work on it, we might be able to get that down to about 2 percent.

I suppose you could argue even then that an absence of French content is no argument for changing the name of a scholarly journal. Think of all the restaurants in the United States that have French names even though the only thing French about them is the Kraft's French dressing they use at the salad bar. I suppose you could argue that, but I'm not about to, because I'm all for this decision. In fact, I feel like dropping into the Pasteur Institute right now and saying, in English, "Stick to your guns, Pasteur Institute."

That phrase itself, by the way, is an example of how much better everything is going to be when the French language finally loses out completely to English. In the French translation, it would mean people literally sticking to their guns—a bunch of people standing there with no one left to shoot but still unable to remove their hands from their guns. Getting rid of that sort of awkward and embarrassing image is going to be a big relief to the French, once they get used to it.

1989

BAGELS, YIDDISH, AND OTHER JEWISH CONTRIBUTIONS TO WESTERN CIVILIZATION

"In Kansas City, where I grew up, Calvin Trillin is a very common Jewish name. My full name is Calvin Marshall Trillin. Marshall is an old family name. Not our family, but an old family name."

Seder Splitsville

For us, the saddest news of the spring holiday season was that our old friends the Levines decided to get a divorce, citing irreconcilable differences over what kind of Passover seder to attend. It seems only yesterday that we were all together at the Levines' for a Freedom Seder—asking that all people oppressed by antidemocratic dictators be freed as the Jews were freed from Pharaoh's grasp, debating the issue of whether the Pharaoh's daughter was trying to co-opt Moses by hauling him out of the bulrushes, and tucking away some of Linda Levine's superb gefilte fish done with a simple béchamel sauce. But when Richie Levine and I had a drink together to talk about the split-up, he reminded me that the Freedom Seder was almost twenty years ago. Since then, he told me, the Levines have observed Passover at dinners that included an Environmental Seder that emphasized the effect the parting of the Red Sea might have had on marine life and a seder done entirely in Reformation dress. It shows you how time flies.

When we had our drink, Richie was in a reflective mood, talking about the seders he used to go to as a kid in Detroit at the home of his Uncle Mo the Gonif. Richie happened to have two uncles named Mo—one of them a failed actor who lived off his relatives, the other a prosperous businessman who had once been accused of embezzlement by his partner—and to keep them straight, the family called them Uncle Mo the Schnorrer and Uncle Mo the Gonif.

"Those were the days," Richie said. "My sisters and I would get a little tipsy on the Passover wine and kid Aunt Sarah about the matzo balls being kind of rubbery: 'I'll just save this one, thanks, Aunt Sarah; we're going to play jacks a little later, and it'll make a good ball.' "

"Simpler times, Richie," I said. "Those were simpler times."

It was an acquaintance of ours we call Harold the Committed who organized the Freedom Seder at the Levines, but Richie didn't seem to blame him for anything that followed. "Hal the C's okay," Richie said. "Sure, I got a little bored when he went into that long spiel comparing Moses' brother Aaron to Ché Guevara, but I figured it wasn't much different from when I got restless waiting for Uncle Mo the Gonif to stumble through all that Hebrew so that I could have another go at the Manischewitz burgundy. Times change."

I nodded, and looked into my drink for a while. "So what went wrong, then?" I finally said.

"Well, nothing right away," Richie said. "Harold the Committed wasn't in town for Passover for a few years there; that's when he was going to Sweden every spring to do that ecumenical Unilateral Disarmament Seder with the schismatic Lutheran peaceniks. Josh and Jenny weren't old enough then to know what was going on, so I guess we just skipped Passover for quite a while, except for that Interfaith Seder at the Mohlers' where we saw you—the one where the priest got blotto and the Methodist minister fainted into the chopped liver."

I remembered the occasion well. The priest polished off the Passover wine supply so quickly that the last two blessings had to be said over apple juice. The Methodist minister started in on the chopped liver with considerable gusto—having had up to that moment no way at all of knowing that he carried in his bloodstream antibodies that would set off a violent chemical reaction to schmaltz.

Apparently, when the kids got old enough to understand what Passover was—Josh was about six and Jenny four—Richie assumed there would simply be a regular family seder every year, but Linda, who had always been intense about causes, was convinced that a seder had to be a statement. After she lost interest in national liberation and gourmet cooking, the Levines went to the Environmental Seder, which Richie remembered as having been "mostly about microorganisms." That flowed into a Natural Foods Seder, whose symbolism irritated Richie. "I mean, let's face it," he told me. "The mortar that the Jews made in Egypt didn't look anything like mung beans, and it's silly to pretend it did."

"So that's what did it?" I asked. "The mung beans for mortar?"

"Oh, no," Richie said. "That was years ago. After that—let me see—we had a seder at a radical feminist collective, where they refused to recognize the killing of the Egyptians' firstborn sons as a curse, which made Josh feel a little uncomfortable, of course."

"So you said you wouldn't go back there the next year?"

"No, no. The next year we went to a seder where the guest of honor was an Indian holy man Linda's pals were very big on at the time. He went on and on about whether plain matzo had inner peace. Finally, I told him I'd promise to stay away from his ashram if he'd stay away from my seders—sort of a reverse interfaith arrangement."

"So that did it?"

"No. What did it is when Linda got involved in finding her roots, and we started going to seders every year in Brooklyn with Hasidim who pray in Hebrew for six or eight hours before you can have a bite of gefilte fish. I have a lot of respect for those people, but they're not the sort of crowd that goes for matzo-ball jokes. So this year, I told Linda that if we're searching so hard for roots, my roots are in Detroit: I was going to seder at Uncle Mo the Gonif's. So she said go. It was great. Uncle Mo the Gonif and Aunt Sarah are getting on, but one of my sisters helped with the cooking, and she even knows how to make those bouncy matzo balls. Uncle Mo the Gonif's Hebrew hasn't improved. He's really a very sweet man, my Uncle Mo the Gonif—as long as you don't leave him alone with the books."

"I hope there's no acrimony between you and Linda," I said.

"It's a very amicable separation," Richie said. "The only problem we're having is who gets custody of the kids on Passover."

1983

Killer Bagels

I was surprised to read that bagels have become the most dangerous food in the country. I've lived in New York—which is to bagels what Paris is to croissants—for a number of years, and I've never been injured by a bagel. When I go back to Kansas City, where I grew up, old friends never say, "Isn't it scary living in New York, what with the bagels and all?" My answer to that question would be that New Yorkers who were asked to name foods they think of as particularly benign would mention bagels as often as chicken soup.

They might talk about that morning in the park when nothing seemed to soothe their crying baby until a grandmotherly woman sitting on a nearby bench, nattering with another senior citizen about Social Security payments or angel-food-cake recipes or Trotskyism, said that the only thing for a teething infant was a day-old bagel. They might talk about the joy of returning to New York from a long sojourn in a place that was completely without bagels—Bangladesh, or a tiny town in Montana, or some other outpost in the vast patches of the world that New Yorkers tend to think of as the Bagel Barrens. They might talk about the days when people used to sit on their stoops and watch the neighborhood kids play roller-skate hockey in the street with a stale bagel as the puck—days spent listening contentedly to the comforting slap of hockey stick against bagel and the inevitable cries, when the action got too close to a drain opening, "Lost bagel! Lost bagel!" They might talk about picking up freshly baked bagels late at night and being reassured, as they felt the warmth coming through the brown paper bag, that they would be at peace with the world the next morning, at least through breakfast.

According to a piece in the *Times* not long ago about how dangerous kitchens have become, that brown paper bag could have been holding a time bomb. "We're seeing an increasing number of bagel-related injuries in the emergency service," Dr. Stephen Adams, associate medical director of the emergency department at Northwestern Memorial Hospital, in Chicago, told the author of the piece, Suzanne Hamlin. It isn't that bagels are considered dangerous to eat in the way that triple bacon cheeseburgers are considered dangerous to eat. It's true that in recent years some bakers in New York have been making bagels with some pretty weird ingredients—oat bran, say, and cinnamon, and more air than you'd find in the Speaker of the House—but not dangerously weird. Nor is there any implication that bagels are dangerous because they are easily flung at people in the close quarters of an apartment kitchen.

The danger comes with people trying to get at bagels. "The hand lacerations, cuts, gouges, and severed digits," it says in the *Times*, "are caused by impatient eaters who try to pry apart frozen bagels with screwdrivers, attempt to cut hard bagels with dull knives, and, more than likely, use their palms as cutting boards."

Ms. Hamlin found no increase in New York bagel injuries. Reading about the havoc that bagels can wreak in Illinois or California, a New Yorker might say, in the superior tone customarily used by someone from Minneapolis describing the chaos caused in Birmingham by a simple snowstorm, "People there just don't know how to handle such things"—or, as the director of emergency medicine at Bellevue said to the *Times*, "Those people just aren't ethnically equipped." The Bagel Barrens have been shrinking rapidly—bagel stores have sprouted in the shopping malls of neighborhoods that baked-goods sociologists have long identified with white bread—so maybe it's true that a lot of Americans are being given access to bagels before they know how to handle them, in the way that a lot of Americans are said to have access to 9-mm pistols or semiautomatic rifles before they know how to handle them.

But there is a more positive way to look at this. Twenty years ago, the bagels in Kansas City were accurately described by one of my daughters as tasting like "round bread." It was impossible to conceive of anybody desperately going to work with a screwdriver to free up one of them for thawing. Could it be that outlander bagels have improved to the point of being something that people truly yearn for? If so, maybe what we're seeing in Midwestern emergency rooms is the price of progress.

1996

So, Nu, Dr. Freud?

According to a quotation carried recently in *The New York Observer,* Jorge Luis Borges, the Latin-American fantasist, was asked during a visit he once made to the New York Institute for the Humanities what he thought of Sigmund Freud. "Never liked him," Borges said. "Too *schmutzig.*"

I was among the readers who found that response surprising. When I was growing up in Kansas City, the few references to Freud that drifted my way gave me the impression that what he wrote was *schmutzig,* or dirty, and this is the first evidence I've come across that in those days I was thinking along the same lines as Jorge Luis Borges on any subject at all. Also, the fact that Borges would use a homey Yiddish word like *schmutzig* required me to make some adjustments on the image of him that I had been carrying in my mind. It was as if I'd been informed that distinguished literary personages who called on Henry James in his London drawing room were customarily greeted with a cheery "Hey, goombah!"

I should say that, now that I'm grown up, I no longer associate

Freud's writings with smut. These days, my views on Freudianism are virtually identical to my views on Presbyterianism: Some people believe in it, I was brought up not to be disrespectful of other people's beliefs, and, for all anybody knows, it could turn out to be right on the money.

I was therefore not someone who took particular satisfaction in the discovery, made some years ago, that Freud had fudged the data in order to come up with his seduction theory, which is central to Freudian thought. I'll admit that I was interested in the controversy provoked by that discovery, in the way I'd be interested in what Presbyterians would have to say if it were discovered that their belief in predestination was the product of an unfortunate misunderstanding at the printer's in 1536.

Either case would bring up what I think of as the Davis Conundrum—how to deal with information that may call into question a tenet that is central to a system of belief. The Davis Conundrum takes its name from a wine-tasting test that I'm told is sometimes given at the highly regarded department of oenology at the University of California at Davis. It turns out that, under blind-test circumstances, the tasters, some of them professional wine connoisseurs, are often unable to tell red wine from white wine. That triggers the Davis Conundrum: Does the failure to distinguish red from white undercut all the learned talk you hear about body and vintage and integrity and which side of the hill the grapes came from?

I assume that there have already been any number of seminars on the question of whether the seduction theory's being based on incorrect data invalidates the Freudian theories that followed. The recent publication of the first volume of *The Correspondence of Sigmund Freud and Sándor Ferenczi* is likely to provoke even more seminars. In these letters to a trusted disciple, Freud, not surprisingly, has some critical words to say about his rival Carl Jung. You might expect him to write, "Jung, of course, is transferring to me his suppressed infantile homoerotic attraction for his Uncle Heinrich," or words to that effect. Not at all. According to what I read in the *Times Book Review,* here is what Freud wrote to Ferenczi about Jung: "Jung is *meshuga.*"

Meshuga, of course, means crazy in Yiddish, and I must say that I was delighted to hear that Sigmund Freud as well as Jorge Luis Borges employed that dazzlingly expressive language, which many German-speaking Jewish bourgeois have scorned. This raises the possibility that Freud's grandson—the renowned artist Lucian Freud, whose paintings of not altogether beautiful people were such a hit not long ago at the Metropolitan Museum of Art—may as a child have called the great doctor *zayde.* For some reason, contemplating that possibility makes me feel better about both of them.

On the other hand, could this actually be Sigmund Freud's diagnosis of Carl Jung—"Jung is *meshuga*"? When the founder of psychoanalysis offered his opinions in a private letter rather than in a paper designed to be read by the profession at large, was this the way he talked? If that's the case, his frank personal opinion of any of his most celebrated analysands might have been (translated from his vernacular to ours) "The man's bonkers—off his squash, nutty as a fruitcake, a cuckoo bird." If so, what's all this talk about sublimation and Oedipus complexes and penis envy? As Borges might have put it, why did we need all that *schmutz*?

1994

Jacob Schiff and My Uncle Benny Daynovsky

> *"The silk-hat banker Jacob Schiff, concerned about the conditions on the East Side of New York (and embarrassed by the image it created for New York's German Jews), pledged half a million dollars in 1906 to the Galveston Project, which helped direct more than ten thousand East European migrants through Galveston into the South and Southeast."*
>
> —*The Provincials: A History of Jews in the South,* by Eli N. Evans

And who is Jacob Schiff that he should be embarrassed by my Uncle Benny Daynovsky? My father's family certainly came to Missouri from eastern Europe around 1908 via the Port of Galveston, and, I'll admit, that route struck me as rather odd every time we read in history class about how all the tired, poor, huddled masses swarmed into this country through Ellis Island. It never occurred to me, though, to explain it all by assuming that Jacob Schiff found my family not only tired and poor and huddled but also embarrassing. I always considered the Galveston passage to be one of those eccentricities of ancestral history that require no explanation—the kind of incident we hear about so often from people who have family trees concocted for themselves by wily English genealogists ("For some reason, the old boy showed up late for the Battle of Hastings and therefore survived to father the first Duke, and that's why we're here to tell the tale"). I have always been content—pleased, really—to say simply that my grandfather (Uncle Benny's brother-in-law) happened to land in Galveston and thus made his way up the river (more or less) to St. Joseph, Missouri, leaving only sixty miles or so for my father to travel in order to complete what I had always assumed to be one of the few Kiev—Galveston—St. Jo—Kansas City immigration patterns in the Greater Kansas City area.

To be absolutely truthful, it occurred to me more than once that my grandfather and Uncle Benny might have caught the wrong boat. I have never heard my mother's views on the subject, but I have always assumed that she would believe that the use by my father's family of a port no one else seemed to be using had something to do with the stubbornness for which they retain a local renown in St. Jo. As I imagine my mother's imagining it, my grandfather would have fallen into an argument with some other resident of Kiev (or *near* Kiev, as it was always described to me, leading me to believe as a child that they came from the suburbs) about where immigrants land in the United States. The other man said New York; my grandfather said Texas. When the time came to emigrate, my grandfather went fifteen hundred miles out of his way in order to avoid admitting that he was wrong. My grandfather died before I was born, but my Uncle Benny is still living in St. Jo; he has lived there for sixty or seventy years now, without, I hasten to say, a hint of scandal. Stubborn, okay. But I simply can't understand how anyone could consider him embarrassing.

"Who is Jacob Schiff that he should be embarrassed by my Uncle

Benny Daynovsky?" I said to my wife when I read about the Galveston Project in *The Provincials.*

"You shouldn't take it personally," my wife said.

"I'm not taking it personally; I'm taking it for my Uncle Benny," I said. "Unless you think that Jacob Schiff's descendants are embarrassed by my moving to New York instead of staying in our assigned area."

"I'm sure Jacob Schiff's descendants don't know anything about this," my wife said.

"And who are they that they should be embarrassed by my Uncle Benny Daynovsky?" I said. "A bunch of stockbrokers."

"I think the Schiffs are investment bankers," my wife said.

"You can say what you want to about my Uncle Benny," I said, "but he never made his living as a moneylender."

I'm not quite sure how my Uncle Benny did make his living; I always thought of him as retired. As a child, I often saw him during Sunday trips to St. Jo—trips so monopolized by visits to my father's relatives that I always assumed St. Jo was known for being populated almost entirely by Eastern European immigrants, although I have since learned that it had a collateral fame as the home of the Pony Express. Until a few years ago, Uncle Benny was known for the tomatoes he grew in his backyard and pickled, but I'm certain he never produced them commercially. A few years ago, when he was already in his eighties and definitely retired, Uncle Benny was in his backyard planting tomatoes when a woman lost control of her car a couple of blocks behind his house. The car went down a hill, through a stop sign, over a median strip, through a hedge, and into a backyard two houses down from Benny's house. Then it took a sharp right turn, crossed the two backyards, and knocked down my Uncle Benny. It took Uncle Benny several weeks to recover from his physical injuries, and even then, I think, he continued to be troubled by the implications of that sharp right turn. One of his sons, my cousin Iz, brought Uncle Benny back from the hospital and said, "Pop, do me a favor: Next time you're in the backyard planting tomatoes, keep an eye out for the traffic."

"First that car makes a mysterious right turn, and now he's being attacked by a gang of stockbrokers," I said. "It hardly seems fair."

...

"There's something very interesting about the Schiffs listed in *Who's Who,*" I said to my wife not long after our first conversation about the Galveston Project.

"I think you'd better find yourself a hobby," she said.

"As a matter of fact, I'm thinking about taking up genealogy," I said. "But listen to what's very interesting about the Schiffs listed in *Who's Who:* The Schiffs who sound as if they're descendants of Jacob Schiff seem to be outnumbered by some Schiffs who were born in Lithuania and now manufacture shoes in Cleveland."

"What's so interesting about that?"

"Well, if Jacob Schiff thought people from Kiev were embarrassing, you can imagine how embarrassed he must have been by people from Lithuania."

"What's the matter with people from Lithuania?" she said.

"I'm not sure, but my mother's mother was from Lithuania and my father always implied that it was nothing to be proud of," I said. "He always said she had an odd accent in Yiddish. I'm sure he must have been right, because she had an odd accent in English. Anyway, *Who's Who* has more Lithuanian Schiffs than German Schiffs, even if you count Dorothy Schiff."

"Why shouldn't you count Dorothy Schiff?" my wife said. "Isn't she the publisher of the *New York Post*?"

"Yes, but why is it that she is publisher of the *New York Post*?"

"Well, I suppose for the same reason anybody is the publisher of any paper," my wife said. "She had enough money to buy it."

"Only partly true," I said. "She is the publisher of the *New York Post* because several years ago, during one of the big newspaper strikes, she finked on the other publishers in the New York Publishers Association, settled with the union separately, and therefore saw to it that the *Post* survived, giving her something to be publisher of."

"Since when did you become such a big defender of the New York Publishers Association?" my wife said.

"My Uncle Benny Daynovsky never finked on anybody," I said.

"Maybe that passage in *The Provincials* was wrong," my wife said when she came into the living room one evening and found me reading intently. "Maybe Schiff gave the money to the Galveston Project just because he wanted to help people like your grandfather get settled."

"I'm glad you brought that up, because I happen to be consulting another source," I said, holding up the book I was reading so that she could see it was *Our Crowd,* which I had checked out of the library that day with the thought of finding some dirt on Jacob Schiff. "Here's an interesting passage in this book about some of the German-Jewish charity on the Lower East Side: 'Money was given largely but grudgingly, not out of the great religious principle of *tz'dakah,* or charity on its highest plane, given out of pure loving kindness, but out of a hard, bitter sense of resentment, and embarrassment and worry over what the neighbors would think.' "

"I don't see what you hope to gain by finding out unpleasant things about Jacob Schiff," she said.

"Historical perspective," I said, continuing to flip back and forth between the Jacob Schiff entry in the index and the pages indicated. "Did you know, by the way, that Schiff had a heavy German accent? I suppose when it came time to deal with the threat of my Uncle Benny, he said something like, 'Zend him to Galveston. Zum of dese foreigners iss embarrassink.' "

"I never heard you make fun of anybody's accent before," my wife said.

"They started it."

"My Uncle Benny never associated with robber barons like E. H. Harriman," I said to my wife a few days later. "When it comes to nineteenth-century rapacious capitalism, my family's hands are clean."

My wife didn't say anything. I had begun thinking that it was important that she share my views of Jacob Schiff, but she was hard to convince. She didn't seem shocked at all when I informed her, from my research in *Our Crowd,* that Schiff had a private Pullman car, something that anyone in my family would have considered ostentatious. When I told her that Schiff used to charge people who made telephone calls from his mansion—local calls; I wouldn't argue about long distance—she said that rich people were bound to be sensitive about being taken advantage of. "One time, he was called upon to give a toast to the Emperor of Japan, and he said, 'First in war, first in peace, first in the hearts of his countrymen,' " I said.

"It's always hard to know what to say to foreigners," she said.

"What about the checks?" I said one evening.

"What checks?" she said.

"The checks Schiff had framed on the wall of his office," I said.

"I can't believe he had checks framed on the wall of his office," my wife said.

"I refer you to page one hundred fifty-nine of *Our Crowd*," I said. "Schiff had made two particularly large advances to the Pennsylvania Railroad, and he had the cancelled checks framed on his wall."

"Did he really?" she said, showing some interest.

"One of them was for $49,098,000," I said.

"That is kind of crude," she said.

"Not as crude as the other one," I said. "It was for $62,075,000."

"I think that's rather embarrassing," she said.

"I would say so," I said, putting away the book. "I just hope that no one in St. Jo hears about it. My Uncle Benny would be mortified."

1975

THE SPORTING LIFE

"I believe it was the legendary Grantland Rice who wrote, 'For when the one Great Scorer marks / Upon his pad just how you played / He cares not if you won or lost. / He rates the deal your agent made.' "

My Team

Benno Schmidt, Jr., the new president of Yale, has been described in the press as a "renowned constitutional-law scholar who is an expert on the First Amendment, race relations and the New York Rangers." The man he will replace, A. Bartlett Giamatti, has been described as "a professor of English and comparative literature and an expert on Dante, Spenser and the Boston Red Sox." It's no wonder I'm never asked to be the president of a major educational institution: I don't have a team.

I used to have a team. When I was growing up, the Kansas City Blues were my team. They were in the American Association, along with the Minneapolis Millers and the Milwaukee Brewers and the Toledo Mud Hens (the league patsies) and several other teams that Schmidt and Giamatti don't know the first thing about.

Because I grew up in Kansas City, people assume that the Kansas City Royals are my team. Not so. My loyalty to the Kansas City Blues was so pure that their demise ended my interest in the national pastime. Oh, sure I could have skipped to the Kansas City Athletics and then to the Royals. I had opportunities. "It's the big leagues," everyone in Kansas City said when the Athletics came in to replace the Blues.

"Big leaguers don't ditch their pals," I replied.

I could see myself running into one of the old Kansas City Blues someday—Cliff Mapes, maybe, or Eddie Stewart, or Carl DeRose, the sore-armed right-hander I once saw pitch a perfect game. Or maybe Odie Strain, the no-hit shortstop. "I guess you follow the Royals now," Odie would say, with that same look of resignation he used to wear when the third strike whisked past him and thwocked into the catcher's mitt.

"No," I'd say. "I don't have a team. My team's gone." A smile would spread slowly across Odie's face.

Meanwhile, I don't have a team. I can just imagine my appearance before the presidential search committee of, say, the Harvard trustees. I'm being interviewed in a private room at the New York Harvard Club by a former secretary of defense, an enormously wealthy investment banker, and an Episcopalian bishop. So far, I feel that things have been going my way. I have analyzed Dante's *The Divine Comedy* in constitutional terms, concentrating on whether any movement from purgatory is federally regulated travel under the Commerce Clause. I have transposed the first ten amendments to the Constitution into Spenserian stanzas, although not in a pushy way.

I can see that the committee is impressed. The former secretary of defense, who at first seemed to be concentrating on some doodling that resembled the trajectory of an intercontinental ballistic missile, is now giving the interview his complete attention. The investment banker has slipped me a note that says "Hold onto Humboldt Bolt & Tube. Sell Worldwide Universal short." The interviewers are exchanging pleased glances and nodding their heads. Finally, as the interview seems to be coming to an end, the investment banker says, "Just one more question. What is your team?"

"Team?" I say.

There is a long silence. Then the bishop, in a kindly voice, says, "You do have a team, don't you?"

"Well, not exactly," I say.

"No team?" the bishop says.

"I used to have a team," I say, "and I still turn on the tennis now and then, just to hiss McEnroe."

The bishop shakes his head sadly.

I am beginning to get desperate. "I know the University of Missouri fight song by heart," I say.

But they are gathering up their papers, preparing to leave. The former defense secretary is carefully feeding his doodles into a paper shredder.

"But why do I need a team?" I say.

Nobody pays any attention, except the bishop who says, "We need a regular guy. Presidents who aren't regular guys frighten the alumni."

"But I *am* a regular guy," I say. "I owe the Diners Club. I had a dog named Spike."

"Regular guys have teams," the bishop says.

Desperately, I begin to sing: "Every true son so happy hearted, skies above us are blue. There's a spirit so deep within us. Old Missouri, here's to you—rah, rah. When the band plays the Tiger . . ."

But now they are at the door. Suddenly, the investment banker walks back to where I'm sitting, snatches his stock tips off the table, and marches out with the rest of the committee. I sit stunned at the table as a club steward comes in to straighten up the room. He glances down at my résumé, still on the table.

"Kansas City, huh?" he says. "You must be proud of those Royals."

"The Royals are not my team," I say. "I don't have a team. If I had a team, I'd be the president of Harvard."

1986

Baseball's Back

Yes, baseball's back. Once more our sporting passion'll
Embrace this game, this hallowed pastime national.
We'll fill the stadium our taxes built
Because the owner threatened he would jilt
Our city, which might die, it was implied,
Without this centerpiece of civic pride.
We'll cheer our heroes when ahead or losing,
Forgetting tales of date rape, drugs, and boozing.
We'll cheer the way they hit and catch and pitch.
We'll cheer the agents who have made them rich.
So, greedy owners, pampered jocks, you all
Are welcomed once again. Okay, play ball!

1993

Chinese Golf

As if we didn't have enough contention in the world, a Chinese academic, Professor Ling Hongling, has gone and upset the Scots by claiming that golf was invented in China.

I know what you're thinking: This is going to remind the Russians that they used to claim they invented baseball, which will provoke the English (who really did invent baseball but got tired a long time ago of arguing with people from Cooperstown) to talk about having invented ice hockey, which will enrage the Canadians (who hardly ever get mad) and provoke the Lithuanians into claiming the invention of darts, and that will lead into a sort of chain reaction of claims and counterclaims until—*powee!*—World War III.

I wish I had some reassuring words about that possibility, but I have to report that—according to a piece in the Toronto *Globe and Mail* by Carl Honoré, which is where I read all about this—the Scots are as angry as hornets. Scottish tabloids have referred to Professor Hongling as "a nutty, Oriental professor" and an "Eastern bogeyman," the *Globe and Mail* article says, and Bobby Burnet, golf historian to the Royal and Ancient Golf Club in St. Andrews, is quoted as calling the whole business "a load of malarkey."

It is only a matter of time, I think, before some Scottish golfer gets mad enough to point out that Professor Ling Hongling's name sounds more like a Ping-Pong match than a round of golf.

Writing in the *Australian Society for Sports History Bulletin*—a journal, I should admit, that I might have missed had the alert Honoré not pointed the way—Professor Hongling concluded from pottery depictions and murals and other evidence that a game very much like modern golf was played in China around the middle of the tenth century, five hundred years before the Scots claim to have invented it. It was called *chiuwan,* or hitting ball—which, you have to admit, is a more logical name for the sport than golf, even though, during my brief fling at it many years ago, I often missed the ball completely.

Burnet tried in the *Globe and Mail* piece to explain away the pottery and murals: "If you take any kind of patterned plate or blanket or stained glass and play around with it long enough, you'll soon find a man holding a club and hitting a ball towards a hole." Being an open-minded person, I tried this theory with an old patterned plate, and it didn't work: After looking at the design for twenty minutes (some of that time squinty-eyed), what I thought I saw was a man in an undershirt eating a herring. What I'm saying is that Burnet's attempt to explain away Ling Hongling's murals may say less about the history of golf than it does about Burnet, or me.

As I understand Ling Hongling's theory, he believes some early traveler to China brought golf back to Europe, the way Marco Polo is said to have brought back to Italy what Italians came to call pasta and the way more recent travelers from the West have brought back hot tips on how a government can get rid of students who are demonstrating for democracy in large public squares.

As you might imagine, this early-traveler theory does not have a big following in Scotland, where, according to *The Globe and Mail,* "Golf sits snugly alongside clan tartan, whiskey and haggis as a symbol of Scottish ingenuity." I should say right off the bat that I have tasted haggis—it is described in my dictionary, rather discreetly, as a pudding "made of the heart, liver, and lungs of a sheep or a calf minced with suet, onions, oatmeal, and seasonings and boiled in the stomach of the animal"—and if the Scots are worried about somebody else taking credit for inventing it, I think I can put their mind at rest on that score.

I think they're also overreacting in talking about the threat this may represent to the industry that is based on foreigners going over there to play golf on Scottish courses. Rich Americans and Japanese do not go to Scotland, wearing funny costumes and lugging golf clubs, because they believe that golf was invented by the Scots; they go there because they like the whisky.

I do believe that if the Scots will just calm down, we can ride this one out. I think it should start with Bobby Burnet apologizing for the harsh language he's used about Professor Ling Hongling. They should meet like gentlemen, perhaps over a round of hitting ball.

1991

On the Marketing of Yankee Grass

A South Jersey grass farm that has supplied turf to Yankee Stadium since the 1960s plans to sell officially licensed grass in the form of sod or seeds.

—Associated Press

You too can have a yard with sod
Like sod upon which A-Rod trod.

One wonders: Has it been suggested
That Yankee Sod and Seed be tested,
In case it's bluegrass that's made bluer
By substances that aren't manure?

2009

The Great Game of Frizzball

I hope the drubbing that movie critics gave a summer gross-out called *BASEketball*—which concerns a homemade game similar to one that the director once actually invented—will not poison the public's mind about hybrid sports created by bozos with nothing better to do. I speak as one of the founders of frizzball.

Even before the release of *BASEketball,* I did not entertain hopes of winning my wife over to the view that frizzball was a serious competitive sport. In the more than thirty years since its invention—at a summerhouse, on a day when it was too cloudy to go to the beach—her kindest description of frizzball has been, "It was the dumbest thing I've ever seen."

"They tried to hit a Frisbee with a stick," she'll say. Not so. It was a broom. The batter, standing in front of an old barn in the backyard, tried to hit the Frisbee with a broom—no cinch, I can attest, when the pitcher's repertoire included an effective slice ball. Imaginary base runners advanced according to a formula having to do with logarithms. After that, the rules got complicated.

The summerhouse, which was shared by several young couples, would have been a friendly enough place except for frizzball. This was at a time when society mandated different cultural norms for males and females—the days before women began following the NFL and men began weeping softly in movies about doomed love or lost pets. The women in the house couldn't understand why anyone would want to spend hours playing frizzball and more hours analyzing each game. They didn't understand how the men could judge someone's character by the way he played frizzball. Cruelly burdened by a culturally imposed sense of perspective, these women were unable to take frizzball seriously.

The progress made in the decades to follow did not completely wipe out such differences between the genders. When the United States invades a tiny country, for instance, women are still more likely to dwell on the disparity in size. Men understand that, regardless of the size of the opponent, combat is combat: You detonate large bombs; you win medals; you could get killed. In that summerhouse, the men understood that regardless of the origin of the game, you still have to analyze the plays. You still have to keep statistics. You still have to play to win. You still have to cheat.

After *BASEketball* came out, I began to regret that no founder of frizzball became a movie director. What a film *Frizzball* would be! You'd set the historical period in the opening scene by simply not having any jokes at all about bodily functions. Everybody would be talking about frizzball—at least all the men. The women would be rolling their eyes.

The climactic scene is a game for the Frizzball Championship of the World—which is, by chance, what we called all our games. The batter resembles me. The pitch is a slice ball. I hit it to the second garbage can—a 7.3-run homer. The game is won. I glance up to see my wife in the stands (well, all right, the backyard). She has been caught up in the excitement of the game. She is cheering wildly.

1998

On Buffalo's Losing the Super Bowl

In Buffalo, they pray for many things—
For big-league ball, for spring, for chicken wings
So good they can be called a sacred blessing

(With celery, of course, and blue cheese dressing),
For leaders who'll bring Buffalo panache,
For shoppers from Ontario with cash.
But most of all, they pray the good Lord wills
One Super Bowl triumphant for their Bills.
The Lord has granted Buffalo a lot:
A population proudly polyglot,
A lake, some chicken wings profoundly great.
And spring comes every year, though sometimes late.
Aside from wings, they've got their beef-on-weck,
And shoppers now are coming from Quebec.
There's so much Buffalo is proud to show.
Just think of polka, beer, and feet of snow.
For all that Buffalonians beseech,
This single game remains beyond their reach.
Though they may think this blemish is unfair,
Perfection might be just too much to bear.

1994

The Gipper Lives On

Most people don't know that the real George Gipp—the George Gipp of "win one for the Gipper" fame, the George Gipp played by Ronald Reagan in *Knute Rockne All American*—is still alive. That's right.

Yes, I realize that in the movie George Gipp died, so that Coach Knute Rockne could invoke the name of the Gipper in the great half-time pep talk that inspired Notre Dame to go out there and wipe up the field with what had been up to then a pretty rugged Rensselaer Polytechnic Institute eleven. But not everything they say in movies is true. That's right. In real life, as it happens, George Gipp survived. In real life—now that we're being absolutely factual about all of this—Notre Dame lost the game. RPI creamed them. In real life, as a matter of fact, George Gipp only went to Notre Dame because he couldn't get into Holy Cross. That happens to be the truth.

How do I know? Because George Gipp told me. I visit him pretty regularly. He lives in an old age home in Massapequa, Long Island, these days, and keeps himself in pretty good shape stiff-arming nurses' aides and dying bravely off camera. His memory is absolutely phenomenal, and he's in good spirits, particularly considering the fact that he's had to go through most of his life being assumed dead. As you might imagine, just about every person he has ever been introduced to says something like, "But I thought you were . . . well . . . uh . . . nice to meet you, Mr. Gipp." Apparently, though, he learned to deal with that a long time ago. He usually just says to the person, rather quietly, "Stick it in your ear, buddy."

He's been particularly cheerful this fall, ever since he started monitoring Ronald Reagan's campaigning for Republican senatorial and congressional candidates. Every night, when the network news comes on, George Gipp and some of his friends can be found in the nursing home's television lounge sitting in front of the twenty-six-incher. He's armed with two or three Magic Markers and a large map that shows the congressional districts of the United States. I happened to be in the lounge several weeks ago on the evening that a clip of Reagan campaigning for a senatorial candidate in Louisiana showed him saying to a cheering crowd something like "So this November I want you to win one for Louisiana, win one for your country, and, if I may add a personal note, win one for the Gipper."

Mr. Gipp and the other people in the lounge started cheering, and a couple of old gentlemen came up to clap Mr. Gipp on the back. Mr. Gipp, smiling broadly, got out one of the magic markers and ceremoniously colored in the entire state of Louisiana. By his count, that made twenty-eight states or congressional districts in which Ronald Reagan had asked the voters to "win one for the Gipper."

I hated to spoil Mr. Gipp's fun, but I felt I had to ask him if it struck him that the president was being just a tad insincere by saying "win one for the Gipper" in twenty-eight different election campaigns.

"Oh, no," he said. "Rockne—the real Rockne—did the same thing. You know, I was pretty sick when he made the original speech—don't let anyone tell you that anything hurts worse than an impacted molar—but I played every game the next year, and every single halftime, Rockne said 'Win one for the Gipper.' He said it with me sitting right there in the locker room. After a while, some of the players started saying, 'Coach, wasn't the Swarthmore game last week the one you told us we were supposed to win for the Gipper?' Sometimes Rockne would say he couldn't remember ever saying that, and sometimes he would remind us that we had lost the Swarthmore game, not to speak of the Kenyon game and the MIT game, so, in fact, we hadn't really won one for the Gipper yet and it was about time we did."

"Excuse me, Mr. Gipp," I said. "But I didn't realize Notre Dame lost to schools like Swarthmore in those days. I've always seen the Notre Dame team of that era referred to as a football powerhouse."

Mr. Gipp smiled. "That was the spin Rockne put on it," he said. "Swarthmore murdered us. But Rockne was careful never to admit that, except to us in the locker room. After the game, he always told the sportswriters how proud he was of the Fighting Irish. By the next September, he'd be saying that it'd be hard to repeat an undefeated season that had seen us whip teams like Michigan and Ohio State and Army. The sportswriters never seemed to point out that we hadn't played those teams and that the teams we had played, like Haverford and Oberlin, had slaughtered us. He was a charming man, Coach Rockne."

"Oberlin!" I said. "Notre Dame was slaughtered by Oberlin!"

But Mr. Gipp, lost in his recollections, seemed not to hear me. "When I read in the paper that Reagan left the summit in Iceland cussing about his failure and two days later decided it was a big triumph, it really brought back those memories of Coach Rockne," he said. "That's exactly how the coach would have handled it. Yes sir, the president learned all that at Notre Dame."

"But the president didn't really go to Notre Dame," I said. "That was just a movie. You're the one who went to Notre Dame."

"Only because I couldn't get into Holy Cross," he said.

1986

SCIENCE, TECHNOLOGY, AND THE HEALING ARTS

"My idea of alternative medicine is a doctor who didn't go to Johns Hopkins."

Molly and the V-Chip

Given the fact that our children were grown by the time debate about the V-chip got cranked up, I hardly paid any attention, except to observe how odd it was that what children watched on television was going to be controlled by an electronic device even though everyone knows that the only people in an American family who understand electronic devices are the children. Then a friend of ours named Molly, who was eleven at the time, confessed to her parents that she had been watching Martha Stewart on television. Picture this: Molly's parents are off at their respective offices, under the assumption that their daughter is doing her homework or at least taking in something broadening on the history channel. Molly, meanwhile, is planted in front of the tube watching Martha Stewart. Molly's parents get home from hard days at work and listen to their eleven year old explain to them how the fall foliage in your backyard can, with a little imagination, be transformed into an attractive centerpiece for that festive Sunday brunch. I don't know if Molly's confession to her parents included handing over something like an exquisite Christmas wreath or the perfect baked apple. The details have never come out.

Molly's parents did not panic. They are pretty cool, even by Molly's standards. Not long after this happened, we all discussed it over Sunday supper not far from where Molly and her parents live, and voices were not raised. The conversation was so lacking in tension, in fact, that I felt it might be all right to ask Molly what she thought of Martha Stewart.

"She seems to have a lot of time on her hands," Molly said.

That remark indicated to me that Molly had almost certainly come away from the experience unscathed. A little later in the meal, though, it was revealed that the same could not be said for her experience with a television advertising campaign against drug use—just the sort of programming that most parents hope their children will watch attentively. Several years before, she'd seen the most famous and widely praised drug commercial in the antidrug campaign. The commercial opens with a shot of an egg, while a voice says, "This is your brain." The egg is then dumped onto a sizzling griddle while the voice says, "This is your brain on drugs." As far as I know, the commercial had no effect on Molly's views about heroin, but she won't eat eggs.

But, you might be thinking, the commercial still did some good for Molly by blunting her interest in eggs: At age eleven, she must have had the lowest cholesterol count in the entire sixth grade. I wouldn't know about that. One of the many pleasant characteristics of my conversations with Molly over the years is that she never talks about cholesterol. No, the lesson I would draw from Molly's problem with eggs is that old one about the doctrine of unintended consequences. It's the lesson that was always drawn from the Soviet propaganda film of

Cold War legend that had been intended to demonstrate the brutality of strike-busting thugs beating peaceful workers in Detroit but apparently left Russian audiences impressed instead with the fact that all the workers seemed to be wearing decent shoes. Even adults can come away with the wrong message—like the garment manufacturer who, according to the old story, remarked while walking from the theater after the opening night of *Death of a Salesman,* "That New England territory never was any good."

1996

Benefit of the Doubt

According to the latest survey on smoking, the percentage of smokers among people who didn't finish high school is now twice as high as among people who have graduated from college. Who says that nobody is doing anything to raise the median level of education in this country? The tobacco industry seems to be on a campaign to kill off the dropouts.

I'm all for raising the education level, but you'd think that the way to reduce the rate of dropouts might be to give the people in question something like incentive programs or tutoring sessions rather than emphysema. I'm not even sure that this falls into the category of employing different methods to reach the same goal.

I'm going to try to look at it that way, though, because these days I'm trying to approach the news with the assumption that people may well have, at least in their own minds, good, constructive, socially useful motives for what they do. It's a sort of New Year's resolution. Before my resolution, I might have assumed from this latest batch of smoking statistics that the tobacco industry, finding its customers declining among those most likely to be acquainted with the overwhelming scientific evidence linking smoking and deadly diseases, started directing its pitch toward those less likely to be familiar with such evidence—another example of the theory that, when it comes to the tobacco industry, the old economic saw that applies is the one that says profits equal marketers chasing victims. That was the old me.

Now, I'm reformed. The other day, for instance, a friend and I passed a billboard that was advertising cigarettes—an outdoor scene showing a couple of those absolutely beautiful and healthy-looking young smokers who can stay on a camping trail or a ski slope all day long without wrinkling their clothes. I noticed a blurry couple of lines in the lower right-hand corner that may or may not have been the surgeon general's warning about the risks that these invulnerable-looking young people are taking of developing lung cancer.

"It appears that anyone who wants to see that warning would have to have the sort of long-range vision usually associated with the pilot of an F-14," I said to my friend. "Perhaps the cigarette company or its advertising agency is trying to encourage regular and thorough eye examinations—an oft-stated public service message, if I'm not mistaken, of the American Ophthalmological Society."

"Have you gone soft in the head?" my friend said.

"It's also possible, of course, that the long-term goal is to play a significant role in the recovery of the American binocular industry, now in a bad way because of overseas competition."

"Why are you talking this way?" my friend said.

"Come to think of it," I said. "I now realize why cigarette companies started sponsoring golf and tennis tournaments, around the time they could no longer advertise on television—because they wanted to encourage all of us to get outside in the fresh air so that every single one of us could look like their models."

My friend glanced around nervously—apparently looking for a telephone, or maybe a policeman.

"This is the new me," I explained.

In that spirit, it occurred to me that if the cigarette manufacturers want to be even more efficient in their efforts to improve the education statistics, they might ask the government to use some longer words in the surgeon general's warning—words that the average high school dropout simply wouldn't understand. If that doesn't work well enough, maybe the warning could be written in Latin.

1989

My Dentist

My dentist—Sweeney Todd, DDS—had his receptionist phone me to say that I should come in for an appointment. I figured Sweeney was having cash flow problems again.

"What is it this time?" I asked the receptionist.

"He says that he was looking at your X rays, and you need a crown in the lower left something or other," she said.

"I don't mean what is it with me," I said. "What is it with him? Did the kid's college tuition bill just come in? Wife redecorate the rumpus room? Would you mind just shouting back there and asking him how much he owes for what? I'd like to get myself prepared."

"I can't," the receptionist said. "He's in the Caribbean until next Tuesday."

"I was afraid of something like this," I said.

"Before he left, he gave me a list of patients to call," she said. "He told me that he'll need you for an hour on the first appointment."

"An hour on the first appointment?" I said. "Sounds like Jamaica. Or maybe Antigua. This is definitely no cheapie to the Bahamas. That time he went to the Bahamas he only needed me for a half-hour session with the dental hygienist. May I ask if he took the wife and kids?"

"And his in-laws," the receptionist said.

"Erghh," I said, with some feeling. "I think we're talking gold crown here. Maybe even root canal. That mother-in-law of his lives high off the hog."

I showed up for the hour appointment anyway. What's the alternative? I could switch dentists, of course, but I've become sort of used to old Sweeney. If you listen closely while he's working on your teeth—you have to listen closely because, being rather clumsy, he makes a lot of noise banging around the instruments—you can hear him mumbling about whatever expense in the Todd family it was that got you into the chair in the first place. After years of that, I suppose I'd feel something was missing if a dentist didn't accompany his drilling with a lot of talk about how much electricians charge for a simple rewiring job these days.

Besides, I don't know any other dentists. I don't admit that to Sweeney Todd, DDS, of course. In fact, I've been telling him for years that some friends of mine are always singing the praises of the dentist they all go to—a relatively recent arrival from Kyoto known to his grateful patients as Magic Fingers Yamamoto.

"They say he's got the touch of an angel," I said of Yamamoto, as I settled into the chair and prepared myself for the assaults of a deeply tanned Sweeney Todd, DDS. I had to raise my voice a bit, since Sweeney, in his effort to recover a mirror he had dropped, had knocked the rest of his instruments onto the floor.

"Open wide, please," Sweeney said. He has never been affected in the slightest by talk of Magic Fingers Yamamoto.

"Also, Yamamoto belongs to some Buddhist sect that believes the exchange of large sums of money corrupts the soul," I continued. "For crowns and bridges, he does wonders with the same material used for the common paper clip. His fees, of course, are nominal. Basically, he seeks his rewards in inner fulfillment. He spits on money—or he would if he weren't so polite."

"Spit, please," Sweeney said.

Sweeney had stopped his banging around and was standing next to his instrument cabinet peering at some X rays. "What do you see there, Sweeney?" I asked. "A new transmission for your BMW? A long weekend with the missus in the Adirondacks?"

Sweeney held the X rays up to the window to get a better look. "Won't be able to get away for the next few weekends," Sweeney said. "We're doing an addition to the kitchen."

"You never cease to amaze me, Sweeney," I said. "I've seen those television commercials that show doctors seeing all sorts of little bitty doo-dads through the miracle of CAT scans—or not seeing them, really, because all of the patients in those commercials turn out to be okay—but you've got to be the only medical man who can look at an

X ray with the naked eye and see an addition to your kitchen. What's your secret?"

"I have a better X ray machine," Sweeney said, knocking over the water glass as he turned toward me. "But it's expensive. Very expensive. Open wide, please."

1989

Backwards Ran the Clock

On a Wednesday afternoon just before Christmas, the wall clock in our kitchen began to run backward. I'm not talking about a literary device here; I'm talking about a clock. Suddenly, this clock's sweep second hand was moving in a direction that can only be described as counterclockwise. There were witnesses. Alice was having a meeting in the living room. The washing machine repairman was present. In fact, there are those who say that he had something to do with the clock's sudden switch in direction, since he was fiddling with the circuit breakers upstairs. But the washing machine repairman is almost always at our house, fiddling with the circuit breakers upstairs. He likes to fiddle with circuit breakers. The only piece of modern technology that repels him is the automatic washer.

The wall clock in our kitchen does not have numbers. It has letters that spell out Hecker's Flour, except for the apostrophe. Having a clock with only letters on it means that my daughters, before they learned to tell time, would occasionally say something like "the little hand's on the *R* and the big hand is just past the *C*," but I do not consider that a strong disadvantage in a clock. The face of our clock can be illuminated by two lightbulbs with a glow so strong that I used to assume pilots were using it at night to take a bead on LaGuardia. We no longer keep lightbulbs in the clock, because my daughters say that would be a waste of energy. As I interpret my daughters' views on the energy crisis, they believe that a patriotic American household should use no energy except that required to power a computer game called Merlin and a Tyco Super-Dooper-Double-Looper Auto Track. In addition to knowing a lot about how much fossil fuel we're wasting, my daughters are already learned on the subject of cholesterol in Italian sausage and carcinogens in beer. Their command of a broad range of such information, in fact, has made it obvious to me why some children in our public elementary schools have difficulty reading and writing: Their teachers spend most of the day teaching them how to depress their parents.

One morning at breakfast, my younger daughter asked me if it would soon be yesterday. I told her it would be if we were talking about a literary device rather than a clock. She asked me why the clock was running backward, and I told her to pay more attention to her cereal eating, my alternative being to admit to her that the only explanation I had been able to think of was that our clock had been invaded by a dybbuk, a bloody-minded cousin of the dybbuk in our washing machine. It happened to be a time when I was feeling the weight of my ignorance more acutely than usual. I had not distinguished myself in the assembling of the Tyco Super-Dooper-Double-Looper Auto Track. I had just been forced to admit to my older daughter that I did not know how to get the square root of anything. All in all, I would have preferred a clock that ran in the conventional direction. Not knowing enough Yiddish to speak to the dybbuk in his native tongue, I tried to reason quietly with him in what I perceived to be English of Yiddish inflection ("So go! I'll pack you a lunch."), but the clock continued to run backward.

In this mood, I went to my next-door neighbor's for a cup of seasonal cheer, and met a friend who said she was worried about the world because Afghanistan had the H-bomb. This was before the Russian adventure, and Afghanistan was not a country often mentioned when holiday discussions ventured from the Brandy Alexander recipe toward sophisticated weapons systems.

"Afghanistan does not have the H-bomb," I assured her.

"They've got it," she said. "I read it in the *Times*."

"There's a progression in these matters," I said. "First a country gets a drugstore. Then it gets the H-bomb."

"I saw it in the *Times,*" she repeated. "The leader of Afghanistan has slicked-down hair and one of those waxed mustaches. I know he wouldn't use it right."

"General Zia!" I said. "That's Pakistan."

She was comforted, and I felt more in control for a while—until I began to wonder what was so comforting about Pakistan's having the H-bomb. Would they use it right? What was the right way to use it?

It was in this mood that I happened to mention our clock to Noam Spanier, who goes to Stuyvesant High School—a seat of learning so high-powered that it offers courses other than Serum Cholesterol 121 and Ravages of Booze 202.

"Your polarity is reversed," Noam said.

"Watch your mouth, kid," I said, taking a quick check of my clothing.

We went next door. Noam unplugged my clock, turned the plug around, and plugged it in again. The clock began to run clockwise.

"Obviously," I said.

Noam nodded.

"It's obvious," I repeated. "You scared the hell out of the dybbuk."

1980

Smart Camera

When we were about to take a trip to Italy, somebody offered to lend me one of those cameras that knows everything. The camera knows how to focus itself. It knows when to speed itself up and when to slow itself down. It knows when to flash its flashbulb. If you point the camera at a mountain, the camera knows that it's pointed at a mountain. If you suddenly swing the camera away from the mountain, point it at your Uncle Harry, and say to the camera, "This is also a mountain," the camera is not fooled. The camera knows your Uncle Harry from a mountain. The camera knows everything.

I told my wife that I was uneasy about carrying around a camera that knows everything. There are certain things I'd just as soon keep to myself.

"The camera doesn't know everything," my wife said. "It just knows more about taking pictures than you do."

I told my wife that I was uneasy about carrying around a camera that knows more than I do. It's bad enough that both of my daughters now know more than I do. If there were a ranking done in our house according to who knows the most, at least I'd come in a strong fourth. (We don't have a dog.) Who wants to be edged out by a camera?

My wife told me that I was being silly. She said to take the camera. I finally took the camera. My wife knows more about these things than I do.

One of my daughters offered to teach me how to use the camera.

"Why do I need you to teach me?" I said. "If this camera knows everything, it can teach me itself."

My daughter told me I was being silly. So I accepted her offer. She knows more about these things than I do. She can set one of those watches that work with tiny buttons on the side and will give you the month and year and the military time in Guam if you know which buttons to push. Sometimes, if there's a lull in the conversation at the dinner table, my daughter will say, "It's eighteen hundred hours in Guam." Or at least she did until the night I responded by announcing, "All enlisted personnel are required to finish their broccoli before leaving the mess hall." That was just before she got so she knew more than I did.

So she taught me to use the camera. She read the instruction booklet (several years ago, I swore off instruction booklets) and studied the camera from a number of angles. Then, this is what she taught me: "Just press the button. The camera does the rest. The camera knows everything."

So I took the camera to Italy. The first thing I did was to point it at a mountain. Then I pressed the button. The camera seemed to know just what to do. It focused itself. It slowed itself down, or maybe speeded itself up. It decided not to use its flashbulb. When I pushed the button, it advanced itself to the next picture with a contented buzzing sound, like a horsefly that has just had a bite of something good.

I felt proud of my camera. "Hey, this camera knows everything," I told my wife.

"Let's hope so," my wife said.

Just to make sure, I pointed the camera at my wife and said to it, "This is my Uncle Harry." But the camera knew better. I could tell by the contented buzz. The camera took a picture of my wife. The camera knows everything.

So I started taking a lot of pictures. I took the usual kind of pictures—shadows falling in quaint piazzas and fishermen unloading their catch and Americans slapping themselves in the head when a waiter in a café tells them how much their two beers and a Coke cost.

The camera buzzed and buzzed. Pretty soon, I was so accustomed to the buzzing that I thought I could detect not just the camera's mood but what it was trying to say. When I took a picture of an old market-vendor selling onions, I thought I heard the camera say "Nice shot!"

Then, as I was taking a picture of a raggedy little boy talking to a splendidly dressed policeman, I thought I heard the camera say "Corny, cor-ny." That afternoon, when I was taking a picture of my wife in front of a statue of Zeus, I clearly heard the camera say "You're cutting off his head, dummy."

So I quit using the camera. I told my wife I had run out of film. She suggested I buy some. "If the camera's so smart," I said, "let it buy its own film."

1988

Ouch!

Not long ago, I ran across a man who pulls his own teeth. As my father used to say, you meet all kinds. I suppose you're wondering how the subject came up. I suspect you think it came up during one of those frivolous summertime conversations on the beach, when people try to be clever as a way of diverting attention from their waistlines. Somebody says something like, "The way the book business is going these days, I half expect to turn on a talk show and see some shrink in a turtleneck sweater pushing a bestseller called *How to Take Out Your Own Appendix and Find the Real You.*" Everyone chuckles, but then one person on the edge of the crowd—a rather intense-looking person who is wearing sandals and black socks and has a thermos full of lukewarm mineral water with him—says, "As a matter of fact, I pull my own teeth and I just signed a contract with a publisher for a six-figure advance." That is not the way it happened at all.

Now that you know that, you probably think I simply read about this in the newspaper, because a lot of newspaper stories these days are about the sort of people who go on talk shows in turtlenecks to discuss taking out your own appendix. "Two years ago," you imagine the newspaper story saying, "nobody could have predicted that Dr. Marvin Smolin, a successful and conventional suburban dentist, was destined to become the leader of a movement advocating that people pull their own teeth. Dr. Smolin then had a prosperous practice in Bergen County, New Jersey, and was widely known in the New York television world as the technical consultant to the long-running network series based on a father-and-son dental practice—*The Extractors.* He was active in the American Dental Association, having served for three years running as chairman of the ADA's Special Committee on Tax Shelters. 'I was Joe Establishment, DDS, but I really didn't know who I was,' Dr. Smolin said yesterday, while in town to conduct a four-day seminar on auto-extractics. 'Just for a start, I thought I was Joe Establishment, DDS, and I was really Marvin Smolin.' " That's not how it happened. Not even close. The subject of auto-extraction came up because I noticed a man who was jumping up and down.

It happened in front of a fruit-and-vegetable stand in my neighborhood. At first, I didn't pay much attention to the man who was jumping up and down, because I assumed he was just reacting to the price of raspberries. That happens a lot in my neighborhood. I've seen a man stomping on his own hat over what an avocado costs these days. I once saw someone who looked perfectly normal—which is not, as it happens, the way most people in my neighborhood look—lying on his stomach in a produce store and banging on the floor with his fists in response to what they had the nerve to charge for one lousy watermelon.

This jumping up and down had nothing to do with the price of fruit and vegetables. The man involved was jumping up and down to demonstrate how he diverts the blood supply from his mouth so there is less pain when he pulls his own tooth. That you never guessed. That is how it happened. He was explaining the entire process to a friend. I overheard everything. He takes some pill; I can't remember the name of it, but from the way he described it I assume it's the sort of thing that might make you feel like having a go at your spleen once you had your infected molar out of the way. Then he jumps up and down, and then—*whammo!*—he pulls his own tooth. Other than that, he looked like an unremarkable fellow, except that he was missing a lot of teeth. I got the feeling he might pull a perfectly healthy one now and then just to keep in practice.

I don't want to talk about the question of whether a man who pulls his own teeth is the one true practitioner of holistic medicine. That's not what this is all about. I know that the local causemeister we call Harold the Committed would have you believe that this just goes to show that Brute Capitalism, which treats the health of the people as a commodity to be bought and sold, has forced auto-extractic practices on decent working men. Sometimes I get awfully tired of Harold the Committed. He may well be right about Brute Capitalism, but as I sized up this fellow who pulls his own teeth—and I'll admit that sizing up a fellow is not that easy to do if he keeps jumping up and down and trying to simulate the effects of a pill that makes you want to have a go at your own spleen—I figured he might be interested in pulling his own teeth even if he could afford the watermelon at my neighborhood fruit and vegetable store.

I don't want to pull my own teeth. I am still amazed, though, at how plausible it all sounded at the fruit stand. I remember thinking that pulling an upper tooth down would be a lot easier than pulling a lower tooth up. I could almost see myself pulling an upper tooth. I belly up to the mirror, open my mouth wide, and say, "Is it just my imagination, or does that bicuspid look a little shaky?" I take the pill. I jump up and down. Then, *whammo!*

1982

Unplugged

A day or two after the Webers' son, Jeffrey, age twenty-six, finally moved out of the house, they realized that they had lost the ability to tape. I heard about this from my friend Horace, who seems to specialize in stories about our contemporaries—people who are in that awkward phase between the end of paying tuition and the beginning of playing with grandchildren. Very few of those people are much good with a VCR.

Until Bennett and Linda Weber discovered the effect that Jeffrey's move had on their taping operation, Horace told me, they had been pleased by his departure. It wasn't that they weren't fond of Jeffrey, who had always been a bright and sweet-tempered boy. It was simply that, as Linda Weber sometimes put it, "If Jeffrey's going to find himself, it would probably help for him to look somewhere other than his own room."

Jeffrey, who sometimes worked as a technician for avant-garde theater productions, had moved into a cheap railroad flat found by his college friend Jason, who was clerking at a record store while he carried on what he sometimes referred to as his true life's work—trying to decide whether to go on to graduate school. Helen, the third roommate, was working as a waitress while she took acting lessons, although she made it clear that the object of the lessons had never been a career in the theater.

Since not just Jeffrey but all three roommates were sometimes described as trying to find themselves, Bennett Weber sometimes referred to them collectively as "The Lost Patrol," the name of his favorite old Victor McLaglen movie—which was, ironically, the movie he was about to copy off one of the cable channels until he realized that Jeffrey was the only person in the family who knew how to tape from the excruciatingly complicated cable box.

"I had a lot of sympathy with his predicament," Horace said. "I don't know if you've ever tried taping off one of those cable boxes without a kid around, but it's no joke. The other night, I figured I'd tape *Charade,* with Cary Grant and Audrey Hepburn, and I found myself trying to hold three different remote-control gizmos, plus the instructions. I finally put everything down and called my daughter in Phoenix."

I counted my blessings: I have a daughter who lives just around the corner. "So what did Bennett do?" I asked.

"He called Jeffrey, of course, who printed out instructions for taping that even Bennett could understand, and took them over there. Jeffrey's okay. I wouldn't call him highly motivated, but he's okay."

"If he has an extra copy of those instructions, I wouldn't mind seeing it," I said. "Just out of curiosity."

"The next time Bennett called Jeffrey," Horace continued, "Jeffrey said, 'What happened, Pop? You lose the instructions and now there's a Perry Como retrospective you want to save for posterity?' The kid's clever. Anyway, that wasn't the problem at all. The problem was that the Webers' answering machine got unplugged, and Bennett didn't know how to reset the access mechanism."

"I think there's a little thing in the back," I mumbled. "The last time that happened to ours, my daughter happened to be home using the washer, so naturally . . ."

"So Jeffrey went right over and reset the access mechanism," Horace said. "And while he was there he showed Bennett how to set the alarm on his digital watch. Bennett can now do it himself perfectly."

"It sounds like Jeffrey might have a gift for helping pre-microchip people survive," I said.

"Exactly what Bennett and Linda thought," Horace said. "And out of that came Jeffrey's company—TechnoKlutz Ltd. He does an in-home course on how to work your machines. Most of his customers are people whose kids have just moved out. He's doing so well he might franchise."

"The Webers must be proud of him," I said.

"They are," Horace said. "In fact, Linda told him that a big executive like him shouldn't be living in a crummy railroad flat. She's hoping that he'll move back home."

1994

FOREIGNERS

"I set the record for consecutive columns by an American columnist on Canada. Two."

Losing China

Daddy, I don't understand what it means that we've finally recognized China. Was it wearing a disguise or something?"

"Yes. For twenty-five years, China pretended to be the Republic of Rwanda. Naturally, we had no idea who it really was, although the disguise was much too small for it, and China bulged out all over, sometimes into Tibet or North Korea. We knew it wasn't the Republic of Rwanda, of course, because there already was a Republic of

Rwanda in Africa. Also, no Chinese diplomat could pronounce the Republic of Rwanda."

"Mommy says she can never get a straight answer out of you either."

"Well, diplomatic recognition is a very complicated question. Why don't you ever ask me the kind of questions other little girls ask their fathers? The capital of North Dakota, how to spell 'disgusting'—that sort of thing."

"What *is* the capital of North Dakota?"

"That's a very complicated question. Do you want more Cheerios?"

"Didn't I hear you talking to Uncle Bill about the time we lost China?"

"I'm pleased that you happened to hear one of our foreign policy discussions. Your mother would have people believe that Uncle Bill and I talk about nothing but sex and violence and exotic flavors of ice cream."

"If China's so big, how could we lose it?"

"We didn't lose it that way. We lost it the way Uncle Bill sometimes says that he had the Giants and ten points, and lost his shirt."

"But if we lost it, we must have had it."

"Well, we had what Uncle Bill would call a piece of the action. Then there was a civil war, and the people we didn't like because they were Communists beat the people we had a piece of, so our people had to take over somebody else's island and call that China."

"You mean there was an island disguised as China?"

"Exactly. The disguise was too big for the island, of course, and we had to keep stuffing it with foreign aid to make it fit."

"So who lost the real China? And please don't start talking about Uncle Bill's shirt again, Daddy. It just mixes me up."

"Your Uncle Bill had nothing to do with losing China. I'll admit that he may do some fiddling with the laws governing New York State sales tax now and then, but basically your Uncle Bill is a loyal citizen."

"Then who lost it?"

"Well, fortunately, there were a lot of hearings and investigations at the time, and it was decided that China was lost by the people who were right about which side was going to win the war. To use a very simple analogy, it's as if Uncle Bill's bookie predicted that the Giants would lose, then the Giants do lose, so the people who bet on the Giants have the bookie jailed for breaking and entering."

"I hate your analogies, Daddy. Just tell me in a regular way: Are the people who lost China the same people who won it back?"

"Oh no. The people who lost China lost their jobs for losing China and had to live in disgrace the entire time that China was disguised as the Republic of Rwanda."

"Then please just give me a straight answer: Who won it back?"

"Richard M. Nixon won it back."

"Richard M. Nixon!"

"See how boring straight answers are?"

"And he wasn't one of the people who lost it in the first place?"

"Certainly not. In fact, he called the other people traitors for losing it, and he insisted for twenty years that only traitors would point out that the disguise of the island we had disguised as China was getting baggy around the knees. Are you sure you wouldn't rather talk about sex and violence and exotic flavors of ice cream?"

"I think I understand. If recognizing China twenty years ago was losing it and recognizing it now is winning it, the people we didn't like there must have become a lot nicer, so now we like them. What have they done since we lost them?"

"Well, they killed a lot of our soldiers in Korea and they called us running dogs of capitalism. Also imperialistic lackeys."

"Then why do we think they're so nice now?"

"Because they also called the Russians running dogs of capitalism. The way our foreign policy works, it's okay to kill people and call people rude names as long as you don't like the Russians, because the Russians are Communists."

"But I thought you said the Chinese were Communists, and that's why we didn't recognize them."

"Are you sure you don't want any more Cheerios? They're stinky with riboflavin."

"Really, Daddy."

"Pierre."

"Pierre's a Communist? Pierre who?"

"Pierre is the capital of North Dakota."

"Daddy, Pierre is the capital of *South* Dakota, you dum-dum."

"Well, it's a very complicated question."

1979

Thoughts on Geopolitics

It seemed like such a good idea.
Oh, when did it begin to sour
And start to be no fun to be
The last remaining superpower?

2003

Bonjour, Madame

When I read *Newsweek*'s cover story on what the world thinks of America and Americans, I happened to be in France, so I naturally took advantage of my morning croissant run to check out the *Newsweek* findings.

"*Bonjour, monsieur,*" Madame LeBlanc, who runs the bakery, said as I walked in the door.

"*Bonjour, madame,*" I said. "Tell me, Madame LeBlanc, what do you think of us Americans at this stage of history?"

Madame LeBlanc looked at me silently for a while, as if considering her response. Finally, she said, "*Comment?*"

"Don't be afraid to speak up," I said. "It's all for research."

Madame LeBlanc looked blank.

"I know you Europeans think we Americans worry too much

about what other people think of us, Madame LeBlanc," I said. "But if we need an example of the problems caused by false impressions of national traits, we need look no further than Maurice Chevalier."

"Maurice Chevalier?" Madame LeBlanc said. Her eyes shot toward the door, and then she peered over my shoulder as if checking to see if someone was standing behind me.

"For years, the impression most Americans had of French people was based on Maurice Chevalier," I explained. "So they expected every Frenchman they met to be a charming, debonair old gent who at any moment might start singing 'sank Evan for leetle gerls.' Naturally, they were disappointed when they came to France and the Frenchmen they met were sour customs officers with scratchy pens and some nasty Parisian cabdriver who pretended not to understand their French when they said '*bonjour.*' "

"Ah, *bonjour, monsieur,*" Madame LeBlanc said, smiling at me in her accustomed way.

"Oh. *Bonjour, madame,*" I said. "As I was saying, American tourists were very disappointed to discover that the only Frenchman who acted like Maurice Chevalier was Maurice Chevalier—and he was in California. So they started going to Italy, where they could still run into somebody now and then who acted like Ezio Pinza, and you fellows lost a bunch of money."

Madame LeBlanc seemed to remember suddenly that the countertop of her display case needed dusting.

"So," I continued, "if a French magazine did a similar survey (although I realize you people don't do that sort of thing; it would be what General de Gaulle used to call 'uncool'), you would probably find out that the reason so many Americans think of the French as petty, mean-spirited functionaries . . . although, God knows, that's not the way I think of you and Monsieur LeBlanc, Madame LeBlanc—you with your ever-present smile and your cheerful *bonjour*—"

"*Bonjour, monsieur,*" Madame LeBlanc said, putting down her feather duster.

"*Bonjour, madame*. What I'm really asking is whether you include yourself among those French people who find us Americans industrious, energetic, inventive, decisive, and friendly. I don't mean to muddy the sample here, Madame LeBlanc, but I might point out that it's pretty industrious and energetic for someone who's supposed to be on vacation to present himself right here in front of your display case every morning at eight-thirty on the dot, friendly as a puppy dog, and I must say that a certain amount of inventiveness was required to discover the baker in town who used the quantity of butter we Americans associate with a week's supply for a family of four in every one of his croissants—"

"*Croissants, monsieur?*" Madame LeBlanc said, reaching for the door of the display case.

"Precisely, Madame LeBlanc," I said. "And I would like to say, concerning *Newsweek*'s finding that the French do not associate Americans with honesty, that the little misunderstanding we had last week about whether it was a ten-franc piece or a twenty-centime piece you gave me in my change was just that—a misunderstanding. Ours is a young culture, Madame LeBlanc, and we're still not real good with old money."

Madame LeBlanc turned from the counter and ducked into the room where the croissants are baked by Monsieur LeBlanc—a petty, mean-spirited functionary I would rate high in industriousness, energy, and butter content.

"Madame LeBlanc!" I called after her. "Madame LeBlanc! I know *Newsweek* found that a lot of French people think having Americans around increases the chance of war, but I'd like to remind you that the question was about American *military* presence. Surely, Madame LeBlanc, a misunderstanding over small change would not lead you to confuse me with some hopped-up G.I. who might decide to lay a ground-to-ground on Leipzig just to put a little zip into a Saturday night . . ."

There was no sound from behind the curtain. I stood silently, wondering whether it would have been appropriate for me to explain that I had nothing whatever to do with the American pop culture that the French people surveyed by *Newsweek* considered so influential. Finally, Madame LeBlanc emerged from the back room. She stood in her accustomed place behind the counter, and looked at me as if I had just walked into the shop.

"*Bonjour, monsieur,*" she said, in her usual cheerful tone.

"*Bonjour, madame,*" I said.

"*Qu'est-ce que vous voulez aujourd'hui, monsieur?*"

"I would like to say, Madame LeBlanc, that when it comes to this Star Wars mickey mouse, not to speak of the Mickey Mouse mickey mouse, I have nothing—"

"*Croissants, monsieur? Brioches? Pains au chocolat?*"

"Nine *croissants, s'il vous plait,*" I said, holding up nine fingers.

"*Très bien, monsieur,*" Madame LeBlanc said, with considerable enthusiasm.

"I notice that you seem to admire my decisiveness," I said, gathering up my croissants. "It's a national trait."

1993

Without His Nurse

Galyna Kolotnytska, described in diplomatic cables as the "voluptuous blond" nurse who accompanies Libyan leader Muammar el-Qaddafi everywhere, has returned to Ukraine.

—News reports

While everybody says, "Just go!"
His countrymen all surely know
Adversity seems more adverse
Without his nurse.

"He's bonkers," people say. "That might
Be why he rants into the night."
His talks gets further still from terse
Without his nurse.

The body count is now quite large.
He's killed a lot to stay in charge.
And all this killing must seem worse
Without his nurse.

It has to bring this man much pain
To bear the crumbling of his reign
And see his fortunes in reverse.
Without his nurse.

Yes, Muammar now has to face
This hatred from the human race
And angry crowds that won't disperse
Without his nurse.

The banks freeze billions of his loot.
His people sorely want to boot
Him out, or put him in a hearse
Without his nurse.

Could Allah show a bit of mercy
And send poor Mu-Mu back his nursie?

2011

Polite Society

Here's what I would like to say to the Rev. Ian Gregory, who has founded the Polite Society to increase the level of courtesy in England: "Buzz off, Gregory. Get lost. Take a walk. G'wan, get out of here."

I think that would get the good reverend's attention. Then I would be able to tell him, without fear of being interrupted by one of his irritating interjections—you have to guard against people like Gregory tossing in comments like "Oh, do go on" or "My, how very interesting"—that there is entirely too much courtesy in England as it is.

The author of the *New York Times* piece that brought the Rev. Gregory to my attention, William E. Schmidt, seemed quite aware that starting a Polite Society in England has a certain coals-to-Newcastle quality to it. He quotes an Italian writer named Beppe Severgnini who "reported in a recent book that Britain is the only nation he has been in where it takes four 'thank-you's' to negotiate a bus ticket."

The most irritating thank-you of the lot is the first one, which the bus conductor utters as he stands in front of the passenger, ready to collect the fare. It's obvious that the passenger has done nothing for which he should be thanked. According to Severgnini, that first thank-you actually means "I'm here." It could also mean that the conductor is giving warning that he means to out-thank-you the passenger in order to make the passenger feel like a mannerless clod.

I suspect the Reverend Ian Gregory would take exception to this interpretation, to which I would reply, "Mind your own business, Gregory." Once that put him in a frame of mind to listen, I would remind him that he lives in a country where a man who did carry coal to Newcastle would, upon arriving at the place where the coal was supposed to be delivered, hand over the bill of lading and say "Thank you."

Get this picture: A large delivery of coal has just been made to someone in Newcastle who is up to his armpits in coal. The air is heavy with coal dust. Every time the person receiving the delivery wipes his brow—which he does pretty often, since he has broken out in a cold sweat trying to imagine what he's going to do with more coal—he leaves a thick black smudge on his head. And the ding-dong who has made the delivery is standing there saying "Thank you."

To be fair to the Reverend Ian Gregory—and I don't know why I should be; call me an old softie—he does distinguish between what he calls "genuinely considerate behavior" and simply littering your conversation with a lot of extraneous thank-yous. What makes the work of the Polite Society necessary, he told Schmidt, was the sort of backsliding in considerate behavior that Margaret Thatcher was referring to when she said, "Graciousness is being replaced by surliness in much of everyday life."

What I would say to that is "In a pig's eye, Gregory." Having thus given him ample notice that I might have a differing view, I would remind him that Margaret Thatcher and genuinely considerate behavior were strangers. She was known throughout the realm, for instance, for bullying and humiliating her own cabinet ministers. What she meant by graciousness was being respectful to people like her.

Genuinely considerate behavior is the sort of thing that might be practiced by an American on a London bus who realizes that answering the conductor's thank-you with another thank-you could start a spiral into violence. Armed with that knowledge, he could actually be doing the bus conductor a favor in the long run if he answered that first absurd thank-you by saying, "Watch your mouth, buddy" or "Listen, Mac, you looking to get your face rearranged?"

The problem is the response he would almost certainly get from the bus conductor: "Thank you."

1991

The Saudis and Their Oil Rigs

(Sung to the tune of "The Farmer and the Cowman" from Oklahoma!*)*

The Saudis and their oil rigs are our friends.
Oh, the Saudis and their oil rigs are our friends.
They can bomb us when they please; we need gas for SUVs.
We're infidels, but we can make amends.

Petrobusiness pals must stick together.
All the guzzlers' gas tanks must be filled.
We'll protect the Saudis' border
While they preach we should be killed.

They teach their kids the Protocols of Zion.
It's jail for women if their hair is showing.
They say that we're corrupt and that we're wicked.
We say, "Whatever. Keep that petrol flowing."

Petrobusiness pals must stick together.
All the guzzlers' gas tanks must be filled.
We'll protect the Saudis' border
While they preach we should be killed.

2002

Capturing Noriega

I think Panama is one of the most interesting countries we've invaded lately. I looked up the population in the *World Almanac*—putting the lie to the notion that I never do any research—and found that it is almost exactly one-hundredth the size of the United States. So it would be like the United States being invaded by a nation of 24 billion. We might still have the edge in military hardware, but think of what they could do with human-wave attacks.

The American Army, which was sent down there to bring military dictator Manuel Noriega back for a fair trial—innocent until proven guilty—went through Noriega's headquarters and used what they found for a report supporting its claim that Noriega was "a truly evil man," a "narco-terrorist," and a "corrupt, debauched thug." The troops going through his quarters found pictures of naked women. I was sorry our boys had to see that sort of thing. And they said he wore red underwear to ward off the evil eye. This was in the report released by a four-star general of the American Army, the first flag-rank officer in American military history to pause in the campaign to discuss the opposing commander's underwear. I might as well admit that I used to know a man in Kentucky once who wore long red underwear to ward off the evil eye, and it seemed to work pretty well for him. The evil eye never got anywhere near him—although that could have been because he chewed a lot of garlic as a sort of second line of defense.

And the Army said that they found fifty pounds of cocaine in Noriega's headquarters, which is a pretty serious charge. Then, a few weeks later, after they finally got around to analyzing the cocaine, they announced that what they thought was cocaine was actually flour for making tamales. You might think that the Army was embarrassed at this disclosure. Far from it. They said that this flour was going to make tamales used in voodoo binding rituals. Until then, I had walked around in full confidence that I knew just about every use you could make of a tamale—eat it, throw it at the guy at the bar who made an insulting remark about your haircut, mold it into tamale art, jam it under a door end-to-end with a lot of other tamales to keep out the draft, pile it up side to side with thousands of tamales to save decent folks' homes from the rising waters of the Chattahoochee River—and I had never heard of using tamales in a binding ritual. Burritos, sure. But tamales!

1990

ISSUES AND OTHER IRRITATIONS

"Learning that the Defense Department may have stored away thirty billion dollars' worth of things it doesn't need made me feel a lot better about my basement."

Complicated Issues

The question about those aromatic advertisements that perfume companies are having stitched into magazines these days is this: Under the freedoms guaranteed by the First Amendment, is smelling up the place a constitutionally protected form of expression?

This is a complicated issue. For instance, let's say that the manufacturers of a chic new perfume called Slap ("When a woman wants to say: 'Go ahead and hit me' ") produce a magazine advertisement that looks pretty much like all magazine ads for perfume look these days; that is, it shows an attractive young woman with a torn blouse being knocked against the wall by an unshaven lout whose agent has been telling him for years that in a certain light he has a striking resemblance to Richard Gere. The manufacturers decide that infusing the ad with the actual smell of Slap would be preferable to attempting a description of it—particularly since the three most poetic phrases mentioned by randomly selected people asked to describe its aroma were "low-tide breeze," "eagle in flight," and "overcooked cabbage."

Let's say that the manufacturers have a constitutionally protected right to smell up the magazine page they have bought and paid for. Fine. But how about the author of the article on the facing page, which now smells strongly of Slap? He has worked for months on a piece extolling the caramelized pastries found in the remote Popolizio region of southern Italy. Now his pastry descriptions are going to be read by people who are at the same time getting a whiff of overcooked cabbage. What about *his* rights?

Let's consider a subscriber to the magazine, a teenager who has always claimed that she is allergic to cabbage. Let's consider the subscriber's father, who, opening an envelope that has spent the day in the mailbox next to the aromatic magazine, discovers that a reminder from the Diners Club about last month's unpaid bill is even more dispiriting if that reminder smells faintly like a large feathered beast. Do these people have rights that are involved here? They may, but those rights seem to be in conflict with Voltaire's famous comment to Helvetius: "I may not like the way someone smells, but I'll defend to my death his right to smell that way!"

Some people may be surprised that I see so many sides to the aromatic advertising issue. They expect me to dismiss aromatic advertising in two or three simple and exceedingly nasty sentences. Why? Because they think I'm a crank. I'm aware of the reputation I've been getting for crankiness. It's all right. I don't mind being thought of as a crank. In my heart of hearts, after all, I know that I am a sympathetic and genuinely sweet-tempered person. What I do mind are people who expect all cranks to rail against certain features of American life that have become designated crank targets—features of American life like aromatic perfume advertisements and tear-out subscription cards in magazines and canned music that plays on the telephone when you've been put on hold.

"I guess I know how you feel about canned music that plays on the telephone when you've been put on hold," one of these people will say to me, once he has been assured that my crank papers are in order.

No, he doesn't. Here's how I feel about it: It's a complicated issue. Let's consider the position of people who believe that a piece of music is something that has to be listened to rather than something that can be used as aural wallpaper. When they're finally put through to the purchasing agent they've been trying to reach for weeks, they might have to say, "Could you please put me back on hold? There are another twelve or fourteen bars to go in the Montavani." But let us also consider the person who spends every second that he's on hold thinking that he might have been cut off—because of some slight congenital displacement of the eardrum, he has never been able to distinguish between the complete silence of hold and the complete silence of having been cut off—and is grateful for any sound that indicates otherwise. This is not a simple issue.

I suppose I'd be decertified as a crank if I admitted that I do not have a simple loathing for tear-out subscription cards. In fact, I use them sometimes. Not for subscriptions. I use them to send little messages to the people who work in what magazines call the circulation fulfillment department. I think it's nice to buck people up now and then—that's not an unusual thought for a sympathetic and genuinely sweet-tempered person—and in this case it doesn't even cost me a postage stamp to do so. The subscription cards always have prepaid postage on them. Sometimes I just send along a simple word of encouragement ("Keep up the good work, fulfillment people") or share an aphorism ("If you can't say something nice, don't say anything at all, creep"). Sometimes I chat about what's in the magazine. Occasionally, I even mention aromatic perfume advertisements—in which case I always say, right at the start, "It's a complicated issue."

1986

Letters to the Solid-Waste Commissioner

FROM HAROLD B. EVANS, SNOMESVILLE—On page 38 of the document entitled *A Simple Guide to Residential Recycling,* it says that "wet newsprint" is organic waste that goes in the Green Cart, with such items as "untinted human hair." However, on page 51 of the same document, there are instructions to place "newsprint" in the Blue Bag, along with recyclables like telephone books from which the binding glue has been removed. Does that mean that if wet newspapers that had been placed in the Green Cart just after a pickup day are likely to dry before the following pickup day, they must be recovered and transferred to the Blue Bag in order to avoid the penalties listed in the section entitled "Grounds for No Collection?" Also, where does the binding glue go?

FROM HELEN MCPHERSON, GATED MEADOWS—We recently had a cross burned in our front yard. Since my husband and I are white Presbyterians who have never been involved in controversy, we think this was simply a mix-up in addresses. (I suspect the cross was meant for the Taylors down the street, since they are a mixed-race couple; he's Canadian.) We've been in anguish, though, about how to dispose of the cross. We figured that the wood, being under the maximum dimensions listed on page 73 of *A Simple Guide to Residential Recycling,* would go into the Green Cart under the category of "small pieces of wood and bric-a-brac." However, would it be necessary to remove the nails first? Also, do you think the Taylors should bear any responsibility at all for the disposal of this item?

FROM JASON TURNER, AGE 9, PARSONS—What are you supposed to do with belly-button lint?

FROM NORTON W. SHACKLEFORD, SHADYVALE—Two weeks ago, a neighbor of mine (to protect his privacy, I'll refer to him as Blockhead) was expecting a visit from his grandchild. My wife and I lent him some toys. When he returned the toys, we weren't at home, so he left them on our porch, in a large pasteboard box. No box had been used to deliver the toys to him; my wife carried the Tooty Train in its own case, while I took the Tiny Pieces Medieval Suburb in an easily recyclable shopping bag.

As you must know, the disposal of pasteboard boxes is one of the most complicated tasks under the new recycling regulations—and not simply because of the recent controversy over the meaning of the phrase "secure with organic twine." Some newlyweds in our neighborhood now inspect every wedding present delivered by UPS and, hazarding a guess based on the name of the store and the weight of the box, refuse receipt of some on the grounds that the present inside is unlikely to be worth the trouble involved in disposing of the box.

When Blockhead stopped by a few days later (to return three of the tiny pieces from the Tiny Pieces Medieval Suburb that had rolled under a couch), I asked him to take back the pasteboard box. He refused. If I turn him in for "trash transference," 1. Will I be given a new identity to prevent retaliation? and 2. Will someone come and pick up the box?

FROM HELENA BRIGHTSON, DONNER SPRINGS—My husband had been an unenthusiastic participant in the county's new recycling plan, but reading Volume Two of *A Simple Guide to Residential Recycling* seemed to spark his interest. At first, he simply became a more conscientious recycler, but gradually he turned into what I can only describe as a zealot. For instance, he was always accusing me of leaving on too much paper when I tore out those little plastic address windows from the envelopes that bills had come in before placing the envelopes in the Blue Bag. He referred to that as "wasting waste." He'd spend a lot of time rummaging around the Black Garbage Bag for the plastic windows, and, as we sat in the parlor after dinner, he would carefully cut the extra paper off them with a scissors, then deposit the paper in the Blue Bag. I took that as a rebuke. When I said that I was having difficulty with some of the changes listed in the "Adjustments and Further Regulations" section of Volume Two—for instance, the change under "Green Cart Items" from "fish intestines" to "fish intestines other than liver and spleen"—he accused me of being a despoiler of the earth.

Eventually, he embarked on what he called "a campaign for thorough separation" and what I called (behind his back) "the final solution." He insisted that I strip the paint off any wood I put in the Green Cart under the category of "small pieces of wood and bric-a-brac." One night, as I was slicing some tomatoes for dinner, he began to shout at me for tossing the end of a tomato in the organic waste destined for the Green Cart without removing that little round sticker that supermarkets sometimes put on vegetables. I still had the tomato-slicing knife in my hand, so I stabbed him in the heart. I put the body in a large freezer we have in the garage, but I know that eventually I'll have to dispose of him elsewhere. Green Cart?

2005

I'm OK, I'm Not OK

First I heard on the radio about a new Happy to Be Me doll, which is thicker at the waist and hips than the idealized doll that we've been accustomed to and also has bigger feet. Then I came across a story I had clipped out of *The New York Times* a couple of months back about how plastic surgeons can now fill out the wrinkles on a patient's face with fat taken from somewhere else on his body—a procedure that a Beverly Hills plastic surgeon called "the epitome of recycling." Sometimes, I have to admit, I wonder about this country.

What I'm wondering this time is how in a single society so many people can make money on the proposition that you are truly fine just as you are (the self-esteem industry), while, at the same time, so many other people are making money on the proposition that there are no limits to the ways you can improve the wreck you find yourself to be (the self-improvement industry).

Every year, two or three different pop psychologists haul in a bundle with self-help books whose titles amount to some version of *You Are the Very Best Person in the Whole Wide World.* Of course, it's perfectly possible that a person who buys one of these books is not, in fact, the very best person in the whole wide world; the cashier at the book store doesn't do any testing. It's perfectly possible, in fact, that a person who buys one of these books is a crumb-bum. Or maybe he's just a perfectly okay person who's a little thick in the waist and has big feet.

But the book is so convincing that the person who buys it—let's call him Harvey—sails along for months, absolutely stinky with self-esteem. He has even begun to feel a little sorry for people who have normal-sized feet and are therefore much more vulnerable to being toppled in a high wind.

At the same time, though, he is constantly being bombarded with suggestions that he is not only not the best person in the whole wide world but a walking disaster area. Every time he turns on the television he is reminded that he is overweight and afflicted with a flaking scalp and occasionally irregular and ignorant of the most rudimentary notions of personal investment strategy. When he goes to the bookstore to browse around for new books telling him how terrific he is, he notices books with titles like *Get That Waistline Down* and *How to Take Inches off Those Feet.* And his morale isn't helped by the fact that any time columnists want to indicate that someone might have low self-esteem they name him Harvey.

So Harvey is on kind of a roller-coaster. One day, he's feeling on top of the world, even though he's having a little trouble getting his pants buttoned over that waist of his, and the next day he feels the self-esteem drain out of him like crankcase oil that needed changing a long time ago.

When he feels like that, he goes back down to the book store and finds something with a title like *There's Absolutely Nobody Better than You,* and gets a little booster shot of self-confidence.

From reading these books, Harvey has learned just how to handle anything that threatens to undermine his belief that there is nobody in the world better than he is. He is quite aware of the possibility that at any time someone might say to him, "Have you ever noticed that you're a little thicker in the waist than a lot of people?" or even, "You know, you've got a wrinkle or two near the mouth there that could be filled out by fat taken from some part of your body where, not to put too fine a point on this, you wouldn't really miss it."

If that happens, Harvey knows to say, "I've been given reason to believe that I'm the very best person in the whole wide world, although I don't like to boast."

If the same person goes on to say, "Are those your feet or is there a ski slope around here I didn't notice?" Harvey knows to say, "I'm happy to be me."

There may be a time, though, when a confrontation like that shakes Harvey's confidence. So he goes over to the mall to look for another book with a title like *You're It, Big Guy*. But the bookstore is closed. For a moment, Harvey is crushed. Then he notices that the toy store next-door is still open. He rushes in and says "Do you have a Happy to Be Me doll?" They do. Harvey is okay again.

1991

Back Where You Came From

(A nativist ballad to twelve million undocumented immigrants, sung to the tune of "Look to the Rainbow")

You have broken our law,
So you'll have to go now.
We will move you all out, and I don't care just how.
As for scrubbing our floors
And for picking our crops,
We will figure that out. I'm now calling the cops.

Go back, back where you came from.
Your kind's not wanted; you cannot stay here.
Go back, back where you came from.
I'll mow my own lawn. Just cross that frontier.
I'll clean my own house. Just cross that frontier.

2008

SEEING THE WORLD

"In the fifties, when my mother began lobbying for a trip to Europe, my father, who had been brought to Missouri from the Ukraine when he was two, said, 'I been.'"

Defying Mrs. Tweedie

Before Alice and I left for a visit to the Sicilian resort town of Taormina, I consulted *Sunny Sicily* for the observations of Mrs. Alec Tweedie, a rather severe travel writer of late-Victorian times who was also the author of *Through Finland in Carts* and, before she caught on to the value of a snappy title, *Danish Versus English Butter Making*. I can't imagine why some people say that I don't have a scholarly approach to travel.

Writing in 1904, Mrs. Tweedie summed up Taormina like this: "The place is being spoilt." It's the sort of comment that can give pause to a traveler who is considering a visit to Taormina somewhat later in the century. Mrs. Tweedie's conclusion that Taormina was being ruined by an influx of English and Americans must have been made, after all, at about the same time the Wright brothers took off at Kitty Hawk—and neither she nor the Wright brothers could have had any notion of the impact of super-saver fares. There was no way for me to know whether or not Mrs. Tweedie had been one of those people who simply seem to take great pleasure in telling you that they can recall the time when the place you're about to visit—any place you're about to visit—was actually okay. ("Pity about the Marquesas. I remember thinking years ago that if that semimonthly prop service from Fiji ever started, that would be it.")

Still, even though Mrs. Tweedie complained bitterly that "the natives have lost their own nice ways," she had to admit that Taormina was "one of the most beautiful spots on earth," an ancient town perched high on a mountain overlooking the Ionian Sea. Also, I had reason to believe that Mrs. Tweedie's standards in matter of spoilage were stricter than my own. She sounded as if she might fit comfortably among those travelers whose measure of authenticity is so exacting that they tend to find even the ruins ruined.

Taormina, in fact, happens to have a noted ruin—a Greek theater where what must have been the cheap seats command such a spectacular view of the sea that I can imagine Aristophanes and Euripides sitting around some playwrights' hangout commiserating with each other on how hard it is to hold a Taormina audience's attention. As a matter of fact, Mrs. Tweedie did find that ruin ruined. The Greek theater, she wrote, "is really Roman, as the Romans completely altered it." I have nothing against the Romans myself. How is it possible to dismiss a culture that handed down penne all'Arrabbiata? Also, I was, of course, traveling with a connoisseur of views. I always seem to be particularly intent on pleasing Alice during Italian vacations, even if that requires taking in what I would think of as a plethora of views. It may have grown out of my custom of calling her the *principessa* whenever we're traveling in Italy. At some point I found that it improved the service at the hotels.

By Mrs. Tweedie's standards, the natives of Taormina must have lost their own nice ways years before she marched briskly into the piazza, wearing, as I have always envisioned her, a tweed suit, sensible walking shoes, and an authoritative expression. At the time of this first inspection, the British had been coming to Taormina for thirty years. A visit by Wilhelm II of Prussia made it popular with European royalty, and, when Mrs. Tweedie was probably still skidding around Finland in a cart, Taormina was picking up a reputation as a place that appealed to writers and artists and assorted genteel bohemians. It almost goes without saying that D. H. Lawrence once lived there. Having had D. H. Lawrence residences pointed out to me all over the world, I can only wonder how he got any writing done, what with packing and getting steamship reservations and having to look around for a decent plumber in every new spot. I suspect, though, that Taormina's reputation for harboring exotics comes less from Lawrence than from a German nobleman named Wilhelm von Gloeden, who arrived at about the same time as Wilhelm II and started taking what became well-known photographs of Sicilian boys—some dressed as ancient Greeks, some dressed as girls, and some not dressed at all.

Late in the evening, as I sat in one of the outdoor cafés on Taormina's principal piazza, where one café uses enlargements of von Gloeden photographs to decorate its walls, my thoughts sometimes turned from Sicilian almond pastry to the possibility that von Gloeden and Mrs. Tweedie met in Taormina. The street that dominates the town—the Corso Umberto, a strolling street that bans cars except during early-morning delivery hours—couldn't have changed much from the days when there were no cars to ban, except that in Mrs. Tweedie's time the industrial revolution had not progressed to the point of providing Corso Umberto shops with souvenir T-shirts that say I MAFIOSI TAORMINA. The piazza, known as Piazza Nove Aprile, is a wide spot about halfway down the Corso Umberto where a gap in the buildings along one side of the street for a few hundred feet presents a stunning view of the sea. The jacaranda trees must have been there then, and I suspect the bench alongside the sixteenth-century church was lined with the very same nineteenth-century old folks, sternly watching the evening strollers as if collecting vicarious sins to confess the next day.

I could easily imagine the encounter. Suddenly a man at one of the cafés stands up, trying to keep his composure while gathering up the bulky cameras and tripod he always carries with him. "I really don't see what concern it is of yours, madam," he says in heavily accented English.

Too late. Mrs. Tweedie is bearing down on him, brandishing the umbrella that made a porter in Palermo sorry that he complained about what had been a perfectly adequate sixpence tip. Von Gloeden bolts from the café, knocking down a portly mustachioed man (Wilhelm II of Prussia) and caroming off an ice-cream vendor as he races down the street. Mrs. Tweedie is gaining on him.

"Shame! Shame!" she shouts as she waves the lethal umbrella above her head. "Shame on you, you wicked, wicked man!"

1981

Weak Dollar Blues

I got them finally got to Paris and the dollar is dropping blues.
I go to all the chic shops, but all I can do is peruse.
There're clothes here that I'd like to hoard,
But a Coke costs as much as a Ford.
I don't know who's to blame, but whoever it is, well, *j'accuse.*
I got them finally got to Paris and the dollar is dropping blues.

1992

Time and Tide

The world's highest tides are in the Minas Basin—at the end of the Bay of Fundy, in Nova Scotia. I've been there. Did I see the high tides? Well, my wife and I certainly showed up at the shore, eager to see what the Minas Basin people had to offer in the way of tides. But how, exactly, do you look at a high tide? If it's in, it just looks like water. If it's out, looking at it is like observing some guy who bills himself as the person who has lost the most weight of anyone in the greater Cleveland area: To make a go of it, he'd pretty much have to have a way to show you what he looked like as a fatty. I don't mean to imply that folks along the Minas Basin would say that a bunch of mudflats are under water at high tide if it weren't true, but you can't be too careful these days.

Usually, something that's the highest or deepest or biggest is easy to spot. If you go to Pittsburgh and you want to see the largest revolving door in the world, for instance, you just ask anyone where it is. Then you can stand in front of it and say things like "Well, that's a big revolving door, all right" or "In Houston, we got a whole mess of revolving doors bigger'n that" or "I wonder if that fat guy in Cleveland could have fit in that revolving door."

But it takes six and a half hours for a tide to change from high to low, or vice versa, and the difference between high and low is actually the attraction you're supposed to observe. I could envision us lined up with other tourists at some lookout point designated by the tourist commission as one of the best places to get a look at the highest tides in the world. The tide is just going out. In six and a half hours, we're going to see a dramatic difference. After about an hour, the man next to me says, "You folks from Indiana?"

"No," I say.

He nods his head, as if my answer made a certain amount of sense.

After a while, he says, "Used to have some cousins in Indiana. Unless it was Illinois." I look at my watch. We've got five and a half hours to go. I try to keep in mind that the word the tourist commission keeps using for these tides is *dramatic.*

My wife broke into this reverie. "It says in the brochure that at high tide on certain days we could look for a tidal bore," she said.

"Not on your life!" I said. I happened to know what the brochure meant by a tidal bore: It's the phenomenon that occurs when a strong incoming tide in a place like the Minas Basin meets the current of a river that is flowing into the sea. But before I realized that, I occasionally passed signs on the highway in Nova Scotia that said TIDAL BORE, and I assumed they were warning motorists about the presence of someone lurking around there waiting to tell you a whole lot more about tides than you ever wanted to know.

Whenever I saw a TIDAL BORE sign, I jammed my foot on the accelerator. Even after the true meaning was explained to me, I couldn't get over the idea that a living, talking tidal bore was just waiting to tell me at great length about the connection of tides and the phases of the moon. I couldn't get over the idea that another sign down the road might say MILES PER GALLON BORE. Then there would be a sign saying TRIP TO EUROPE BORE, and just off the road, half hidden by a clump of bushes, he'd be there, waiting. What's that in his hand? A carrousel full of slides!

I wasn't about to look for a tidal bore, and it occurred to me that we had another problem: We had arrived at half tide, meaning that seeing the extremes of high and low would require us to spend more than nine hours at the lookout, denying all the time that we were from Indiana.

I took another look at the water. "I think, in a manner of speaking, we've sort of seen it," I said to my wife. "It was interesting."

"Somehow, I don't feel it was very dramatic," she said.

"Someday," I promised, "I'll take you to see the biggest revolving door in the world."

1990

Low Visibility

I haven't seen any of the mountains I was meant to see. That doesn't sound right. That sounds like somebody saying, "Alas! I was born to see mountains, yet I have spent my entire life within the environs of Ottumwa, Iowa." That is not what I mean. I mean that I have been in places where you're supposed to see certain mountains, and I have not been able to see them. When I am in parts of France where the Alps are visible on a clear day, for instance, it is not a clear day. In Japan, I did not see Mount Fuji. I missed Mount McKinley in Alaska. From a splendid perch on the top row of an ancient amphitheater in Taormina, Sicily, I failed to see Mount Etna in the distance. In Tanzania, I was unable to make out Mount Kilimanjaro. There might have been snows on Kilimanjaro and there might not have been snows on Kilimanjaro. For all I know, Gregory Peck and Ava Gardner were still up there. I couldn't see a thing.

There is no question that in each case I was in a spot from which the mountain is, in theory, viewable. When I realized that I was not going to see Mount Rainier, in fact, I was standing on the porch of the Mountain View Inn. Also, I would like to dispose at once of the notion that I might have actually seen the mountains in question and not recognized them as mountains. I know where that kind of talk comes from. It comes from people who know that I have never been able to see constellations. It is true that every time someone has said to me "There—can't you see Orion's Belt, starting with that bright star over on the left?" I have said "No, not really." I have never seen Orion or his belt. I'll admit that I wasn't looking very hard for a while, since I thought for years that Orion was O'Ryan, and I considered the possibility of an Irish constellation unlikely. Even after I knew Orion's name, though, I couldn't see him. I don't think the people who are always pointing him out to me can see him either. I think the constellation business is purely arbitrary. I think there are just a bunch of stars up there. I think that if you said to one of the constellation people (in a sufficiently authoritative tone) "Good view of Athena's dirndl tonight over there; you can even see where the hem's coming loose," he would nod sagely and say something about the natural wonders of the universe.

All of which leads me to turn the tables on this talk about whether I can recognize a mountain when I see one: It may be that the people who are always saying that they saw the mountains did not really see them. People are like that. I think it's possible that a lot of people—the same sort of people who say they see belts and pots and all sorts of knickknacks in the sky—just look squinty-eyed through the fog toward the mountain and say, "Hmmm. Yes. Lovely."

Maybe some of them don't like to admit that they missed the mountain. Let's say that a man named Thistlethwaite returns from the trip to Japan that he has looked forward to for years, and his brother-in-law—the boorish brother-in-law who's always saying that Thistlethwaite paid too much for his car and went to the wrong discount store for the grass edger—says that Mount Fuji must have been quite a sight, even for someone who might well have been preoccupied with having paid the straight coach fare to Tokyo when he could have put together a charter-and-excursion package through Honolulu. Is Thistlethwaite really going to say "Actually, we didn't see Fuji, what with the low-lying clouds"? Does he want to hear his brother-in-law say "Hey, Marge—did you hear that? Did you hear they dropped a bundle going over there to Japan and missed the main mountain?"

I think not. I think Thistlethwaite is more likely to shake his head in wonderment and say "Yes, quite a sight, quite a sight." What does he have to lose? He isn't likely to be questioned closely on what the mountain looked like, and even if he is, it's the simplest thing in the world to fake: "Tall. It was tall. And pointy at the top. Tall and pointy."

I want to make this clear right now: I am not complaining. You won't find me grabbing people by the lapels at parties and saying "Why is it that everybody gets to see the mountains but me?" For one thing, it is not true that everybody gets to see the mountains but me.

My wife, for instance, doesn't get to see them. She is usually with me, standing in the fog. I'm not complaining and I'm not being defensive. There is nothing defensive about pointing out that all the inspirational stuff about mountains does not apply in this case. The nun in *The Sound of Music* keeps telling everyone to climb every mountain. Well, fine. But you can't climb them if you can't see them, Sister. Also, there is the matter of George Mallory, the great English mountain climber, who answered the question of why he wanted to climb Mount Everest by saying "Because it's there." But what if he had been asked what he would do if the mountain was not, in fact, there? He'd have said "Well, then, I wouldn't climb it, you silly twit! Is this your idea of a joke, or what?" So much for the inspirational stuff.

1984

Phone Pals

"I'm telephoning, sir, to inform you that you have been preselected by computer to win a trip to Hawaii for only $1,198, including air travel and hotel room—that's double occupancy—and a free Mahu Lahani cocktail upon arrival."

"How nice of you to call! As I was just saying to a gentleman who phoned to tell me I'd been chosen as someone who could benefit greatly from a cattle-ranch mutual fund, it's always comforting to hear the telephone ring around dinnertime and know that people with a large computer at their disposal have been thinking of me."

"Then I take it, sir, that you'd like to redeem your exclusive, limited-time offer to take advantage of this special award?"

"And you'll be interested to hear that, by coincidence, my Uncle Harry has this weird obsession about visiting places that end with the letter *i*. I'll admit that the young woman who phoned last night to tell me that I had been selected for a specially priced series of tango lessons didn't seem absolutely entranced by Uncle Harry's travel theories, but then, she wasn't in the trade the way you are. You see, Uncle Harry's from Missouri, and he got the idea that it would be appropriate to visit any place whose name ends similarly."

"Sir, if I could just get your decision on this, you can charge it conveniently on your MasterCard or—"

"Oh, there were some he collected right away, of course. He and Aunt Rosie drove through Bemidji, Minnesota, one summer on the way to the lakes up there. And it wasn't long before he managed to score what he called his first double: Biloxi, Mississippi. It's on the Gulf Coast—but I guess you knew that, being in the travel business. Although, you'd be surprised: The man who phoned the other night to tell me I'd been preselected for eight days and seven nights in Cancun had never heard of Biloxi."

"This offer is for Hawaii, sir, and it includes—"

"Biloxi's just down the coast from Gulfport, which has a lovely motto: 'Where Your Ship Comes In.' "

"Sir, Hawaii is a land of enchantment, where many cultures have—"

"You might say I collect mottos, the way my Uncle Harry collects places that end in *i*. Do you collect anything yourself?"

"Uh. Well. Actually, I do have a lot of poodle-dog ornaments. But about this Hawaiian trip, sir—"

"Underrated dog, the poodle, and I suppose that goes for the ornaments, too. But you didn't phone to discuss poodle dogs. Listen, my Aunt Rosie, who considers Biloxi just about far enough from home, called all worried one day to say that Uncle Harry was talking about the two of them going to Africa so he could visit Mali. Well, I told her that Uncle Harry just likes to talk about the more exotic places—Haiti, say, or Bari, Italy, or Lodi, New Jersey. So she didn't have to worry about dragging herself all the way over to Bamako. That's the capital of Mali, by the way: Bamako. I had a friend who was sent there by the foreign service. I remember at the going-away party somebody sang a song called 'I'll Be Your Bamako Baby, You Be My Mali Dolly.' It must be interesting doing what you do—calling people around dinnertime and finding out capitals of foreign countries that happen to end in *i*."

"Sir, when I say this offer is a limited-time offer, I really have to—"

"I know: You really have to get to the point. Of course. I can see that. The point is this: Uncle Harry has always talked about going to Hawaii, a one-word double. He figured that even if he didn't get to Tahiti and Fiji and Funafuti while he was out that way, he might spend his time in Hawaii in the town of Kahului on the island of Maui. I think if he did that, Uncle Harry would be a happy man. Although I have to say that Aunt Rosie disagrees with me. She says that no matter where he went, Uncle Harry would be a stubborn, mean-tempered old coot. Of course, Aunt Rosie—"

"Sir! Sir!"

"Yes?"

"Maybe your Uncle Harry would like to take advantage of this limited-time offer for a trip to Hawaii."

"But Uncle Harry hasn't been preselected by computer. I'm the one who's been preselected by computer."

"Well, I think just this once . . ."

"Oh, he would never be party to anything like that. I guess I've told you before what Aunt Rosie always says about Uncle Harry being as flexible as a tree stump. Take his theory that Christopher Columbus's first New World landing was in Kansas City, near what is now the corner of Eleventh and Walnut. Why, he . . . Hello? . . . Hello? . . ."

1987

NATIONAL HOLIDAYS

"Those who persist in thinking that I don't take enough interest in my wardrobe are apparently not aware of how much effort goes into the selection of my Halloween costume."

Eating with the Pilgrims

This Thanksgiving, our family was finally able to sit down together and give thanks over a meal of spaghetti carbonara. It has been several years, of course, since I began my campaign to have the national Thanksgiving dish changed from turkey to spaghetti carbonara—I love spaghetti carbonara—but until now invitations to have Thanksgiving dinner at friends' houses prevented our family from practicing what I preached. This year, nobody invited us over for

Thanksgiving dinner—my wife's theory being that word got around town that I always make a pest of myself berating the hostess for serving turkey instead of spaghetti carbonara. In my defense, I should say that my daughters do not believe that our lack of invitations has anything at all to do with my insistence on bringing the spaghetti carbonara issue to the attention of the American public at any appropriate opportunity. They believe it may have something to do with my tendency to spill cranberry sauce on my tie.

I'll admit that my campaign might have been inspired partly by my belief that turkey is basically something college dormitories use to punish students for hanging around on Sunday. I'll admit that early in the campaign I brought up some advantages that are only aesthetic—the fact, for instance, that the President would not be photographed every year receiving a large platter of spaghetti carbonara from the Eastern Association of Spaghetti Carbonara Growers. As King Vittorio Emmanuelle once said to his Chancellor of the Exchequer, "Spaghetti doesn't grow on trees." I'll admit that I would love to see what those masters of the float-maker's art at the Macy's parade might come up with as a three-hundred square-foot depiction of a plate of spaghetti carbonara. I'll admit that I'd find it refreshing to hear sports announcers call some annual tussle the Spaghetti Carbonara Day Classic.

My campaign, though, has been based also on deeper historical and philosophical considerations. Nobody knows if the Pilgrims really ate turkey at the first Thanksgiving dinner. The only thing we know for sure about what the Pilgrims ate is that it couldn't have tasted very good. They were from East Anglia, a part of England whose culinary standards are symbolized by the fact that any number of housewives there are this week serving Brussels sprouts that were put on to boil shortly after the Pilgrims left. Also, it's all very well to say that we should give thanks by eating the meal our forebears ate, but, as it happens, one of the things I give thanks for every year is that those people were not my forebears. Who wants forebears who put people in the stocks for playing the harpsichord on the Sabbath or having an innocent little game of pinch and giggle? In fact, ever since it became fashionable to dwell on the atrocities of American history—ever since, that is, we entered what the historians call the Era of Year-Round Yom Kippur—I have been more and more grateful that none of my forebears got near this place before 1906. We had nothing at all to do with slavery or massacring Indians or the slaughter of the American buffalo or the assorted scandals of the Spanish-American War. It used to be that an American who wanted to put on airs made claims about how long his family had been here. Now the only people left for a first-generation American to envy are the immigrants who arrived in the last half-dozen years. They don't even have to feel guilty about the Vietnam War.

Naturally, the whole family went over to Raffeto's pasta store on Houston Street to see the spaghetti cut. It's important, I think, to have these holiday rituals. As the meal began, I asked the children if they had any questions about our forebears.

"Was Uncle Benny responsible for the First World War just because he was already in St. Jo then?" my younger daughter asked.

"Not directly," I said. "He didn't have his citizenship."

"Is it really true that your grandparents got mixed up about American holidays and used to have a big turkey dinner on the Fourth of July and shoot fireworks off in the park on Thanksgiving?" my older daughter asked.

"At least they had nothing to do with snookering the Indians out of Massachusetts," I said. "Be thankful for that."

Then, as is traditional, I told the children the story of the first Thanksgiving:

In England a long time ago, there were people called Pilgrims who were very strict about making sure everyone observed the Sabbath and nobody cooked food with any flavor and that sort of thing, and they decided to go to America where they could enjoy Freedom to Nag. The other people in England said, "Glad to see the back of them," and put on some Brussels sprouts to boil in case any of their descendants craved a veggie in 1981. In America, the Pilgrims tried farming, but they couldn't get much done because they were always putting each other in the stocks for crimes like Suspicion of Cheerfulness. The Indians took pity on the Pilgrims and helped them with their farming, even though the Indians thought the Pilgrims were about as much fun as a teenage circumcision. The Pilgrims were so grateful that they invited the Indians over for a Thanksgiving meal, and the Indians, having had some experience with Pilgrim cuisine in the past, took the precaution of bringing along one dish of their own. They brought a dish that their ancestors had learned many generations before from none other than Christopher Columbus, who was known to the Indians as "the big Italian fella." The dish was spaghetti carbonara—made with pancetta bacon and fontina and the best imported prosciutto. The Pilgrims hated it. They said it was "heretically tasty" and "the work of the devil" and "the sort of thing foreigners eat." The Indians were so disgusted that on the way back to their village after dinner one of them made a remark about the Pilgrims that was repeated for generations and unfortunately caused confusion among historians about the first Thanksgiving meal. He said, "What a bunch of turkeys!"

1981

Harold the Committed and Halloween

A couple of weeks ago, Harold the Committed asked me again if I wanted to see civilization as we know it destroyed in a nuclear holocaust, and I had to admit that I didn't. He always asks me that question, and I always give him the same answer. I can't imagine what led him to think that my position on the destruction-of-civilization issue might waver. What kind of person does Harold the Committed think I am? Sure, there are days when things don't go quite the way I had hoped they would. Occasionally I go through what I think of as a multi-motor day: The automobile repairman says we need a new motor, the dishwasher repairman says we need a new motor, the clothes-dryer repairman says we need a new motor. Even on a multi-motor day, though, I don't sit down with a drink when it's all over and say to myself, "Well, if that's the way it's going to be, I would like to see civilization as we know it destroyed in a nuclear holocaust." I'm much more likely to say something like, "But didn't we just *get* a new motor for the dishwasher?"

I didn't go into all of that with Harold the Committed, of course. What I said was, "I've given this issue a lot of thought, Hal the C, and I remain firmly opposed to the destruction of civilization as we know it in a nuclear holocaust. You can count on me on this one."

"What are you doing about it?" Harold the Committed said.

"As it happens, you've caught me at a bad time, Harold the Committed," I said. "You know I'm not very political just before Halloween."

I wasn't just spinning an alibi for Harold the Committed. Just before Halloween, I always have a lot on my mind. For one thing, I have to decide on a costume for the Halloween parade. Are people getting tired of my ax murderer's mask? Should I take advantage of my uncanny ability to bark like a dog by going as an unhappy Airedale? Harold the Committed finds it difficult to understand how I can spend so much time agonizing over a costume for the Halloween parade; he goes every year as an unemployed coal miner.

My Halloween responsibilities go well beyond my own costume. I have to be a consultant to my daughters in the matter of their costumes, since my wife's attitude toward Halloween, I regret to say, borders on the blasé. I have to take part in serious discussions about the possibility that my daughters and I might encourage my wife to wear something more appropriate than a token witch hat.

"Daddy, I don't really think you're going to be able to persuade Mommy to wear that long, crooked witch's nose with the warts on it," one of them is likely to say.

"Well, how about these individual, rubberized, easy-to-remove face warts?" I say hopefully.

"Halloween can be approached as an opportunity," Harold the Committed was saying. "Like any other public event, it can be used as a platform for making a political statement."

The last time Harold the Committed started talking about Halloween that way he ended by suggesting that my ten-year-old daughter, Sarah, go to the Halloween parade costumed as Emma Goldman. She decided to go as a chocolate-chocolate-chip ice-cream cone with chocolate sprinkles instead.

"What's your daughter Sarah going as this year?" Harold the Committed asked.

"She's leaning toward the idea of going as a jar of Hellmann's mayonnaise, Hal the C," I said.

"She really doesn't have a lot of political awareness, does she?" Harold the Committed said.

"It's not her awareness she's worried about, it's other people's," I said. "Last year not everybody was aware that she was supposed to be a chocolate-chocolate-chip ice-cream cone with chocolate sprinkles. A couple of people thought she was a tube of toothpaste. She figures a mayonnaise jar would be a little more explicit."

I knew what was coming next, and, sure enough, Harold repeated a suggestion he seems to make every year: "Maybe your daughter Abigail could go as the dangers posed to our society by the military-industrial complex."

"We don't have anybody at home who can sew that well, Hal the C," I said. "Abigail's going as an M&M." Abigail has never been much impressed with Harold's costume suggestions, particularly since he persuaded his niece to go as a peace dove and everyone thought she was supposed to be Donald Duck.

"It's a matter of paying lip service or making a political statement through every aspect of your life," Harold the Committed said. "Everyone must make a decision."

"I've decided, Hal the C," I said. "I'm going as an ax murderer again after all."

1982

Christmas in Qatar

(A new holiday classic, for those tiring of
"White Christmas" and "Jingle Bells")

VERSE:

The shopping starts, and every store's a zoo.
I'm frantic, too: I haven't got a clue
Of what to get for Dad, who's got no hobby,
Or why Aunt Jane, who's shaped like a kohlrabi,
Wants frilly sweater sets, or where I'll find
A tie my loudmouthed Uncle Jack won't mind.
A shopper's told it's vital he prevails:
Prosperity depends on Christmas sales.
"Can't stop to talk," I say. "No time. Can't halt.
Economy could fail. Would be my fault."

CHORUS:

I'd like to spend next Christmas in Qatar,
Or someplace else that Santa won't find handy.
Qatar will do, although, Lord knows, it's sandy.
I need to get to someplace pretty far.
I'd like to spend next Christmas in Qatar.

VERSE:

Young Cousin Ned, his presents on his knees,
Says Christmas wrappings are a waste of trees.
Dad's staring, vaguely puzzled, at his gift.
And Uncle Jack, to give us all a lift,
Now tells a Polish joke he heard at work.
So Ned calls Jack a bigot and a jerk.
Aunt Jane, who knows that's true, breaks down and cries

Then Mom comes out to help, and burns the pies.
Of course, Jack hates the tie. He'll take it back.
That's fair, because I hate my Uncle Jack.

CHORUS:
I'd like to spend next Christmas in Tibet,
Or any place where folks cannot remember
That there is something special in December.
Tibet's about as far as you can get.
I'd like to spend next Christmas in Tibet.

VERSE:
Mom's turkey is a patriotic riddle:
It's red and white, plus bluish in the middle.
The blue's because the oven heat's not stable.
The red's from ketchup Dad snuck to the table.
Dad says he loves the eyeglass stand from me—
Unless a sock rack's what it's meant to be.
"A free-range turkey's best," Ned says. "It's pure."
"This hippie stuff," Jack says, "I can't endure."
They say goodbye, thank God. It's been a strain.
At least Jack's tie has got a ketchup stain.

CHORUS:
I'd like to spend next Christmas in Rangoon,
Or any place where Christmas is as noisy
As Buddhist holidays might be in Boise.
I long to hear Der Bingle smoothly croon,
"I'm dreaming of a Christmas in Rangoon"—
Or someplace you won't hear the Christmas story,
And reindeer's something eaten cacciatore.
I know things can't go on the way they are.
I'd like to spend next Christmas in Qatar.

1994

Iran for Christmas

For Christmas, I took over Iran for Alice. I don't mean I went there with a band of mercenaries recruited from the better Manhattan saloons, took over the government, and presented Alice with all of the rights and privileges accruing to the Peacock Throne. I try to avoid travel during the holiday season. What I mean is that I took over keeping up with what was happening in Iran, giving Alice a little extra time to devote to the Middle East peace talks and the January sales.

On Christmas, there was a moment when I feared that I had not chosen well. As I watched her open the package containing Iran—I had wrapped it in some rather colorful paper whose print, it seemed to me, suggested a Persian rug if viewed in that spirit—I thought I saw the flicker of a frown on her face. "She was hoping for the SALT talks," I said to myself.

I had thought about getting her SALT instead of Iran. I knew she despised protracted negotiations. Once, having heard on a talk show that presenting surprise gifts for no particular occasion was one secret of keeping the romance in a marriage, I had returned from the office on a rainy, uneventful Tuesday and announced to Alice that she need no longer concern herself with a British coal strike then in its third week. She was ecstatic. SALT, I realized, was a drearier subject than Iran—lacking even the stimulation of a story now and then about some particularly revolting act of conspicuous consumption by the Shah and his family. But the papers had not been carrying much about the SALT talks, and there were thousands of words daily to read about Iran. Somehow, SALT had seemed a smaller gift.

"Actually, I thought about getting you the SALT talks," I said tentatively.

"Oh, no. This is much nicer," Alice said. "It was just that the wrapping seemed a little tacky."

"You said a few weeks ago that you hated worrying about how to pronounce Ayatollah Khomeini. Was that a hint?"

"Well, it's certainly true, anyway," Alice said. "Also, plowing through those oil production figures was a bore, and all of those endless speculations about whether or not 'American intelligence was caught napping' just made me sleepy. This is perfect. Really. I love it. Just think of not having to concern myself anymore about knowing whether the Shah is about to leave and where he might go! I was beginning to feel like a travel agent."

"Probably the United States, although Gstaad has also been mentioned by informed observers in Tehran," I said.

"What?"

"I was just telling you what's in the paper this morning," I said. "The gift has begun."

Alice started it all some years ago by giving me Cyprus for my birthday. I was delighted—and only partly because I had somehow got it into my head that she was planning to give me an orange vinyl tie. For some years, I had been thinking that the task of being a well-informed citizen was particularly onerous when it came to Cyprus. On the Cyprus question, I craved ignorance. I was tired of the Bishop. The history of Greek and Turkish settlement failed to fascinate. Any analysis of the effect a Greek-Turkish conflict might have on NATO caused me to long for the Arts & Leisure section.

Sometimes, Cyprus seemed to disappear from the papers for years, only to surface in an even more desperate crisis, full of pathetic refugees and ponderous United Nations debates. Cyprus had begun to remind me of some dreadful old uncle who is always alarming the family with emergencies that are invariably described as beyond solution: Something must be done immediately before Uncle Jack's behavior drives Aunt Thelma to violence. How long can a man continue to shoot at postmen with a crossbow before tragedy occurs? Can a fanatic Christian Scientist and a homicidal podiatrist live together for another day? Then, people in the family become distracted by their own problems, everyone forgets about Uncle Jack for months, and suddenly he reemerges—with problems just as insoluble as ever. Who solved the insoluble emergencies in the meantime? Should citizens who already have Uncle Jacks be expected to worry about Cyprus as well?

"DON'T GIVE IT ANOTHER THOUGHT," Alice's birthday gift to me had said, printed in colorful letters on a map of the dread island. "LEAVE IT TO ME."

"Could that really be?" I had asked incredulously. I was almost overcome with gratitude—not to mention a little guilt for having thought, even for a moment, that a woman who could think of such a gift might have stuck me with an orange vinyl necktie.

"You just tell me now at which point you care to be informed," Alice said. "I can let you know when it appears that they're going to start fighting again, for instance, or I can let you know when it's getting to the point at which the NATO alliance might be seriously weakened."

I thought about it for a while. "Worldwide nuclear conflagration," I finally said. "If it appears that, because of Cyprus, worldwide nuclear conflagration is imminent, I would appreciate being informed. If not, I'll just give it a skip, thank you very much."

After all of those years of freedom from the wretched Cypriots, I found it gratifying, of course, to begin a Christmas Day by presenting Alice with a gift that would lift from her shoulders the daily strain of distinguishing between General Gholam ali Oveissi and General Manuchehr Khosrowdad. I was filled with Christmas warmth as I opened my own gift. It was a map. I recognized it immediately from my research: Iran. DON'T GIVE IT ANOTHER THOUGHT, the printing on it said. LEAVE IT TO ME.

1979

The Fruitcake Theory

This was the year I was going to be nice about fruitcake. "Just try to be nice," my wife said. My younger daughter—the one who is still in high school, and talks funny—said the same thing. Actually, what she said was, "Cool it, Pops. Take a chill on the fruitcake issue." That's the same thing.

They were right. I knew they were right. It's not that I hadn't tried to be nice before. It's not my fault that some years ago I happened to pass along a theory about fruitcake I had heard from someone in Denver. The theory was that there is only one fruitcake, and that this fruitcake is simply sent on from year to year. It's just a theory.

But every year, around this time, someone calls up and says something like, "I'm doing a story on people who make fun of the holiday symbols that so many Americans hold dear—symbols that do so much for warm family life in this great country of ours and remain so very meaningful to all decent people. You're the one who maligns fruitcake, right?"

"Well, it's just a theory," I always mutter. "Something someone in Denver said once."

Who in Denver? Well, I can't remember. I'm always hearing theories from people in Denver. People in Denver are stinky with theories. I don't know why. It may be because of the altitude, although that's just a theory.

Anyway, I can't be expected to remember the name of every single person in Denver who ever laid a theory on me. I've had people in Denver tell me that if you play a certain Rolling Stones record backwards you can get detailed instructions on how to dismantle a 1973 Volkswagen Rabbit. A man I once met in a bar in Denver told me that the gases produced by the drying of all these sun-dried tomatoes were causing the Earth to wobble on its axis in a way that will put every pool table in the Western Hemisphere nearly a bubble off level by the end of this century. Don't get me started on people in Denver and their theories.

The point is that nobody ever interviews the person who gave me the theory about fruitcake, because nobody wants to start picking through this gaggle of theory-mongers in Denver to find him. So I was the one called up this year by someone who said he was doing a piece about a number of Scrooge-like creatures who seemed to derive sadistic pleasure out of trashing some of our most treasured American holiday traditions.

"Well, come right over," I said. "It's always nice to be included."

He said he'd catch me the next afternoon, just after he finished interviewing a guy who never passes a Salvation Army Santa Claus without saying, "Hiya, lard-gut."

When he arrived, I remembered that I was going to try to take a chill on the fruitcake issue. I told him that the theory about there being only one fruitcake actually came from somebody in Denver—maybe the same guy who talked to me at length about his theory that dinosaurs became extinct because they couldn't adapt to the personal income tax.

Then, trying for a little historical perspective, I told him about a family in Michigan I once read about that brings out an antique fruitcake every Christmas—a fruitcake that for some reason was not eaten at Christmas dinner in 1895 and has symbolized the holidays ever since. They put it on the table, not as dessert but as something somewhere between an icon and a centerpiece. "It's a very sensible way to use a fruitcake," I said. I was trying to be nice.

"You mean you think that fruitcake would be dangerous to eat?" he asked.

"Well, you wouldn't eat an antique," I said. "My Uncle Herbert used to chew on an old sideboard now and then, but we always considered it odd behavior."

"Would a fruitcake that isn't an antique be dangerous?"

"You mean a reproduction?"

"I mean a modern fruitcake."

"There's nothing dangerous about fruitcakes as long as people send them along without eating them," I said, in the nicest sort of way. "If people ever started eating them, I suppose there might be need for federal legislation."

"How about people who buy fruitcakes for themselves?" he asked.

"Well, now that you mention it," I said, "nobody in the history of the United States has ever bought a fruitcake for himself. People have bought turnips for themselves. People have bought any number of Brussels sprouts for themselves. But no one has ever bought a fruitcake for himself. That does tell you a little something about fruitcakes."

"Are you saying that everybody secretly hates fruitcakes?" he asked.

"Well, it's just a theory."

1988

Oh Y2K, Yes Y2K, How Come It Has to End This Way?

Now every day, to our dismay,
We're told of yet more disarray
That Y2K may put in play.
A double zero on display
In some computers could convey—
Since they are lacking thought, per se—
A false impression they'd obey,
Concluding in a faulty way
Which century it is that day,
And thus unleash, without delay,
The cyberbug called Y2K.
Then life won't be a cabaret.

Oh Y2K, yes Y2K,
How come it has to end this way?

If circuits sizzle and sauté
The cables into macramé,
Those passengers then in Taipei
With reservations for Bombay
Could find themselves in Saint-Tropez
Or on the road to Mandalay.
And ferryboats to Monterey
Would dock on time, but in Calais.

And in a brief communiqué
The Pentagon might have to say
It cannot fight the smallest fray
Because it's lost the dossier
Of soldiers to be told that they
Must leave the service, come what may—
The list that lists each Green Beret
Who privately has said he's gay.

Oh Y2K, yes Y2K,
How come it has to end this way?

The lobbyists who work on K
See all their loopholes go astray
And benefit the EPA
And, thinking this is like Pompeii—
A doomsday in the USA—
Militiamen in full array
Go underground, and say they'll slay
Whoever tries, through naïveté,
To take the food they've stored away
Or criticize the NRA.

The ATMs begin to spray.
Fresh twenties fall like new-mown hay.
The traffic lights all go to gray.
A celebrator slurs "Olé!"
As cars begin to ricochet

Like balls caroming in croquet
And, slyly slowing his sashay,
He just escapes a Chevrolet.

There's darkness on the Great White Way.
Nearby, a fussy, smug gourmet
Who's had some quail and duck pâté
And finished with marron glacé,
Sips cheap Hungarian rosé
That in the dark the sommelier
Mistook for rare Courvoisier,
And says—in French, of course—"*Parfait!*"

Oh Y2K, yes Y2K,
How come it has to end this way?

But maybe it will be okay—
As peaceful come this *Janvier*
As water lilies by Monet,
As lyrics sung by Mel Tormé
Or herds of grazing Charolais.
For just such peacefulness we pray.
We say, "Oh, *s'il vous plait,* Yahweh."
But, still, we're scared of Y2K.
There's no one who remains blasé.
No awesome monster's held such sway
Since King Kong grabbed the fair Fay Wray.
We try to keep our fears at bay.
But one fear makes us say, "Oy vey!"
And here's the fear we can't allay:

God's thinking of pulling the plug,
And not with a bang but a bug.

1999

ABOUT THE AUTHOR

A longtime staff writer at *The New Yorker,* CALVIN TRILLIN is also *The Nation*'s deadline poet. His bestsellers range from the memoir *About Alice* to *Obliviously On He Sails: The Bush Administration in Rhyme.* He lives in Greenwich Village, which he describes as "a neighborhood where people from the suburbs come on weekends to test their car alarms."

ABOUT THE TYPE

This book was set in Sabon, a typeface designed by the well-known German typographer Jan Tschichold (1902–74). Sabon's design is based upon the original letter forms of Claude Garamond and was created specifically to be used for three sources: foundry type for hand composition, Linotype, and Monotype. Tschichold named his typeface for the famous Frankfurt typefounder Jacques Sabon, who died in 1580.